THE ARCHITECTURE
OF BRITISH
SEASIDE PIERS

PIER POINT TACKLE AND BAIT

FISHING TACKLE
FRESH AND FROZEN BAIT
CLOTHING
ACCESSORIES
SEA FISHING TRIPS
KAYAK SALES & HIRE

TEL: 01492 877678

01492 877678 SHOP · MOBILE 07719 556092

THE ARCHITECTURE OF BRITISH SEASIDE PIERS

FRED GRAY

THE CROWOOD PRESS

First published in 2020 by
The Crowood Press Ltd
Ramsbury, Marlborough
Wiltshire SN8 2HR

enquiries@crowood.com

www.crowood.com

British Library Cataloguing-in-Publication Data
A catalogue record for this book is available from the British Library.

ISBN 978 1 78500 713 2

Frontispiece: Llandudno Pier, May 2013. (Fred Gray)

Every effort has been made to trace and acknowledge the holders of the copyright of the illustrations used in this book. The author and publisher would be pleased to hear from copyright holders concerning any error or omission.

For CG, JHG and HKLG

Typeset by Sharon Dainton Design
Printed and bound in India by Parksons Graphics

Contents

My earliest vivid pier experience was during a holiday to the Isle of Wight one summer in the late 1950s. My older brother and I hired a pedalo from Shanklin beach (or perhaps from the neighbouring resort of Sandown). Too young to control the unfamiliar vessel we got stuck amid the struts, ties and braces under the pier. Much to the amusement of the spectators peering over the railings above, the pier's performing diver climbed down to rescue us. The details are hazy and just perhaps more imagination than accurate memory.

Living and working in Brighton from the mid-1970s, the town's two piers provided a fascinating architectural backdrop whenever I visited the seafront. More significantly much of my teaching for the University of Sussex's Centre for Continuing Education was about the seaside and seaside architecture, past and present. Adult students throughout Sussex shared my increasing passion for the subject and I benefited greatly from their knowledge and experiences. Teaching led to research, writing and organizing exhibitions about seaside architecture. Holidays and working visits abroad revealed intriguing new dimensions about the nature and shape of coastal built form in other parts of the world. When from the mid-1990s I became honorary historian and archivist for the Brighton West Pier Trust, I came to understand much more about the life history of one remarkable pier.

Across the decades since my pedalo adventure my personal and professional pier experiences have, of course, been shaped by broader social and economic changes to the seaside holiday and seaside resorts. The extraordinary architectural and engineering confections that make for the best of seaside piers have reflected these societal developments. And yet seaside piers have provided countless individuals with deeply personal memories and experiences; in this sense piers have as many meanings as there are people who have walked on the decks above the waves.

I was delighted when The Crowood Press asked me to write a book about the architecture of seaside piers. The task was more demanding than I originally envisaged, taking me on unanticipated excursions including, for example, the entwining of architecture with other aspects of design and engineering.

The book that follows does not provide an architectural history of all of Britain's seaside piers: it would be impossible to do so. Some piers are mentioned briefly if at all. Instead the approach taken here is to focus on broader themes in the architecture of seaside piers, illuminating these trends, developments and changes over more than two centuries, with examples from specific piers at particular times. Much has depended on the (often uneven) information available. My favourite pier, Brighton West, has provided a touchstone allowing me to contrast what happened there with piers in other places.

Piers are made for enjoyment, and the intention of this book is to explore the design processes and their consequences that have allowed people to walk on water in such diverse and delightful ways.

Left: Blackpool North Pier, June 2018. (Fred Gray)

Chapter One

WALKING ON WATER: INTRODUCING BRITISH SEASIDE PIERS

BEGINNINGS

Of all the architectural delights of the British seaside, the most astonishing and idiosyncratic is the seaside pier. Often providing a remarkable visual spectacle, piers also represent an extraordinary architectural and engineering feat.

Piers are rooted on dry land but then take an intrepid journey across the seashore and out over the sea. The architecture and engineering of piers is often extreme and often outrageous. The hostile and marginal coastal zone presents unique challenges of making a structure that is safe, secure and sustainable. But piers also need to lure visitors to venture on a journey over the sea and away from land-based entertainments. The architectural challenge has been to make piers 'must see' and 'must experience' attractions.

The essential foundations of all piers are piles, fixed into the shore and seabed, designed to provide security and support for the structure above. The piles are part of the substructure, of columns and arches, ties and braces, girders and associated lattice work, functioning to carry a pier's superstructure safely above the many perils of the sea below. In turn, superstructures range from simple open decks with protective pier-edge rail-ings to the grand pavilions, huge entertainment halls and associated paraphernalia of pleasure and amusement piers.

The experience of strolling on a piled seaside pier is unlike walking along a harbour arm or promenade wall. While waves glide around a pier's piles and columns and seawater flows beneath its decks – at least, that is the intention of pier designers – the sea smacks or smashes against hard barriers.

What is nowadays often acknowledged as the first seaside pier, at Ryde on the Isle of Wight, was, according to Simon H. Adamson, technically the first major piled passenger pier.[1] Early piers did indeed function as landing stages and select promenades, perhaps with a stand or shelter for musicians to entertain promenaders, but with few architectural embellishments. Today, the grandest of British seaside piers are architectural and engineering confections designed for leisure and pleasure over the sea.

Piers are moveable feasts, their architecture and engineering evolving and changing over time in response to the challenges of nature and the demands of society. Although designed for permanency, piers have often been the most precarious and transitional of built structures. Each pier developed its own particular life

Left: Dreams of pleasure, past and present. The Palace Pier and West Pier, Brighton, April 2011. (Fred Gray)

The life history of the Brighton West Pier

The promenade pier shortly after opening, c.1870s. (Brighton West Pier Trust)

The fully-fledged pleasure pier with pier-head theatre and concert hall, c.1920s. (Brighton West Pier Trust)

The pier in transition: the miniature race track was installed in 1927. (Brighton West Pier Trust)

The closed and ruined pier, 1997. (Fred Gray)

The Funfair Pier, c.1950s. (Brighton West Pier Trust)

Metamorphosis: the West Pier in August 2019 with pier-head skeleton and a replica 1866 toll house, part of the i360 observation tower complex. (Fred Gray)

The West Pier as skeleton, 2006. (Fred Gray)

history, reflecting local and regional circumstances and events, as well as broader national and international changes in seaside holidaymaking and architecture. We can trace how piers begin, develop, are sometimes transformed or renewed, but on other occasions are ruined and, literally, disappear. In the latter circumstances, construction is eventually followed by deconstruction. Some piers started short but finished long. Others started long but ended up short.

Although there are many variations and exceptions, it is possible to distinguish three overall varieties of seaside pier: first, the earliest and simplest promenade pier; second, the entertaining pleasure pier emerging more than a century and a half ago; and, finally, the amusement and funfair pier of the twentieth century and today. While some of the earliest promenade piers have remained just that – and are nowadays cherished as a civic asset – others have been transformed, in stages, into pleasure piers and subsequently into amusement piers. As to the number of seaside piers, while it depends on the particular definition used, approximately 60 piers survive from around 100 that were constructed in the nineteenth and early twentieth centuries.[2]

As cultural artefacts, piers may be seen as a material product of the evolving relationship between society and nature on the coast. These artificial structures above the sea enable the seaside to be experienced in a more intense manner than simply being on the shore or a seafront promenade. The senses – including touch

The architecture of pleasure: Llandudno Pier in early May 2013. (Fred Gray)

Llandudno Pier in early May 2013. The pier-head pavilion was built in 1905. (Fred Gray)

and feel, sound, taste and smell – are all assailed more vividly away from the land. Piers transport people to other environments and, at their most powerful, may suggest other worlds, places and times.

The seaside pier and its architecture are also full of symbolism, about the relationship between society and nature, and of the past, present and future. These varied meanings are reflected in how piers have been represented in the art and literature of the coast. The popular significance of piers is indicated by the huge variety of Victorian and Edwardian seaside souvenirs carrying images of the structures and the deluge of pier postcards sent to family and friends by twentieth-century holidaymakers. Piers became an important and often essential feature of many English and Welsh seaside resorts (there were very few in Scotland). At times the architecture of piers is used to characterize seaside resorts and society or nature more generally. The Victorians viewed their new piers as modern, enterprising

Llandudno Pier was constructed in the mid 1870s. It was remarkably vibrant in early May 2013. (Fred Gray)

and forward-looking. Since the 1960s, images of decayed or destroyed piers have often been used to represent the decline of coastal resorts or society's ills more generally.

Themes and structure

This book is about the architecture of British seaside piers. Architecture is defined broadly, to include many aspects of design from the style of pier buildings to both engineering and interior design and decoration. It is also about the design process and how the use, purpose and very idea of piers have evolved over time and from place to place. No attempt is made to list and describe each of the seaside piers that have graced British seaside resorts. Instead, drawing on examples, the emphasis is on the ideas, issues and themes that explain the emergence of seaside piers, the rich diversity of their development and the varied processes of change over time.

The remainder of this introductory chapter places piers in the broader context of the development of the British seaside, coastal resorts and seaside architecture. One focus is on piers as an architectural expression of the evolving relationships between society and nature at the seaside. The chapter concludes with a brief look at the export of the idea of piers to other Western countries.

Chapter 2 turns to key themes in the making of piers. It centres, in particular, on the construction of piers during the crescendo of building taking place in the period from 1860 to 1910. One focus is on the key groups of people involved in the making of piers and

The Chain Pier at Brighton, shortly after opening. Print made by John Bruce, c.1826.
(Yale Center for British Art, Paul Mellon Collection)

another on materials and techniques.

The third chapter explores how, in the late eighteenth and early nineteenth centuries, stone harbour arms and timber jetties, designed for other functional purposes, also appealed as promenades to leisured visitors to the seaside. The chapter traces the development of simple piled landing-stage piers, designed to allow passengers safe and comfortable movement between ship and shore. Such piers quickly adopted a promenade role. The distinctive Chain Pier in Brighton, while a spectacular and unique structure, also presaged future possibilities.

The story then turns in Chapter 4 to the revolutionary impact of iron, both cast and wrought, for the design and making of piers. Most of these early iron piers were simple promenade and landing-stage structures. One person, Eugenius Birch, stands out as the most original and important pier designer, whose work was to prove influential for the remainder of the

nineteenth century.

Chapter 5 moves to the extraordinary golden age of pier building in the last decades of the nineteenth century. It was a remarkable boom time for the British seaside, and a remarkable period for piers, with dozens of new pleasure piers completed and many older promenade piers transformed by the addition of pleasure pavilions, winter gardens and other entertainment buildings. Although never dominant, seaside Orientalism as a design style was in full flow. Piers also developed a distinctive vernacular architecture for using the sea, for music and dancing and for artificial amusements and funfair rides. The death of Queen Victoria coincided with a slowing in the number of new piers. The golden age drew to a close.

The focus of Chapter 6 is on piers during the interwar years of the twentieth century and the growing popular enjoyment of the sunny seaside. It was sometimes difficult for piers, with a leisure architecture

A cold Sunday on Blackpool's North Pier, c.1920s. (Fred Gray collection)

from the past, to be adapted to meet the transformation in holidaymaking expectations. During the 1930s, however, some innovative and streamlined Modernist pier entertainment buildings were produced. And then came another World War. The chapter concludes by describing the profound consequences for seaside piers of a world at war.

Once the war had ended, British resorts and holidaymakers heaved a sigh of relief. Chapter 7 begins by exploring how the demands of pier reconstruction and reopening were followed by early post-war vitality. But then, from the 1960s, and reflecting the declining fortunes of British resorts, many piers experienced an often traumatic and unpredictable journey of optimism, disappointment and decline. This malaise, however, was only part of the story and as one century ended, and another began, there were also signs of hope and renewal.

The concluding chapter outlines significant pier developments in the first two decades of the present century. The focus is on looking forward and using these illustrations to tease out the prospects for piers in the not-too-distant future.

THE CHANGING SEASIDE

The British invented the modern idea of the seaside as a place of health, leisure and pleasure. It became a great, if often unacknowledged, British export, spreading to coasts, especially hospitable ones, around the world. The first small, select resorts emerged three centuries ago. Subsequently, dozens of resorts, large – sometimes huge – and small, developed around the coasts of Britain. They became the most tangible products of the British fascination and love affair with the seaside.

A distinctive architecture of the seaside emerged to adorn and embellish coastal resorts, making them stand out both from each other and from more ordinary inland places. Seaside architecture, broadly defined, ranges from flamboyant shoreline entertainment pavilions to tiny seafront shelters and the minutiae of promenade railings and lamp posts, through grand hotels and cheerful guest houses, to Regency terraces and Modernist flats. It includes Victorian seawater baths and streamlined interwar lidos, and the planned open spaces of seafront promenades, parks and gardens. It is piers, however, where seaside architecture is at its most extreme and excessive. The twin challenges for the pier makers are to build in and over the sea, in the inhospitable and marginal coastal zone, and to produce a spectacular architecture that delights and attracts.

The sublime seaside

The emergence of seaside resorts in the eighteenth century allowed the sea, newly discovered by the leisured classes as a site of pleasure and health, to be consumed by individuals and social groups. Central to this new form of consumption were the assumed therapeutic and health enhancing qualities of seawater. Previously, elite groups had largely ignored nature at the margin between land and sea. Alain Corbin's path-breaking history of the discovery of the Western seaside between 1750 and 1840 roots the emergence of seaside resorts in the Enlightenment.[3] He details the 'revolution' that occurred in how people understood and appreciated nature and their own bodily consciousness.

Gradually the seaside became a 'sublime' awe-inspiring and terror-inducing place that was perceived to offer therapeutic remedies for the excesses and ailments of the ruling classes. In contrast to the malevolence of the cities and the overcrowded, dissolute inland spas, the seashore resorts offered a new closeness to nature, because, as Corbin argues:

The ocean represented indisputable nature which

Insignificant spectators, dwarfed by monumental stone harbour arms, wonder at the terror of the seas. George Chambers, *Port on a Stormy Day*, 1835, oil on canvas. (Yale Center for British Art, Paul Mellon Collection)

was more than just scenery, and which remained unaffected by falsehood … the sea became a refuge and a source of hope because it inspired fear. The new strategy for seaside holidays was to enjoy the sea and experience the terror it inspired, while overcoming one's personal perils. … The sea was expected to cure the evil of urban civilization and correct the ill effects of easy living, while respecting the demands of privacy.[4]

The untamed, natural sea came to be seen as a source of society's salvation and medical opinion galloped to aid and abet the discovery of the seaside. Doctors proclaimed the extraordinary medicinal virtues of seawater both for bathing and drinking.

From the late eighteenth century, however, elite society's perceptions of the sea and shore began to change. There was a growing belief that the seaside should be appreciated for its beauty, for the visual delights it offered, for the nature it revealed, for the exercise and relaxation it could provide, and for the quality and purity of its air. Visitors were no longer so apprehensive of the sea. They learnt instead how to understand, admire and enjoy it. There was also a growing appreciation that the seaside's joys and benefits would be made more intense by not just being beside the sea, but by promenading over it.

Early in this transitional period, existing stone harbour arms and wooden jetties, designed for other purposes, were adopted as promenades for appreciating and contemplating nature and mixing with polite society. Then, in the early nineteenth century came the first promenade piers. They were part of what Corbin describes as a process of 'attuning space with desire'.[5] With none of the disadvantages and dangers associated with boats, whether seasickness or the possibility of capsizing or even drowning, piers enabled visitors to leave the landward side of the sea and venture out over the water itself.

The growing interest in both marine aesthetics and the developing importance of the sea in the visual imagination led to views, panoramas and perspectives

Bathers and bathing machines close to Sandown Pier, c.1880s. The nature writer, Richard Jefferies (1848–1887) thought the pier promenade experience tedious. He did, though, enjoy looking from the deck of a pier to female bathers below. (Fred Gray collection)

within a resort for invalids suffering particular complaints. In the last quarter of the nineteenth century the cult of sea air became dominant. It was sea air and sea bathing that was thought to restore and transform.

Ozone as an element of sea air became a powerful recommendation of the coast, repeatedly analysed by doctors, vigorously promoted by the seaside authorities and endlessly debated in respectable society. Ultimately, though, its use and value were imagined rather than real and it was vainly hunted for by invalids searching for good health.[7] The restorative value of sea air and its role in blowing away the malaise of work and the city continued to be acclaimed for much of the twentieth century, although it was to be rivalled and ultimately vanquished by the cult of the sun.

The Victorians and piers

British seaside piers were one of the most remarkable and idiosyncratic artefacts produced by the Victorians. The vast majority of Britain's piers were constructed during Queen Victoria's long reign from 1837 to 1901 and, indeed, toward the end of the period there was a fondness to name a new pier after the Queen. A mere seven were built before she came to the throne, and just a dozen in the century after her death.

Before the introduction of the steam engine and rail transport technologies, few resorts were within reach of anyone other than 'persons of high rank and fashion'. It was expensive, of money and time, to visit the seaside. In Britain, Gravesend and Margate on the Thames estuary, with cheaper and comparatively easy access by water from London, were among the exceptions.[8] It is in resorts such as these that the first seaside piers appeared.

In the mid-nineteenth century however, the coming of the railway permitted faster, easier and cheaper trips to the coast, eventually undermining the previous class basis of many resorts. As the cost of using the technology fell, an ever-increasing number of middle-

of the sea and coast being increasingly prioritized. By the middle of the nineteenth century, esteem for the glories of the sea view was deeply embedded in society's consciousness. The horizon, for example, became an important part of the Victorian visual imagination, suggesting, 'futurity, the space into which the imagination and inner vision may travel: it connotes expansiveness'.[6] There was a sense, too, that the sea, or at least its coastal margin, was being tamed, domesticated and subjugated.

Increasingly during the nineteenth century, rather than just proclaim the virtues of bathing, the medical profession and the published guides and manuals also emphasized the value of sea air, coastal climate and the benefits of swimming. Doctors took to pronouncing on the climatic advantages of one region or resort compared to another, and even on the best location

At least the rain stopped. A damp and cool experience on Blackpool's Central Pier. The open lattice seat backs were replaced by more substantial decorative cast-iron backs. (Rijksmuseum, Amsterdam)

and working-class visitors were carried by train to the expanding resorts, as day-trippers or to holiday by the sea for a week or more.[9] In many resorts 'railway mania' led to 'pier mania'.

The pier-building mania of the last four decades of the nineteenth century depended on the application of Victorian technology – often rapidly developing – to an extreme environment. In some ways it was ludicrous to attempt to build in and over the hostile margin between land and sea, particularly when a primary purpose of the new piers was as a place of leisure and pleasure. Technology was tested to its limits and in unsuitable locations, piers were quickly destroyed by natural forces.

But Victorian pier designers, promoters and entrepreneurs had the confidence – often tinged with arrogance – that their plans would be successful and, in turn, yield a substantial financial gain. The very notion of seaside piers was bound up with what Victorians thought about society and nature both at home and overseas. Piers transformed many Victorian seaside re-

sorts and, for those Victorians able to venture to the coast, the experience of being beside the sea.

Piers provided a platform and associated architecture for consuming nature, improving health, enjoying leisure and engaging with society. Walking on to a pier was to be transported ever closer to the natural environment, heightening both the sense of admiration of nature and the accomplishment of the individual making the visit. Moreover, sea air was surely purer and more beneficial when breathed in over the sea before it was tainted and adulterated by the land. And there was the camaraderie to be enjoyed by walking on water with like-minded people. There were new panoramas of the coast to view, storms and sunsets to marvel at and horizons to contemplate. The pier, as a platform from which to view the horizon, allowed people to reflect on themselves, other places and other times. Although it was of course an illusion, the pier was remarkable in seeming to enable people to journey a little closer to the unobtainable.

By 1860 there were just a dozen piers in British resorts, most serving both as landing stages and promenades. And yet by 1900 Britain's seafront architecture had been transformed. By that date, there were eighty piers, with some resorts having two or even three of the structures.

The first wave of this deluge of pier building in the 1860s and 70s was of promenade piers proper; structures some harbour authorities described as 'not made for trade'.[10] These piers became fashionable and select extensions to seafront parades and drives. The inevitable band apart, promenade piers had little in the way of artificial entertainment. As John Walton suggests, they were an 'established recreational institution with pretensions to gentility and even "rationality".[11] In reality, promenade-pier builders underestimated the continuing radical transformation of many resorts and the business of being beside the sea.

Over the following decades, rising standards of liv-

Gazing at promenaders on Clacton's timber pier from the first-floor balcony of the 1893 pavilion. (Rijksmuseum, Amsterdam)

Clacton's pier-head pavilion in 1997. (Fred Gray)

The Palace Pier, Brighton, opened within weeks of Queen Victoria's death. (Fred Gray collection)

ing and improved holiday entitlements allowed an ever-broader range of people to holiday by the sea for a day or more.[12] The broadening of the potential class make-up of resorts, facilitated by significant technological changes in transportation, had major implications for seaside towns and their architecture.[13]

The new seaside visitors with new demands were a major factor in the transformation of seaside piers in the last two decades of the nineteenth century. Although the ubiquitous enjoyment of a stroll over the sea was still available, in many resorts the traditional landing-stage function for anything other than pleasure trips on the sea disappeared. And, by the end of the period, the open-deck promenade pier had also disappeared from the largest and most popular resorts. From the 1880s, a second wave of new fully fledged pleasure piers engulfed the coastal resorts.

The pleasure piers – either newly constructed or transformed from earlier promenade structures – were sites of artificial entertainments and amusements. Many echoed and developed what was to be found in inland cities, including opera, theatre, orchestral music, music hall and variety, dancing and roller-skating. Pleasure piers burgeoned with pavilions and theatres, concert halls and winter gardens, refreshment rooms and shops.

The business of piers

The new piers were represented as modern and community ventures in which a resort and its inhabitants had an important stake. Piers were usually speculative private enterprises. Shareholders included wealthy people mostly living locally or regionally, and also others of much more modest means, owning just a few shares.[14] Other financial models included both the construction of piers as part of much larger coastal development schemes for new resorts, and the involvement of local government boards wishing to enhance resort facilities.

The completion of a new pier was invariably a cause of civic pride and the opening an occasion for public celebration and rejoicing. One of the earliest of the many spectacular events marking the opening of a new pier was in Blackpool in May 1863. Almost 20,000 people flocked into the town – it had fewer than 4,000 residents – to join the 'magnificent festival … to celebrate the opening of the pier', the emerging resort's first.[15]

Two decades later, in 1885, a perceptive commentator described Margate, one of London's great seaside leisure sites, as 'a great business, the gross receipts of which total about a million a year received from visitors.'[16] Piers were a critical part of the infrastructure and commercial success of the largest and most vibrant resorts; they were part of the process through which the seaside was commodified.

There was money to be made by enabling people to walk out above the ocean. Apart from entrance tolls, the pier companies found other ways to generate income. New entertainments were invented, and large pier buildings provided a wealth of attractions. Exterior architecture and interior design were important parts of the process and pier buildings were designed to attract and entice, using various leisure motifs and

The celebrations for the opening of Blackpool Pier. (*The Illustrated London News*, 30 May 1863)

Frolicking in the sea at Hastings, May 1920. The increasing accumulation of buildings on the pier was designed to increase the pier company's profits. (Fred Gray collection)

symbols. The most successful pleasure piers became architectural spectacles in their own right while also offering dazzling entertainments.

Piers became extraordinary make-believe worlds and an essential feature of the most successful resorts. There were ways in which the seaside location was used to provide a unique experience. Most pleasure piers hosted a plethora of maritime entertainments ranging from steamer excursions – providing, for the majority of voyagers, otherwise unobtainable views and panoramas – through aquatic entertainers and performing divers, to water fetes and bathing facilities. It was this combination of maritime entertainments and other indoor and outdoor pleasures over the sea that made piers such an important feature of the British seaside experience to the mid-twentieth century.

The economic historian John Clapham, looking at the pier building obsession of the last decades of the nineteenth century from the vantage point of the early 1950s, thought Victorian piers 'were as symbolic of what archaeologists call a culture as are axe-heads and beakers … There they stood. No visitor to the island could miss them. From them the least seafaring of the islanders could watch his ships go by with the joy of

vicarious ownership.'[17]

Despite the proliferation of new piers the pier development process was not always plain sailing. Sometimes proposals were abandoned because resorts were too small, finance inadequate or local political opposition too great.

Existing vested interests, antagonistic to pier proposals, attempted to delay or foil them. A new pier might threaten the livelihoods of boatmen ferrying passengers between ship and shore. In the early 1840s the watermen at Gravesend, resorting both to law and riot, delayed the building of Britain's first iron pier by four years. In 1864 Deal's boatmen, whose businesses were jeopardized, denounced the new pier. One commentator saw it otherwise, describing 'those predatory gentlemen' with exorbitant charges, who shot passengers out of their boats 'on a shingle beach up to their knees in water.'[18]

The class character of a resort also had consequences for pier enterprises. In one extreme example, in 1874, Portsmouth's antagonistic class and political relations resulted in riots over the control of land by the entrance to the first pier at Southsea. The pier company wished to enclose the land, thereby excluding the local working people, and turn it into an exclusive and private space reserved for respectable pier visitors. The several nights of protest by the traditional local users of the common land included the burning of newly erected fences, attacks on the pier – the angry crowd pelted the promenaders and pier buildings with stones – and the quelling of the unrest by police, volunteer assistants and troops.[19]

Some select and late-developing resorts in counties such as Devon eschewed piers because of the fear that such developments 'would drive away affluent visitors who wanted to avoid both noisy, flashy amusements and the working-class excursionists they attracted.'[20] There was no such concern in high-class and exclusive Eastbourne, a resort under the patronage and control

A golden pier for the 'Empress of Resorts' glowing in the late afternoon winter sun. The 1925 shore-end pavilion was destroyed by fire in 2014. (Fred Gray)

Local councils were crucial in advertising the delights of a resort; piers were a major attraction. (Geoffrey Mead collection)

of the Duke of Devonshire. In what was called the 'Empress of Watering Places', 'the pier, with its bands and its theatre, only offered the highest class of entertainment.'[21] In contrast, Blackpool's eventual three piers were able to accommodate different degrees of respectability and popularity. Over time many of even the most socially exclusive resorts bowed, at least to some extent, to the growing demands of working-class visitors. Entertainments and amusements responded in kind.

Even though dominant landowners continued to have a formidable influence in some British resorts, from the middle of the nineteenth century seaside town councils became progressively more interventionist.[22] The resort public authorities frequently saw piers as crucial assets. If the privately owned enterprise was threatened – perhaps because a pier was making a loss or had suffered major damage through storm or fire – town councils intervened surprisingly often to take it into municipal ownership.

The municipal authorities increasingly judged and determined the architecture of the seaside and what should be built. This eventually extended to funding and designing individual seaside buildings, such as new pier pavilions, and producing the design and architecture of the principal open spaces, particularly the important mood-creating and tone-setting seafront promenade and public gardens. The resort and its architecture, including piers, were then vigorously promoted through official guides and other advertising mechanisms.

The coming of the sun

Despite the abiding appeal of the seaside and seaside resorts – the fascination with the sea, the lure of the beach, the extraordinary array of both natural and artificial seaside pleasures and entertainments, the wonder of being away from work and domestic duties and actually on holiday – the British seaside had been in a state of continual flux. Whether it was everything that made a seaside resort or the very visitors enjoying its pleasures, nothing stayed the same for long: everything evolved.

'Getting away from it all' had always been one of the chief attractions of the seaside. But in fundamental ways the notion was an illusion. Seaside resorts and

Relaxing on Brighton's West Pier, August 1922. The photograph reveals the signs and paraphernalia of the public bathing station below. (Fred Gray collection)

Cover of Southend Pier's musical entertainments programme, early June 1934. The architecture of the pier's late Victorian pavilion was partially hidden by the 1931 Art Deco entrance structure. (Fred Gray collection)

the pleasure piers always reflected and responded – albeit sometimes in a distorted or limited fashion – to an array of societal change.

The first four decades of the twentieth century were a period of acute change. Particularly in the largest resorts, the seaside market broadened and became ever more popular. New groups of people, including many from the working classes, enjoyed the seaside for the first time. They were carried to the coast by railway trains, powered by steam or electricity, or by motor coach or charabanc using the improving road network. As the technologies of rail and road travel developed, so one of the old roles of the earliest seaside piers – as landing stages for visitors carried to the seaside by ship – faded away. Whether day trippers or staying visitors, the new seaside holidaymakers expected new forms of amusement and entertainment.

From the late nineteenth century, the sun emerged first as an accompaniment to sea air and then, by the 1930s, as the dominant natural force shaping what people searched for, did and built at the seaside. As with other uses of seaside nature, it is difficult to untangle popular movement from expert prescription in the developing interest in the sun.

In the early part of the twentieth century, the medical profession promoted the therapeutic use of the sun, particularly in combating tuberculosis – consumption – then still a scourge of many parts of the Western world. By the 1930s the medical benefits of the sun were widely acknowledged.

The sun, though, seized more than the medical imagination. It had class and gender dimensions. Previously, the social and economic elite preferred white skins for the indication of both status and health; the suntan was distasteful in part because of its connotations with degrading physical activity.[23] Similarly, until the 1920s, the feminine ideal of wealthy women stressed pallor, fragility and whiteness. The coming of the sun, however, inverted these existing values. A suntan became a 'distinguishing trait' for the elite and 'a

At Hastings the increasing popularity during the 1930s of swimming at the seaside was combined with new illuminations on the pier; night-time swimming was one result. (Steve Peak collection)

Shown here in May 2001, although in a truncated form, Cleethorpes Pier survived into the twenty-first century. The pavilion dates from 1905. Put to a variety of entertainment uses including as a night club, in 2019 the pavilion was a fish and chip restaurant, claimed to be the largest in the country. (Fred Gray)

The joys of hunting under a pier. Cleethorpes, May 2001. (Fred Gray)

The rival attractions of the sunny beach, Paignton, June 2017. (Fred Gray)

new symbol of modern times, an external manifestation of prosperity.'[24]

The value placed on the sun extended to other parts of society. For social reformers, architects and town planners of the period, a 'dream of health, sunlight and the body reformed' was bound up with a quest to transform existing society into a new and modern social order.[25] There was also a more broadly based popular appreciation of health, physical activity and pleasure in the sun and open air. People loved the sun! These impulses led to new ways for holidaymakers to use and enjoy the seaside. The seaside builders responded to these demands with new types of resort buildings including lidos and open-air pools, sun decks and sun terraces, and minimalist hotels and pavilions.

British seaside piers, with their architecture of the past, were for the most part ill equipped to react to such fundamental changes. There were exceptions, and at times piers were able to embrace and meet the challenge of the sun.

The debate was interrupted by the Second World War – the conflict led to the closure and increasing dereliction of many piers – and was then largely stifled as resorts responded to the need for a post-war reconstruction project and the revitalized demands of the holidaymaking public.

From the 1960s, as increasing numbers of holidaymakers flew to new and sunny seasides overseas, British resorts experienced enormous trials and tribulations which, in places, have continued into the twenty-first century. There were complex, and sometimes dramatic, consequences for the architecture of seaside piers. And yet many piers survived and, into the new century, signs emerged of a reinvented seaside and new roles for seaside piers.

THE SEASIDE PIER EXPORTED

From Britain, the modern seaside, coastal resorts and seaside piers were all exported to other Western coun-

Opened in 1901, the pier at Scheveningen, the Netherlands, was destroyed during the Second World War. (Rijksmuseum, Amsterdam)

A modern Italian pier: the 285-meter Pontile Bellavista Vittoria, Lido Di Camaiore, opened in 2008 and photographed in 2009. The pier head featured a double deck, a stylish café and canvas sunscreens. (Fred Gray)

tries. Seaside piers came to adorn the coasts of countries such as France, Germany, Italy, the Netherlands, the United States of America and Australia. Once implanted on coasts elsewhere, piers developed in intriguingly different and original directions.

France

A late nineteenth-century bout of pier building on mainland Europe reflected the British influence. As early as 1868, the great Eugenius Birch designed a spectacular pier with pagoda-style kiosks and a monumental pier-head casino – far larger than any previous proposed pier building – for Nice, on the French Riviera coast.[26] The design was unexecuted, although two decades later Birch's ideas were reworked and another exotic casino pier was built in the fashionable resort, jutting out from the Promenade des Anglais. The location was appropriate given the pier was designed by a prolific Victorian British engineer, and erected by a British company. Disaster then struck, with a fire destroying the building a few days before the planned opening.

The replacement Casino de la Jetée, completed in

1891, was both taller and more explicitly Oriental in design, with minarets and a large dome topped by a trident-carrying siren plated in gold.[27] The pier was much disputed. It was unwanted by the municipal authorities and criticized by some local people for obstructing the view of the bay. Many architectural commentators abhorred it: for example, as a copy of St

Nice's Casino de la Jetée was topped by a trident-carrying siren plated in gold. (Rijksmuseum, Amsterdam)

The Jetée was a place of varied performance: the apparatus for tightrope walking can just be glimpsed at the seaward end of the pier. (Rijksmuseum, Amsterdam)

Sophia in Constantinople, it was a 'dreadful travesty'.[28] It was one of the most extreme of the resort's Belle Epoque buildings. By the inter-war period, however, it was an established feature of the Nice seafront. As a symbol of the resort, it was continually represented on postcards and posters and was much painted by artists such as Raoul Dufy. The German occupying forces destroyed the pier in the latter stages of the Second World War.

Germany

There was also a spate of pier construction on the German Baltic coast. It followed the emergence of a unified German state in the 1870s and the rapid development of mostly small-scale and respectable

seaside resorts. As the name *seebrücke* (seabridge) suggests, like their British promenade-pier counterparts, many German piers were open-deck structures functioning primarily as promenades and as landing stages. A few carried substantial buildings including, perhaps, a restaurant, dance hall, shops, a casino or a Kursaal. Originally a word used to describe a spa building or assembly room, Kursaal (a direct translation from German is 'cure hall') was subsequently transformed into a term for a seaside leisure building. It was particularly popular in English resorts before the First World War. The Baltic piers were mostly wooden structures, resting on pointed timbers driven into the seabed. While the engineering challenge was reduced because of the minimal tidal rise and fall of the land-locked sea, the

Baltic Sea provided an alternative natural hazard in the form of sea ice with potential to crush a pier to destruction.[29]

By the early years of the last century, piers had become an essential attraction of most Baltic resorts. With the Second World War and the subsequent communist regime, however, the existing Baltic piers declined and eventually vanished from the seaside landscape. Sometimes the immediate reasons were traumatic events such as fire or adverse weather, but the political and economic complexion of what by then was East Germany had no place for piers, a seaside architectural form from a rejected past.

And yet in the last decade of the twentieth century they were to miraculously reappear. Following German reunification, a remarkable pier building mania occurred with seventeen new piers constructed between 1989 and 2000. It was as though the wheel had turned full circle, back to the original enthusiasm for pier building of a century before. Part of the wholesale rejuvenation of the Baltic seaside resorts, the new piers were used as the focal point of the seafront; key resort attractions given an economic and political significance and even symbolic value. The piers and their renewed resorts were an act of faith that, after two wars and two totalitarian states, the seaside should be an integral part of a modern democratic society.

The United States

In the United States, from the late nineteenth century many established resorts on both the east and west coasts developed distinctive amusement piers. The primary purpose was to entertain visitors to the seaside while ensuring they paid for the pleasure. The competition to attract and keep visitors led to spectacular architectural responses and equally spectacular and distinctive entertainments. Piers in resorts such as Atlantic City vied to provide the most extreme, impressive, unique and innovative attractions. Size – of a ride, a dance hall or theatre – and fame – of the entertainers

Sellin Pier, Germany, 2000. (Fred Gray)

Heringsdorf Pier, Germany, 2000, the new pier on the right, the remains of a much older timber pier on the left. (Fred Gray)

The original American maritime pier converted for leisure purposes. Pier 39, San Francisco, California, 1998. (Fred Gray)

or entertainments – mattered, and piers often represented modernity, technology, excess and pleasure at the seaside.

A new Californian form of pleasure pier form emerged in the last decades of the twentieth century. Echoing the early nineteenth-century British use of breakwaters and harbour arms as promenades, former commercial shipping or fishing wharves – essentially maritime commercial structures from the past – have been rejuvenated and transformed into major tourist destinations, often advertised as heritage sites, but in practice dominated by retail outlets, eating places and visitor attractions. A series of new fishing piers has also been built along the Californian coast.

The 1989 Imperial Beach Fishing Pier, California, October 2017. (Fred Gray)

A state historic landmark and the oldest surviving concrete pier in California, Manhattan Beach Pier on a sunny day at the end of 2017. (Fred Gray)

Sterns Wharf, Santa Barbara, California, April 2019. (Fred Gray)

MAKING PIERS: PEOPLE, MATERIALS AND TECHNIQUES

BRIDGING BOUNDARIES

This chapter explores the making of piers, the key groups of people involved in design and construction, and how materials and techniques have changed over time. The focus is on the vital period of pier-building in the half century from 1860, although there is discussion of what went before and what came after.

Although the first British seaside pier was constructed more than two centuries ago, the fundamental design challenges are abiding. In the context of the hostile coastal zone, the marginal and ever-changing transitory area between land and sea, the major task is to make seaside piers secure and sustainable. A related issue revolves around ensuring piers are fit for purpose. Even for the earliest and simplest landing-stage piers made of timber, the difficulties were considerable: how to make a pier long and stable enough to provide a safe passenger bridge between ship and shore. The task increased once seaside piers gathered other roles; as promenades, as sites of health, pleasure and amusement, and as places of profit. At their most developed, piers needed an architecture of performance and spectacle designed to lure visitors and entice them to spend money.

Particular vocabularies are associated with seaside piers. There is a technical engineering language associated with the substructure including, for example, main-lattice girders, cross-bracing girders, ties and bracing bars, and joist and beam sections. It is usual to distinguish between the piles, fixed into beach and seabed and providing the foundation engineering, from the columns attached to the piles and supporting the structure above. The varied techniques for fixing piles have also acquired their own vocabulary.

Some of the phrases used to describe piers hint at organic characteristics implying, almost, that a pier is a living organism: 'root end', 'pier head' and the narrower pier 'neck' or 'stem'. The analogy is useful since most piers, like living creatures, evolved and developed over time. The architectural and engineering boundaries were in a state of flux. For any individual pier, a vastly speeded-up visual chronology would reveal the birth, periods of growth and stability, change and development and, often, decline, shrinking and, perhaps, death and disappearance. The paucity of information means that the chronology of a pier's changing colour is immensely difficult to reconstruct. Despite individual divergences, at a generic level the surviving information suggests that in their Victorian heyday piers

Left: Blackpool North Pier, June 2018. (Fred Gray)

were rich in contrasting colours, both light and dark. Lighter and pastel shades dominated with the coming of the inter-war sun while, post war, white became commonplace.

The defining question

Pier aficionados delight in debating what is or isn't a seaside pier. A short definition is that it is a structure, fixed into the shore and seabed with piles, extending out over and above the sea, and designed for pleasure, whether a simple promenade or more elaborate entertainment or amusement. Piers begin on the land, travel over the intertidal foreshore and then, to a varying degree, complete a journey into the inshore areas sometimes permanently covered by seawater.

Of course, it is more complicated than that, and there are exceptions and variations. Some piers do not extend to permanently submerged zones. Occasionally, piers are not directly rooted into the land. The now demolished New Brighton Pier was an example of an island pier and the entrance to Brighton's Chain Pier was, unusually, directly from the beach. Lowestoft South Pier is a conundrum; despite its core being a solid harbour breakwater completed in 1846 (and so falling foul of it being piled) it has a long history as a

A crowded pier, Lowestoft. The sender of the postcard, posted on 21 August 1907, comments that 'this is our favourite pier'. (Fred Gray collection)

structure with all the architectural paraphernalia of a pleasure pier. At another extreme, the bridge-like Royal Victoria Pier at Tenby was designed to ensure people could reach a pleasure-steamer landing stage located off the rocky shore; the pier head, however, embellished with decorative cast-iron railings, was used for concert performances, while the pier overall performed as a venue for angling competitions.

Despite the work of the National Piers Society, founded in 1979, there is no single definitive register of British seaside piers, past and present. The surviving seaside piers in coastal resorts provide an accepted core list of over fifty surviving piers, from the slightly more than 100 that once existed. Beyond the core, there is a periphery open to debate and interpretation.

Depending on the definition used, and sometimes whim and fancy, specific piers may be included or excluded. In Scotland, for example, the present-day structures at Dunoon, Fort William and Tighnabruaich may or may not be counted. Even given its delightful architecture, is the pier at Wemyss Bay anything more than a railway and ferry interchange? Some experts omit Gravesend's two early iron piers as the town, on the banks of the River Thames, is deemed not sufficiently of the seaside. The entrance-building remnants of Weymouth's Bandstand Pier, including a

Promenading pleasures on the stone and timber Beaumaris Pier. (Geoffrey Mead)

Margate's three piers, c.1960s. In the foreground, the 1920s Bathing Pavilion, later renamed as the Sun Deck. In the distance, Margate Pier – a stone harbour arm – and behind it a glimpse of Margate Jetty, the resort's pier proper. Only the stone structure survived into the twenty-first century. (Fred Gray collection)

single surviving row of four concrete piles on the beach, is frequently accepted as an extant pier. In contrast, the much larger Worthing Lido, currently a 'family entertainment centre' full of arcade games and children's rides, is never recorded as a pier, although it is built on piles driven into the beach. Similarly, is the structure protruding into the Bristol Channel from the promenade at Burnham-on-Sea best classified as Britain's shortest seaside pier, and the last to be completed (in 1911) before the First World War, or is it an entertainment pavilion that just happens to be on concrete piles fixed into the shore?

Various other piled structures were designed for

The shortest pier? Worthing Lido 2002. (Fred Gray)

leisure and entertainment at the seaside. They included the Marine Terrace Bathing Pavilion on Margate's Main Sands. This 1920s structure was planned to include 362 changing cubicles, four kiosks, a café, accommodation for an orchestra and what was described as a 'promenade pier', 132ft long by 45ft wide.[30] As holiday fashions changed the building was rebranded as the Sun Deck; it was demolished in 1990. Other piled structures at Margate included the deck promenade and bathing station at nearby Walpole Bay. Eastbourne's Birdcage Bandstand was carried on piles driven into the beach. Brighton could once lay claim to an astonishing moving pier, in the form of the Brighton and Rottingdean Seashore Electric Railway with tracks covered by seawater except at extreme low tide. The 'Daddy Long Legs', as it was nicknamed, was in sight of the ornate cast-iron Madeira Terrace. Founded into the reclaimed foreshore, this engineering and architectural confection clothed and disguised the stark chalk cliff face, providing a spectacular pier-like promenade running parallel to the beach and sea. At the time of writing, Madeira Terrace is fenced off and closed as unsafe.

Being too obsessive with precise pier definitions limits appreciation and understanding of seaside piers, and pier-like structures, in all their fascinating variety.

PEOPLE AND PROFESSIONS

Despite the extreme engineering and sometimes outrageous architecture, piers were a product of British society and economy at particular times. Piers, when they were built and as they changed over time, reflected technological, economic and cultural possibilities, ambitions, sensitivities and limitations. Similarly, pier designers worked with the freedoms and opportunities, constraints and restrictions, opinions and values, provided by the professional and design (and

nowadays, regulatory) context of the times.

Material wars

The golden age of pier building depended on iron. It was a material pier engineers became increasingly comfortable and confident with for both structural and ornamental purposes. And yet iron was loathed by many architects.[31] The leading and opinion-forming critic of iron was John Ruskin (1819–1900). The arguments against iron included a number of related propositions. Unlike architectural materials, such as stone, which were rooted in history, iron buildings had no history and could not be considered architecture. Structures made of iron were nothing more than ahistorical parodies. They lacked truth, taste, refinement, substance and value and were, instead, false, tasteless, vulgar, shallow and worthless.

As Paul Dobraszczyk observes, Ruskin and his followers believed iron used in a building 'offended the eye because of qualities inherent in its materiality': it was simply not solid enough and was too thin to appear as architecture should.[32] Iron structures lacked beauty. Seaside piers, with their spindly and seemingly insubstantial legs sticking into the sea, were particularly susceptible to the criticism. It was partly for this reason that seaside piers were disliked by some commentators. The early iron pier at Margate was described as 'unquestionably ugly', while the thin iron legs of another early pier, at Worthing, were said to have made the structure look like a giant centipede. No wonder, perhaps, that some iron piers were swept away by storms. Pier promoters, attempting to allay such criticism, were frequently eager to stress that what was proposed was 'substantial'.

The sins were compounded when iron was decorated. Ruskin, as a critical arbiter of taste, bemoaned decorative cast iron as 'these vulgar and cheap substitutes for real decoration'.[33] The problem, from this perspective, was partly that cast iron was mass produced,

Cast-iron decorative detail displayed on Torquay's late Victorian Princess Pier. A wet April morning, 2009. (Fred Gray)

Despite the critical storm, the structural and decorative use of cast iron for seaside buildings became standard. Iron was far too important for the seaside and pier builders to be bypassed. It became a necessity in constructing the expanding resorts. There were massive cost and design advantages of mechanical reproduction and the repetition and duplication enabled by the cast-iron making process. The sheer range of prefabricated structural and decorative elements made for extensive design possibilities.

However, the mid-nineteenth-century hostile architectural criticism of cast-iron structures and decoration at the seaside was to cast long shadows over the future. Well into the twentieth century, piers and other forms of iron seaside architecture continued frequently to be disparaged as insubstantial and of little value; somehow not proper architecture and instead frivolous and unimportant. The debate ripples to the present day with consequences for expert (rather than popular) perceptions of the heritage value of piers and other iron seaside buildings.

The professional context

Individual pier designers proposed the overall concept and detailed structure of a new pier. Decisions were required about the appropriate dimensions, components, style and decoration. Materials and construction techniques needed to be specified. Those individuals and companies, and local authorities, commissioning for a new pier, or the redevelopment of an existing structure, would also have had opinions, perhaps strong ones, on what they wanted to see built. A design would be negotiated. The contractor building a pier had a part to play too, particularly where they were experienced in pier work.

The nature of the resort and local circumstances were also important. Contextual factors included the funding available, the nature of the site, the tidal range and the characteristics of the littoral zone to be piled

made by machine and industrial processes rather than being crafted and handmade according to long-established design ideas.

A minority of professional voices attempted to end the vehement material and stylistic war between architects and engineers. For example, the architect Charles Henry Driver (1832–1900) searched for common ground and proposed a synthesis of divergent views. Although an architect, Driver was a well-known expert on ornamental cast iron and worked with several engineers on a number of piers. Until the end of the century, such collaboration between the two professions was unusual.

– for example, whether the seabed was sand, mud, gravel, rock or a combination of different materials. Constructing a pier was a learning process, with the ease or difficulty of the site only becoming apparent as work proceeded.

Pier engineers

Pier designers also learnt from each other and, as the nineteenth century advanced, from the expanding canon of pier work. The professional engineering context for the proliferation of seaside piers in the last four decades of the nineteenth century is not well understood. There were some locally and regionally based engineers who produced pier designs for nearby resorts. More often, pier engineers were based in London and worked across the country (and abroad). Pier work was just one aspect of what was usually a wide engineering portfolio. Even the prolific Eugenius Birch was involved in much non-pier design and engineering.

Many engineers had their offices in or close to Westminster in the heart of the capital city. The central London neighbourhood was the home of the influential Institution of Civil Engineers (ICE), founded in 1818 and with premises in Great George Street, a brief stroll from the Palace of Westminster. The ICE was a critical organization, providing a forum for the exchange of knowledge and for learning and debate. Two ICE presidents, Sir Robert Rawlinson (1810–1898) and Sir James Brunlees (1816–1892), designed early iron piers. A Westminster location, in the same neighbourhood as the various organs of the British government, was also immensely valuable. The colossal and transformative engineering schemes of the period, both at home and in varied parts of the empire, ranging from railway lines to urban sanitation schemes and from docks and harbours to water supply projects, were either sponsored or approved by the British state. The Westminster base was useful for political lobbying of

pier proposals, and Acts of Parliament and harbour revision orders associated with individual piers. An indication of the importance of Westminster in pier terms is the 1879 competition for a design for the proposed Skegness Pier. Forty-four entries were received with twenty from Westminster-based engineers.[34]

James Brunlees

Looking at the pier work of James Brunlees and some of his professional relationships reveals the complexity of the interactions that existed between different individual professionals.

Brunlees, although a prolific railway and dock engineer in Britain and abroad, was also involved in pier design over three decades. His first pier (and the second iron pier on the sea coast) at Southport was completed in 1860. The very long pier was piled using the technique of jetting – using water under high pressure to sink piles – invented by Brunlees while he was building railway viaducts across the sands of Morecambe Bay. The contractor for that railway line, Alexander Brogden (1825–1885), assisted Brunlees in the development of the jetting method. A third individual was also involved, with John Dixon (1835–1891), an entrepreneurial contractor, civil engineer and iron merchant, carrying out the Southport Pier piling for Brunlees. So at least three professionals with complementary skills and expertise were involved in inventing, refining and using the jetting technique.

John Dixon was one of the engineers supporting the architect Charles Driver's attempt to resolve the vitriolic professional dispute over cast iron. Dixon also introduced the shock-absorbing wooden dolly used in driving cast-iron piles. He was both designer and contractor for the 1869 Iron Pier at Douglas on the Isle of Man; the pier was relatively short lived, being demolished in 1894.[35] Dixon was famed outside the engineering profession for conceiving and implementing the intrepid scheme to transport an Egyptian obelisk,

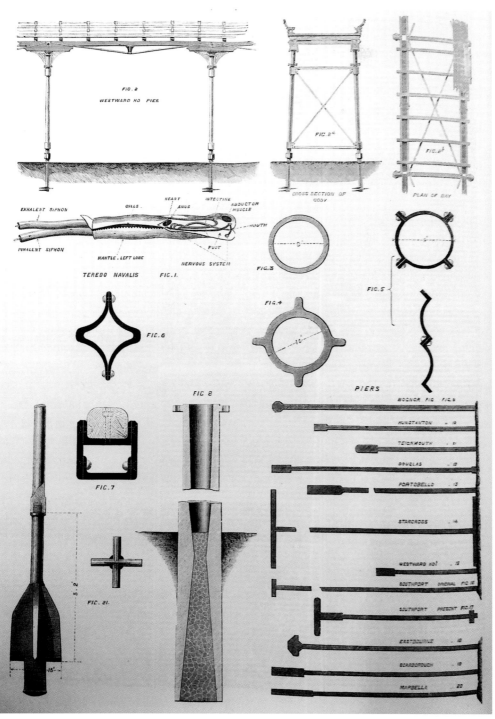

Illustrations for an article on the construction of piers. (*The Engineer*, 12 March 1875)

Cleopatra's Needle, from Alexandria to London in 1877–8. After Southport, Brunlees designed the 1867 Rhyl Pier and two ferry – not promenade – piers for New Brighton and New Ferry, on the River Mersey.[36] The contractor for Rhyl was Robert Laidlaw, the most prolific of the early pier constructors and responsible for building many of Eugenius Birch's piers. As was often the case for the early experimental promenade piers, the designs for Rhyl were technically flawed. By September 1866 almost half of the 3,200ft structure had been completed but, on the 11th of the month, 900ft was destroyed in a storm. Brunlees was replaced and the pier reconstructed 7ft higher and with stronger piling.[37] When the pier eventually opened in 1867 its facilities, perhaps inspired by Birch's West Pier, included a bandstand, shops and even a café.

Brunlees was the lead designer of the 1878 Llandudno Pier (the contractor was Dixon) and a decade later was the engineer for the new Southend Pier. In between he designed the large ornamental casino pier at Nice on the Côte d'Azur, although that pier, the Jetée-Promenade de Nice, was destroyed in a fire shortly before it was completed.

Brunlees' last three piers, beginning with Llandudno, were a collaboration with his son-in-law, Alexander McKerrow (1837–1920), with the assistance of Charles Driver. As we have seen, unusually for the period, Driver was an architect who worked closely with engineers and was a 'recognized authority on ornamental cast ironwork'. It seems that Driver, working with another architect, Charles H. Rew, was responsible for transforming Brunlees' and McKerrow's initial unambitious and rather ordinary Llandudno designs into something far more exotic and 'a combination of Islamic and naturalistic ornament'.[38]

Driver subsequently designed the 1893 pavilion on the head of Brighton's West Pier for Robert William Peregrine Birch (1845–1896). This Birch, unrelated to Eugenius, was a noted sanitary engineer, responsible for the huge extension to the West Pier that helped its metamorphosis into a fully fledged pleasure pier.

The picture emerges of the development and execution of a pier design often being a collaborative affair, with the design engineer working closely with other professionals and the executing contractor. It was the art of the possible, with contractor and engineer responding to local circumstances and conditions, which turned a design on paper into a real structure. Occasionally, as in the case of some of John Dixon's work, contractor and engineer were one and the same person. Occasionally, too, a contractor was unable to execute a design; the failings of the contractors ap-

Damage to Southend Pier caused by the vessel *Marlborough* slicing through a recently renewed section of the pier on 23 November 1908. (Fred Gray collection)

Another Victoria Pier, at Colwyn Bay, 1900s. (Library of Congress, Washington, D.C.)

pointed to construct both Brighton's Chain Pier and Margate Jetty led to the designing engineers completing the projects.

Architects

Exceptionally, some pier engineers – Eugenius Birch is the obvious example – appear to have been multi-talented designers and confident architects of pier buildings. However, we do not usually know whether they drew on other professionals with specific architectural and interior design expertise.

Towards the end of the century, the pattern emerged for professional architects to be employed whenever a new pavilion, theatre or concert hall was required. Although some pier architects worked across the country, many were involved in designs for resorts close to where they worked. To give just one example, the St Annes-based architect, Arnold England (1876–1942) designed the 1910 Floral Hall on his home-town pier. England was also a surveyor and estate agent in the resort and his architectural output was small, although he did prepare an unexecuted 1928 pier proposal for a new pavilion for nearby Lytham Pier.[39]

There was also a cluster of Manchester-based architects working on piers on the Lancashire and North Wales coasts.[40] The large Manchester practice of Mangnall and Littlewood designed the extravagant Oriental 1897 pavilion on the Central Pier at Morecambe and the Victoria Pier and its pavilion at Colwyn Bay, completed in 1900. The firm of Darbyshire and Smith, also based in the city, designed the 1891 Grand Pavilion built at the root end of Rhyl Pier.

The Bolton-based Richard Knill Freeman (1840–1904) was the designer of the grand pavilion at the shore end of Southport Pier opening in 1902, with an auditorium seating 1,500 people. He was the architect of the White Pavilion added at the entrance of Blackpool's Central Pier in 1903. The Manchester-born John Dent Harker (1860–1933) designed the 1893 Grand

The 1893 Grand Pavilion on Victoria Pier, now the South Pier, Blackpool. (Fred Gray collection)

Pavilion on Blackpool's Victoria Pier (now the South Pier) and the 1896 pavilion on Morecambe's West End Pier. In 1899, Harker was the architect of the large entrance building and offices for St Annes Pier; by that date he had decamped from Manchester to live in the resort.[41]

Contractors

The extreme and inhospitable marginal seaside location frequently made building a pier a daunting, challenging and often time-consuming process. Some regionally based contractors built just one or two of the structures, typically at nearby local resorts. But there were also specialist pier builders working nationally. The firm of Robert Laidlaw & Son was particularly dominant in the 1860s, constructing five Birch-designed piers and building Blackpool's second pier and another at Rhyl. At its Glasgow works, the company specialized in making cast-iron pipes for gas, water and steam; constructing the piles and columns required for seaside piers would have been an ideal diversification.

Joseph Emerson Dowson (1824–1868) was another early pier contractor and also inventor of patented wrought-iron piles and columns. He built the Aberystwyth Royal, Bognor and New Brighton piers. His unexpected death led to his work on Eastbourne

Mumbles Pier, mid-1990s, displaying its ornate iron railings. A few years later the fibreglass male gorilla was 'kidnapped' and then returned unharmed although its gender changed. (Fred Gray)

The safety of railings, Mumbles Pier. (Fred Gray)

and Scarborough piers being completed by the firm of Head Wrightson. This Stockton-based company, a large and diverse enterprise, with activities including engineering, iron founding, bridge building and machine making, quickly became an important pier contractor. Head Wrightson continued to build piers into the 1890s, including the new St Leonards Pier early in the decade and the rebuilt and extended Herne Bay Pier, completed in the final year of the century.

Other companies, sometimes working together, came more to the fore toward the end of the golden age of pier building. The Widnes Foundry, another pipe founder, built piers at Morecambe, Mumbles, Colwyn Bay and Great Yarmouth. Alfred Thorne of Westminster was involved in a variety of pier work, building both new structures, for example at Dover, Tenby and, with John Dixon, Shanklin, and constructing extensions and additions to existing piers such as Brighton West, Eastbourne and Llandudno. Another London-based firm, Mayoh and Haley, were both engineers and contractors. The company designed the unexecuted Bexhill Pier of 1898 and, in the first years of the new century, the second Britannia Pier at Great Yarmouth. As contractors, Mayoh and Haley were responsible for building some of the finest late pleasure piers including, for example, Brighton Palace, Morecambe West End, Penarth and Western-super-Mare Grand, the last great pleasure pier, completed in 1904.

MATERIALS

Timber

Designing and building seaside piers depended on the construction materials available. The first seaside piers were built of timber: piles, braces, girders, decking, railings and the first small toll houses and shelters were all made of wood. Although it had iron towers and chains, even the idiosyncratic 1823 suspension pier at Brighton depended on wooden piles. Timber was relatively cheap and readily available. Using it to build a pier required basic technologies and moderately low skills. As a pier engineer commented in 1875: 'this material is more readily procured than others, and the manipulation of it being so much more generally understood and easily accomplished'.[42]

Timber is an elastic material that copes well, except in extreme circumstances, with the power of waves. Most early timber piers were piled into sand or mud. Indeed, the purpose of such piers was to provide a pas-

Renewing the timber landing-stage piles, Worthing Pier, 2014. (Aarsleff Ground Engineering Ltd)

Taking the exceptional opportunity of an extremely low-tide to renew landing-stage piles, Worthing Pier, 2014. (Aarsleff Ground Engineering Ltd)

senger bridge across the intertidal zone that was so difficult to traverse at low water. The resultant structures were usually simple and uncomplicated. Despite the advantages, some major weaknesses were also apparent. They were piled into ground that was liable to shift, change and so threaten the stability of the structure. The strength of timber piles might be rapidly eroded by the actions of marine borers, such as the gribbles and shipworms, literally eating away the substance of the wood. Wooden piers lacked the resilient qualities to withstand savage coastal storms. The underlying difficulty was that timber piers often lacked

permanence: they needed to be continually repaired or remade.

Nevertheless, wood remained an important component of most piers. Used for the walls of buildings, for example, it was cheap, lightweight and reasonably easy to repair. Wood came into its own for pier decking: it was an ideal surface for promenaders to walk on and could be regularly renewed. Landing stages, too, were often made of timber; its elastic qualities, allowing for the safer berthing of vessels, came to be valued over unyielding metal. Timber continues to be used where pier landing stages are actively renewed.

Iron

And then came iron.

Iron at the Victorian seaside

The material was the making of Victorian seaside resorts. Iron rails and iron steam engines carried visitors in increasing numbers to the coast. Iron was used to construct the physical infrastructure of the burgeoning resorts mushrooming around the coastline. It became an indispensable element in creating new promenades, seafront shelters and bandstands, fountains and clock towers, protective railings and the lamp standards used to light seaside parades. Iron was also a principal building material for many new seaside entertainment buildings from the smallest kiosk to the most elegant winter garden or concert hall.

Not simply a functional structural building material, cast iron could be turned to ornamental use, allowing seaside architecture to be embroidered with symbolic decoration.[43] Apart from lamp posts and railings marked by the obligatory resort crest or shield, cast-iron seaside decoration used an eclectic blend of elements, sometimes drawing on standard pattern books from iron foundries, but determinedly ornamental and often Oriental in its design and purpose. Even the smallest iron bracket or stanchion would be

Eastbourne Pier. Identical seat backs were used on the earlier Brighton West Pier. (Fred Gray)

Blackpool Central Pier seat back unrestored, July 2016. (Fred Gray)

Blackpool North Pier, June 2018. The original seats backs were of plain open-lattice work. (Fred Gray)

And restored, July 2016. (Fred Gray)

The maker's mark. 'W. MACFARLANE & Co GLASGOW' on cast-iron seat back, Blackpool North Pier, June 2018. (Fred Gray)

Mumbles Pier, 1993. (Fred Gray)

Unnecessary decoration? A corroding detail on St Annes Pier, June 2018. (Fred Gray)

embellished and enhanced with moulded cast iron. Iron structures and iron decoration clothed the expanding resorts, providing for a large and often diverse holidaymaking population rather than the small and elite clientele of the past.

Iron in piers

From the mid-nineteenth century, iron, seemingly immensely strong and resilient and with other attractive qualities, increasingly became the pier designer's material of choice, used for both structural and ornamental purposes. New iron pleasure piers, so different from the select promenade piers of earlier decades, became a defining feature of the innovative and modern seaside architecture that emerged in the last part of the nineteenth century.[44]

The cast-iron manufacturing process was ideal for the cheap production of identical elements. Prefabrication was key. It might take place many hundreds of miles away from the construction site, at the modern foundries where iron was cast. Prefabricated cast iron – combined with essential wrought-iron elements –

revolutionized the design and making of seaside piers. Designers were freed from many earlier constraints in making a bespoke timber pier. Iron allowed the rapid – in theory at least, if not always in practice – construction of tall and wide load-bearing piers carrying extensive promenade decks and, by the end of the nineteenth century, large entertainment buildings. Limited only by the characteristics of the specific site, designers working in iron had far more control over all the dimensions and the shape of a pier.

Once the moulds were made, piles, columns, railings, seat backs and associated pier paraphernalia could all be endlessly replicated as and when required. The catalogues of manufacturers, such as the famous Walter Macfarlane & Company, based at the Saracen Foundry, Glasgow, illustrate the diversity of prefabricated cast-iron structures and the richness of decoration. A pier designer might choose components from an iron manufacturer's catalogue or work with an iron founder on bespoke designs. Once an element had proved its value on one pier, it might be duplicated and used again on another. Even today, there is a delight to be had in spotting identical cast-iron elements on surviving seaside piers. The ease of decorating cast iron meant that the usually hidden-from-view columns used in a pier's substructure might still display ornamental capitals and other decoration.

Substructure

A pier's piles and columns were the essential element on which everything else depended. The technology for making pipes, whether for gas, water or steam, was applied to produce the hollow, cylindrical columns used in the substructure of iron piers. These components were economical to produce and immensely strong in bearing compressive loads. Another advantage was that cast-iron cylinders provided a minimal resistance to the water and waves, which flowed around rather than smashed against a pier's columns.

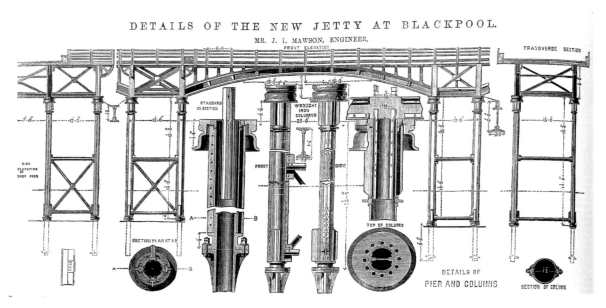

DETAILS OF THE NEW JETTY AT BLACKPOOL.

MR. J. I. MAWSON, ENGINEER.

Engineering details of Blackpool Jetty. (*The Engineer*, 23 April 1869)

Both cast and wrought iron used together were critical in the construction of pier substructures. The two types of iron displayed different qualities, strengths, advantages and disadvantages. Iron that is cast has been melted, poured into moulds and allowed to solidify. Iron that is wrought has been heated and then worked with tools into required shapes. While structural cast iron has great compressive strength, it has relatively weak tensile strength. It is brittle. Unlike wrought iron, it will not readily bend or stretch. Struck in the wrong place, say along the length of the cylinder, it may fracture. In contrast, wrought iron will not take a structural load but it will flex and accept movement. It is malleable. In building a pier's substructure, the load or weight-bearing elements were usually cast iron, but malleable wrought iron was typically used to tie, brace and fasten the cast-iron substructure, securing it together and providing overall stability, and for lattice-girder frameworks carrying decking.

Steel and concrete

Although iron was the pre-eminent pier-building material of the Victorian period, its dominance was not sustained. It was first challenged and then surpassed by steel and concrete. During the twentieth century these two materials, either individually or combined, became dominant for making and remaking piers and, indeed, the built fabric of seaside resorts more generally.

The emergence of steel and concrete in pier building paralleled the use of the two materials in many other types of construction. Their growing importance was partly a result of technical invention and change. The rolled steel section became the most used structural component in civil engineering projects by the 1890s. Steel was cheaper and easier to mass produce than iron and its greater strength and load-bearing capacities meant that less of the material was required. Structures could be lighter and therefore more efficient and less costly to produce, both ideal qualities for sea-

The Electric Theatre, American Palace Pier, St Leonards-on-Sea, c.1909. (Steve Peak collection)

side piers. At much the same period cement, in particular Portland cement, underwent a similar process of development. The two materials were combined to produce reinforced concrete, the archetypal twentieth-century construction material.

Pier designers began to grasp the potential of the two materials. Small amounts of concrete had been used in iron piers from early on. Attempting to improve their strength and stability, Birch filled the hollow iron columns of his 1863 Blackpool pier with concrete.[45] Reinforced concrete was also used to encase damaged iron piles. From the 1880s steel, too, began to be used on pleasure piers. For example, and although much cast iron was to be used in its making, the 1888 plans for St Leonards Pier specified that the main joists were made of rolled steel. Four years later, in 1892, steel was used for the deck beams of Blackpool's new Victoria Pier. It was subsequently used on the Palace Pier at Brighton and for the frame of the 1903 pavilion of the Wellington Pier at Great Yarmouth. Because of the cost and weight advantages, steel-framed pier buildings quickly became standard.

Despite its benefits, steel suffered a major disadvantage: the marine environment exposed the material to significant corrosion. In an article published in 1934, Noel Ridley, a long-established pier engineer, argued that some wrought-iron joists and girders on Brighton's West Pier were still in good condition over

Under the pier, Walton-on-the-Naze, June 2019. The remains of the original timber piles nest amid the later concrete structure. (Fred Gray)

Nothing lasts forever. Although a resilient material, reinforced concrete is subject to decay, aggravated by the coastal location. Walton-on-the-Naze, June 2019. (Fred Gray)

sixty-seven years after the pier had opened; in contrast similar components in steel had to be replaced after only twenty or thirty years.[46] Indeed, some of the West Pier's original cast-iron elements remained in a salvageable condition in the year 2000.[47]

Pier builders optimistically hoped and anticipated that some new technical or material development would provide a miraculous solution. For example, in 1927 the substructure at the head of Boscombe Pier was reconstructed using high alumina cement (HAC), a product developed two years earlier by the cement producer Lafarge. Over the following half a century HAC was widely used in structural concrete for piers, and in other marine applications. Claimed to be unaffected by seawater, it was promoted 'for important work where great strength, rapidly attained, is essential'.[48] The wonder material – 'hardens in a day – lasts for ever' – promised a revolution in construction and maintenance. The hopes eroded away as, if exposed to water for lengthy periods, the crystalline structure of the cement was prone to change and the concrete weakened.

Concrete and reinforced concrete were both increasingly used on piers, particularly for substructures

and decks. An early example of the use of concrete is the pier-like structure at Burnham-on-Sea constructed in 1911: the concrete piles made using Cornish granite chippings proved extremely resilient and, remarkably, survive today. On the south coast at Weymouth, the two new 1930s piers were made with pre-cast concrete piles. During the inter-war and early post-war period concrete was used extensively to remake the old wooden piers at Felixstowe, Walton-on-the-Naze and Clacton-on-Sea – each a short pleasure steamer trip from the other. The pier at Felixstowe was shortened after the war and reconstructed with concrete piles and decking. The material was also used widely at Walton to change the pier from a wooden into a concrete structure, although the neck of the pier stretching into the sea continued to be decked in timber. During the inter-war period, and while the pier head was left relatively unchanged, a huge amount of reinforced concrete was used to transform Clacton Pier into a radically different enterprise.

Except where the substructure was enormously strong (as it was at Clacton), the heaviness of concrete precluded its extensive use for pier buildings, and pier architects searched for lighter-weight solutions. Building frames were typically of prefabricated and sometimes pressed steel components. As for walls, there were modern alternatives that could be fireproofed – a necessity given the predilection for pier buildings to burn down. They included hollow concrete blocks, plywood, fibre board and, storing up problems for the future, asbestos sheeting. Sometimes however, designers resorted to tradition, employing timber cladding for a pier building's walls.

EXPERIMENTAL TECHNIQUES

Particularly during the innovative and experimental early phase of iron pier construction, designing and

The busy pier head at Ryde, the key link between the Isle of Wight and the mainland, in c.1910.
(Geoffrey Mead collection)

erecting a seaside pier was an uncertain engineering enterprise. Issues included how to securely fix a pier to the seabed, ensure it was of sufficient height to remain unharmed in rough seas, and guarantee the stability of the structure. The iron pier engineers, grappling with such questions, developed a variety of approaches and answers. Often, however, our pier-building hero, Eugenius Birch, was at the experimental forefront.

Fixing

An enduring issue for pier designers has been how to fix or found a pier securely to the seabed, foreshore and beach. The piles attaching a pier to the strata beneath it also need to carry the remaining substructure and superstructure soaring above. Piles can be banged (driven), screwed, dug or sunk, the technique chosen according to the material forming the seabed and intertidal zone. Where possible, piling occurred when the littoral zone was uncovered at low tide. In other circumstances, piles were inserted from a barge or raft, or from a platform extending from the end of the pier as the construction progressed away from land.

Banging

Inserting a pile by driving or hammering is the most obvious and the simplest piling technique. It was used in the construction of early timber piers and is used

today for modern piling with hollow steel tubes inserted using pile drivers. Driving cast-iron piles risked fracturing them, which would result in the expenditure of time and resources to rectify the problem. The solution was provided by the engineer John Dixon, who was behind the use of the shock-absorbing wooden dolly. The dolly was placed above the top of the pile, fitted into the interior and rested on a 'ring of indiarubber [sic], or some other yielding compressible substance … to deaden the concussion. By this means it is found that these piles may be safely and successfully driven to a great depth.'[49]

Extending the railway on to Ryde Pier required a heavy-duty piling solution. The two-track railway jetty constructed in 1879–80 was piled using both wrought-iron 'Hughes piles' filled with concrete and cast-iron screw piles, 'driven up to 50ft penetration through quicksand'.[50]

Screwing

The most famous piling technique for seaside piers was the use of the screw or helical pile, having the form of a helix or spiral at its business end. The inventor was the remarkable Alexander Mitchell (1780–1868) who was totally blind from the age of twenty-three. In 1833 Mitchell took out one of the earliest civil engineering patents, for a method of screw piling to be used in moorings and foundations. The engineer became

'Madras Pier, on screw-piles, the invention of Mr Alexander Mitchell, C. E.' (*The Illustrated London News*, 28 February 1863)

Although cast iron was usually used for piling, Birch sometimes used wrought-iron piles with cast-iron columns attached above. This pile was recovered from Brighton West Pier, c.2000. (Fred Gray)

known by the nickname of 'Screw-Pile Mitchell'. With the exception of solid rock, his piles could be used in most types of seabed. Mitchell's initial use of the technique was to provide the foundations for two lighthouses, one on the treacherous Maplin Sands and another in Morecambe Bay.[51] In 1847 Mitchell extended an existing pier at Courtown, Wexford, Ireland, using screw piles. Then, in 1859, he designed the substantial commercial pier at Madras in India using solid wrought iron piles.[52]

Although Mitchell was the inventor, the major innovator in the use of screw piles for seaside piers was Eugenius Birch. He first used them in the construction of the 1855 Margate Jetty. The author of an article in the professional journal, *The Engineer*, explained how by the mid-1870s 'perhaps the most ordinary construction of modern piers consists of circular hollow

A rare photograph of screw-piling underway, location unknown but perhaps St Leonards Palace Pier. (Steve Peak collection)

cast iron screw piles, supporting cast iron hollow cylindrical columns, braced diagonally or otherwise by wrought iron bracing, in compression or in tension; these in turn sustain a timber superstructure.'[53]

Although Birch is renowned for his use of screw piling, he did not use a single standard pattern of pile; instead the piles and techniques varied according to local circumstances. The screw piles providing the foundations for the head of Margate Jetty were of solid wrought iron, 5.5in in diameter and 20ft long with cast-iron screws 30in in diameter. For Brighton's West Pier two types of pile were employed. Some were similar to the ones used at Margate but hollow cast-iron piles with integral moulded screws were also used; both types of pile were recovered from the pier in the 1990s. Intriguingly, for his pier at Scarborough, Birch resorted to wooden screw piles fixed to cast-iron columns.[54] At Aberystwyth and Eastbourne screw piles seem to have been rejected in favour of 'rock sockets'. In the Welsh resort the piles were inserted into concrete bases embedded into the seabed while, for the Sussex pier, the piles 'were to sit in special cups in the rock bed to enable movement in bad weather'.[55]

It wasn't until the first piles were fixed that the ease of construction became known. There were often delays in the completion of Birch's piers, with opening ceremonies frequently taking place months or even years before the structure was finally finished. According to Birch, the building of Hastings Pier had been held up for more than a year because of 'the extraordinary nature of the foundation, and the state of the elements'. The unanticipated problem was the difficulty of screw piling into the clay at the seaward end of the pier because the material included the submerged remains of huge tree trunks from an ancient forest. In consequence, the builders were 'obliged to use a double screw, 2ft 6in in diameter, to secure a hold'.[56]

Although screw piling was subsequently largely vanquished by improvements and cost efficiencies in driving steel piles, it is still retained as a technique for occasional use. For example, in the early twenty-first century, screw piles were employed in the delicate refurbishment of part of the head of Brighton's Palace Pier.[57]

Digging

In some circumstances neither driving nor screwing was possible and instead the pile was inserted into a previously excavated hole in the seabed. Although this sounds simple, on occasion the process required immense ingenuity. Constructing the pier at the small north Devon resort of Westward Ho! in the early 1870s precluded the use of normal piling techniques because of the hard and rocky ground conditions and the seabed over which large boulders '... are constantly rolled about in all directions by the actions of the waves, which in the calmest weather are almost constantly in motion, and assume frequently gigantic proportions during stormy weather, the rollers coming in with great force from the Atlantic.'[58]

Instead an iron cylinder made in halves was lowered over the site to be piled and a jumper tool almost 5ft long was repeatedly banged into the ground, using winch, pulleys and a portable steam engine. The process excavated a foundation hole into which a pile was lowered and fixed into place by a diver, working in between 6 and 30ft of water, using wrought-iron wedges and concrete.

The engineer describing the Westward Ho! pier in 1875 thought the pier demonstrated how at times it was necessary 'to bring into subjugation the forces of nature, and even to say to the sea, "Thus far shalt thou come and no farther"'. Following repeated storm damage and the 'great force from the Atlantic', the pier was closed in February 1880 and was soon demolished. Nature was not subjugated! Close to the shore the ruined remains of more than a dozen piles are still to be seen at low tide.

Sinking

Another much commented on although little used piling method was jetting. Screwing or driving piles was not particularly suitable for Southport's soft and deep sands and, on the pier's 1860 opening, commentators stressed how the 'bearing-piles were sunk to the necessary depth by a peculiar process' known as jetting. The bottom of the pile was covered with a disc with a small hole in the centre. Gas tubing was then passed down the pile, through the hole, and into the sand. Water under pressure was jetted through the tubing and 'forced the sand from under the disc, thereby enabling the pile to sink by its own weight.'[59] The naturally compacting sand effortlessly filled voids created by the jetting process, leaving the pile securely positioned. The method was speedy, and a pile could be sunk to the required 15 or 20ft at the rate of 1ft every one or two minutes.[60]

Jetting was used on one other occasion, for the piling of Blackpool's South (Victoria) Pier, the resort's third pier that opened in 1893. A steam fire pump was used in the process, with each pile sunk in twenty minutes.[61] Jetting may also be used to supplement and enhance normal driving techniques.[62]

Height

A fundamental test of the quality of a pier design was storm. Surprisingly, given Eugenius Birch's undoubted talents, his piers were sometimes insufficiently high to cope with the fiercest storms and highest waves.

Margate Jetty was liable to damage in rough seas. During the construction of the first Blackpool pier 'a fearful storm' revealed that the design was too low. The 'sometimes angry … waves of the Irish Sea' washed over the deck that had been completed.[63] The height of the pier needed to be increased by 3ft, with the cost of erecting the structure rising from £1,600 to £13,100.

The lessons of Birch's first two piers being 'erected at too low a level' went unheeded. Stormy seas washed over the shore end of Eastbourne Pier, weakening the structure and necessitating remedial work. Then, five years after completion, on 1 January 1877, a violent storm destroyed the root end of the pier. Massive waves rushing up the shallowing seabed and on to the beach ripped the pier apart. The landward end of the pier was subsequently rebuilt to a higher level and the problem solved. Scarborough Pier, another Birch structure, was repeatedly and often seriously damaged in violent North Sea storms. Plans were made to ameliorate the storm damage issue by increasing the height

Margate Jetty's devastated decking, the morning following the storm of 29 November 1897. (Geoffrey Mead collection)

THE PIER; NORTH BAY.   SCARBOROUGH.

The pier at Scarborough. It was finally destroyed by storm in 1905. (Fred Gray collection)

of the pier by 6–8ft. But before they could be implemented the combination of a fierce gale and exceptionally high tide destroyed the pier in early January 1905. The isolated pier-head pavilion lingered forlornly on for a few months longer.[64]

Stability

Another structural issue emerged on the Brighton West Pier. Despite claims made on the pier's opening that the engineering provided for the 'greatest amount of stiffness', one potentially ruinous flaw in the early years was the instability of the structure. In early August 1868, for example, panic broke out among the crowd on the pier head who feared the structure would collapse. One letter writer to *The Times* explained there were:

> … *several thousand present at the head of the pier, many seated round, while others were standing and promenading during the performance of a band. There was a sudden commotion among the company, who endeavoured en masse to make for the shore end of the pier, ladies fainting and children screaming, some trodden upon, many of whom, I fear, must have been seriously injured. The cry having been raised that the pier was giving way was the cause of what might have proved a great calamity.*[65]

There were various ideas about the cause of the problem. Perhaps a squall had lifted the pier's planking. Or the commander of a steamer, using the pier as a spring to turn the vessel, caused the pier to oscillate when the hawser between ship and pier was suddenly released. Possibly the large crowd on the pier head began to march in time to the band music, leading to an undulating ripple over the decking. Conceivably, it was simply a case of a sudden moment of mass hysteria.

Whatever the explanation, Birch argued 'the construction of the pier is not upon the principle of absolute rigidity, but provides for deflection, as essential to the security of such a structure'.[66] In illustrating the weaknesses of devising a new architecture and built form using cutting-edge technology, the incident threatened to undermine public confidence in the pier as a place of pleasure and business. Remedial work to rectify the problem occurred over the following two decades.

TIME AND TIDE

Piers proved to be flexible and evolving architectural and engineering forms. In the most commercially successful resorts, piers were repeatedly extended and enlarged. Destruction by fire or storm, both persistent threats, would sometimes be seized as an opportunity to rebuild in a contemporary style or for a contemporary purpose. As the demands of seaside visitors changed, so existing pier buildings were put to new uses. What was originally designed as a winter garden for musical entertainments might become a rifle range or roller-skating rink, and then be transformed into an amusement arcade. Each transition might also involve an architectural and interior design makeover or, at least, a new coat of paint. Ornate Victorian decoration might be hidden away behind a 1950s Modernist façade. If existing buildings could not be adapted or

Eastbourne Pier shortly after the 1 January 1877 gale with salvaged timber and cast-iron columns stacked next to the surviving entrance booths and gates.
(Fred Gray collection)

Eastbourne Pier showing the pair of original entrance booths, the landward section of the pier rebuilt at a higher level and the plain pier-head pavilion added in 1888. (Rijksmuseum, Amsterdam)

The original entrance buildings were replaced by three Gothic-styled kiosks in 1912. The sender of this card, posted on 4 August 1916, wrote that they were 'having a lovely time but it's awfully hot. My neck and face are getting blistered and you can guess it hurts.'
(Fred Gray collection)

The end of an era. Preparations underway for the demolition of the Modernist entrance.
(Fred Gray collection)

The architectural pretence of the 1991 entrance building on a wet and windy morning in early November 2018. (Fred Gray)

were deemed old fashioned, they could be swept away and replaced with new structures designed for modern amusements and pleasures. Ironically, late on in the twentieth century, some streamlined Modernist structures fell from favour and were removed; the replacement new buildings were sometimes designed as a nostalgic Victorian pastiche.

The brilliance of a new pier is soon tarnished by natural processes. Both in the past and today two fundamental issues are the rusting of iron (and the iron alloy, steel) and the decay of wood.

Iron seaside piers are in preposterously adverse locations. Iron exposed to oxygen and water will, over time, be turned into rust. Piers at the seaside are subjected to water and air in bucket-loads. But the corrosive perils are massively increased when salt is present. The salt in seawater, and carried by the spray and spume whipped up by wind and waves, intensifies the rusting process. Rust, an iron oxide, will eventually crumble and then disintegrate. Rusting may lead to structural failure and, in extreme situations, the partial collapse of a pier. The iron and steel reinforcing the concrete used in a pier's structure will also be open to rust attack and destruction. The irony, of course, is that the iron oxide extracted from iron ore is used to make iron and steel which, as the rusting process takes place,

The archaeology of the stranded 1891 landing stage, St Annes Pier, June 2018. The channel to the end of the pier silted up and the last steamer called in 1910. (Fred Gray)

The return to nature: St Annes Pier, June 2018. (Fred Gray)

The astonishing sculptural art of the remains of St Annes Pier landing stage, June 2018. (Fred Gray)

turns back to iron oxide.

Used on a seaside pier, wood, too, is an unstable material. Whether under or above the sea, a process of degradation begins as soon as wood is installed as part of a pier. An additional threat to timber in seawater is the destructive action of marine borers such as ship-worms and gribbles. If left to natural forces, wood, like iron, will disintegrate and eventually disappear.

Together with the hostile seaside environment, the attendant perils of coastal storms and rough seas compound the hazards. Storms, sometimes aided and abetted by a drifting vessel transformed into a battering ram, have been involved in the destruction of the majority of Britain's lost seaside piers. But many other destructive processes are at work. In the adverse littoral zone traversed by piers, sand, pebbles and stones are thrown around by the swirling sea, acting to abrade wooden or metal piles. If the seabed is eroded away, piles may be left hanging useless, suspended in water. Temperature fluctuations lead to thermal movement and fractures caused by the repeated expansion and contraction of component parts. Columns may split, crack or break. The load-bearing capacity of piles and columns may weaken. The critical ties, trusses and braces holding a pier together may fail. No longer sup-

A rare example of snow and ice impacting on south coast piers: Brighton, February 2009. (Fred Gray)

ported by the substructure, buildings on the deck of a pier may tumble into the sea.

Except in the most extreme circumstances, many of these issues can be addressed through technical engineering interventions. For example, piles are particularly prone to damage and fracturing where they enter the seabed. A standard solution, to be seen today on many piers at low tide, is to encase metal piles at their most susceptible and at-risk points with a protective sheaf, perhaps made of concrete or steel.

The patchwork of repairs and renewals to the substructure of Blackpool Central Pier, June 2009. (Fred Gray)

A small boy is fascinated by the machinery of pier maintenance: Paignton, summer 2008. (Fred Gray)

Although the ideal response to the challenges posed by time and tide is a regular programme of proactive maintenance, repair and renewal, after-the-event remedial work is also frequently required. Modern engineering materials, techniques and equipment may ease some of the difficulties in maintaining piers, although the enduring issues remain of working on precarious structures in a hazardous and marginal environment.

There are significant new challenges too. As they age, historic pier structures accumulate new and more acute and extensive maintenance and renewal needs. Addressing such issues may require financial resources far in excess of standard maintenance budgets.

Global warming, and its attendant threats including rising sea levels and the increasing height of storm waves, expose piers to additional dangers.

Contemporary seaside piers are also jeopardized by accelerated low water corrosion (ALWC), an alarmingly aggressive and localized form of steel decay occurring in the low water zone of tidal waters.[67] Although first identified in coastal metal structures around the UK in the 1960s, ALWC was not widely reported until the 1980s. It is now viewed as a major risk to steel structures such as pier piling. Because of the inaccessible locations where it often occurs, it may be difficult to identify. ALWC is evidenced by a bright orange bloom or a black deposit and significant and rapid metal loss. This form of corrosion seems particularly prevalent in polluted waters and is 'microbially induced': it is the result of bacterial activity. The chilling headline conclusion is that steel piers are threatened by being eaten by microscopic organisms in much the same manner that timber piers are at risk of marine borers.

If for whatever reason they are left unmaintained, seaside piers will eventually deconstruct through natural processes. A ruined pier is in a state of active collapse, although the process of disintegration is typically uneven: extended periods of minutely slow decay interrupted by sudden traumatic failure. The tragic sight of closed piers, unattended for years, reveal the outcomes of processes of decay and disintegration. Once proud piers are reclaimed by nature.

Accelerated low water corrosion may attack even the most well-maintained pier, July 2019. (Fred Gray)

Chapter Three

AGREEABLE PROMENADES AND PIONEER PIERS

PROMENADES ON THE SEA

As older coastal towns evolved into resorts, existing structures designed for functional maritime purposes gained a new role as places to walk over the sea for pleasure. Harbour arms and stone piers, providing a sheltered haven for ships, sailors, fishermen and associated maritime activities, also offered possibilities for the romantic contemplation of nature by like-minded individuals. Wooden landing stages and jetties, primarily intended to facilitate movement of people and goods between ship and shore, similarly presented opportunities for promenading by fashionable visitors. We can trace the emergence, from these beginnings, of seaside piers proper.

Lyme Regis and the Cobb

In *Persuasion*, written in 1815–16, Jane Austen describes the 'old wonders and new improvements' of the Cobb, an ancient stone breakwater forming the harbour wall at Lyme Regis, Dorset.[68] The stone pier, of indeterminate age but with origins dating back to at least 1300, formed one of the earliest artificial harbours in Britain. Today it is the oldest surviving breakwater in Britain. Because of the hostile marine environment,

the Cobb was repeatedly severely damaged and sometimes destroyed by storms. However, the structure was essential for the town to function as a maritime centre, and this meant it was usually speedily remade and sometimes reshaped. It was originally made of local materials including timber and Greensand boulders found on the beach, called 'Cowstones'. From the 1780s, however, the Cobb was 'a rigid, heavy and carefully shaped structure, designed by military engineers and built with precision by masons from massive skins of costly imported dry-bedded Portland Stone tied with oak dovetails and iron cramps.'[69]

By the early nineteenth century, as the town was developing as a resort, the remade Cobb had become a genteel promenade. It was one of the chief 'charms' to be enjoyed by visitors. Austen makes use of the Cobb for a critical turning point in her story, the first in a rich literary tradition using piers as sites of leisure and happiness but also unforeseen danger or denouement. One of the novel's characters, Louisa Musgrove, jumping down 'from the high part of the new Cobb', misses the safe hands of Captain Wentworth, to fall and be 'taken up lifeless'.[70]

A history of Lyme Regis, published in 1823, confirmed the romantic appeal and natural attractions of

Left: John Butcher's mid-1790s portrayal of Great Yarmouth's Jetty. (Copyright Norfolk Museums Service, Great Yarmouth Museums.)

the stone pier for leisured visitors to the town. Accordingly, the Cobb:

… furnishes an agreeable promenade in serene weather: in summer evenings it is much frequented by company for the sake of the prospect and coolness of the air. By moonlight the gentle heaving of the waves, the passing of boats, and the calm and pleasing, though sometimes melancholy, reflections, endured by a survey of the wide expanse of water, render it one of the most delightful spots.[71]

An enduring promenade: the sinuous form of the Cobb, Lyme Regis, August 2019. (Fred Gray)

Promenading on Ramsgate Harbour, mid-nineteenth century. Engraving. (Fred Gray collection)

Evidence from other early seaside resorts, including Ramsgate, Scarborough and Weymouth, confirms the stone harbours and piers, designed for other purposes, being used for promenading by leisured seaside visitors. Walking out along a stone pier must have added a frisson of excitement to the almost mandatory resort activity of promenading. Apart from the constant attraction of meeting with one's social equals or betters the experience of the sublime was surely more intense so close to the unfathomable sea. The sense of danger must have been heightened by the absence of a safety wall on some of these stone structures. A violent gust of wind or a rogue wave threatened to sweep the unwary to an untimely and unromantic end.

Promenading on Whitby's West Pier, February 2019. Repeatedly rebuilt and improved, the two piers guarding the entrance to the harbour have been an enduring feature of Whitby. (Fred Gray)

Margate's stone pier

As Austen was penning her fiction, at Margate a new stone 'pier' was being built to replace an earlier piled timber structure destroyed in an 1808 storm, which also wrecked part of the town. This structure was designed by noted engineers Josias Jessop (1781–1826) and John Rennie (1761–1821), the namesake and father of another distinguished marine engineer. The new solid pier formed a harbour arm accommodating both maritime and promenade functions and was designed partly as a defence against the sea again inundating parts of Margate.

Construction began in 1810 and was completed in 1815. Although appearing to gently curve away from the coast, the structure was made of five straight sections, each at a slight angle to the adjacent ones. Jessop and Rennie used timber piles as a foundation, although the principal construction materials were white sandstone blocks quarried from Aislaby near Whitby in Yorkshire. While this tough erosion-resistant stone formed the exterior of the structure, the interior was infilled with chalk blocks and an aggregate of chalk rubble and gravel.[72]

The chief attraction for leisured visitors was the parade, designed by a local builder, Thomas Edmunds, making use of the wide protective sea wall, high above the working quay. The safety of visitors was ensured by iron railings on the inner, harbour side of the pier and a 'handsome stone parapet' on the sea side. There was a gallery for a band to play and the parade was subsequently lit by a row of iron lamp standards. The result was a 'marine walk … unrivalled by any in the kingdom'.[73] An early instance of promenading over the sea involving a monetary transaction; on payment of a penny entrance toll visitors to Margate pier had access to a private, exclusive and separate space. Not everyone

The exclusive promenade, Margate Pier c.1867. (Fred Gray collection)

Margate Pier left high if not dry, March 2009. (Fred Gray)

was happy, and the introduction of the admission fee reportedly led to riots.[74] Money and architecture were means of separating the unwanted, including those people working in the harbour, from polite society.

In contrast to the necessarily strong, stone harbour walls and breakwaters designed to rebuff the sea and provide sheltered water, the principal function of landing stages and jetties was to get people and goods between ship and shore safely, easily and reasonably cheaply. Constructed of wood and built speedily at relatively low cost, the design challenge was to provide a bridge into deeper water where vessels could moor and people embark or disembark simply by walking along a wooden walkway.

The Jetty at Great Yarmouth

Although not primarily designed for passenger traffic, some earlier wooden structures had acquired a promenade role during the eighteenth century. The Jetty at Great Yarmouth was originally built in 1560 to facili-

tate fishing and mercantile trade. Frequently damaged or destroyed by storm, on each occasion it was remade. During the Napoleonic Wars the structure was used in victualling the naval fleets anchored in the sheltered Yarmouth Roads and Lord Nelson, the great naval hero, alighted on the Jetty on 1 July 1801 when returning from the English victory at the Battle of Copenhagen. Located adjacent to the town's resort facilities, including hot and cold baths, hotel, lodging house and a ballroom, by the end of the eighteenth century the Jetty had also emerged as a place of promenade for visitors to the town.

A painting by John Butcher (c. 1736–1803), presented to Great Yarmouth Corporation in 1796, portrays the Jetty being used to transport people and goods in small boats between the land and ships offshore. Despite the absence of protective railings along its sides, Butcher's painting also shows the Jetty thronged with promenaders in Regency dress. There were tensions in the contrasting roles performed by the

Jetty and the diversity of its users, ranging from seamen and fishermen to members of respectable society. Early in the new century a guide to the town described how the pier, at that stage 330ft long, was not quite as respectable as polite company might wish. The Jetty presented 'a lively and interesting scene, and was it under proper regulations, no place would be better calculated to afford a relaxation from the severe application of the mind; and the heat of the summer softened by the refreshing breezes from the sea.'[75]

Following extensive storm damage in 1805 the Jetty was rebuilt. The new structure, completed in January 1809, extended 450ft into the sea and was 24ft wide. The deck of oak planks rested on wooden piles driven into the seabed and in turn was 'guarded on both sides by a strong railing nearly breast high.' The railings were an indication that promenading on the Jetty was growing in significance and needed to be catered for in the design of the structure. An 1817 guide to Great Yarmouth described how:

Its length, breadth, and security, the constant change of objects moving in the ocean within a few yards of its end, and the cool refreshing sea breezes which are equally enjoyed here as on the bosom of the ocean, conspire to render the Jetty of Great Yarmouth a most interesting walk, and entitle it to the honour of being the first structure of the kind in the kingdom.[76]

Great Yarmouth's 'free pier', the Jetty, c.1890s. (Library of Congress, Washington, D.C.)

A decade after its opening it had become 'a very agreeable promenade for the ladies and gentlemen visitors, of all ages, who assemble here in gay crowds, almost every fine summer's evening, to inhale the refreshing sea breezes.[77]

The Jetty was lengthened twice more during the nineteenth century. In the 1890s the resort's borough surveyor, J. W. Cockrill, proposed ambitious plans to transform the Jetty into a pleasure pier with a new pier head, including a large entertainment pavilion.[78] The varied Oriental designs, some with strong Islamic motifs, were all unrealized. In contrast to Great Yarmouth's remade toll-charging piers to the north and south, the Jetty remained essentially undeveloped. An Edwardian guidebook described it as 'a free pier' for holidaymakers to stroll above the waves and use the 'comfortable seats and shelters'.[79] Further changes included a glass roof added in the 1920s and the timber structure replaced by a steel one in the early 1960s. In 2012, however, and after years of decay and the inability of the local authority owners to fund a restoration, the Jetty was demolished. Subsequently the site and long history of the Jetty – arguably the world's first promenade pier in function if not name – was marked by a seafront plaque. A few of the Jetty's salvaged timber beams were reused in a seafront landscaping project.

Jarvis's Landing Place, Margate

Another seaside town, Margate – again – and another jetty. It was quickly evident that the 1815 stone Margate Pier was an inadequate means of ensuring the necessary access by sea to the resort. Passenger vessels could only use the pier when the tide was reasonably high. The solution was another structure, made of oak and 1,120ft in length, reaching further into the sea. In 1824 Jarvis's Landing Place was built close to the root end of the stone pier. Designed by Dr Jarvis, chairman of the Pier and Harbour Company, the low-lying wooden jetty's primary purpose was to allow passengers 'to reach the shore when the water is too low for vessels to enter the harbour'.[80]

Despite the intent, an 1841 guide described how it 'is deservedly considered one of the most inviting marine walks which fancy can imagine, or experience realize'.[81] The promenade, though, only functioned between low and mid-tide, as the structure was completely submerged at high water. Visitors were often stranded on the slightly higher pier head, leading either to alarm from those in danger of an unwanted sea bath or hilarity from those observing the scene from dry land and the marooned frequently being rescued on the backs of local sailors.[82]

RYDE AND THE FIRST SEASIDE PIER

Unusually, promenaders were able to use Jarvis's Landing Place free of charge. The promoters of such ventures elsewhere increasingly saw promenading as a useful subsidiary income-generating function. An early and prime example of these new dual-purpose piers was the 1814 pier at Ryde on the Isle of Wight. Ryde Pier is nowadays widely acknowledged as being the UK's first seaside pier,[83] although more accurately, 'it was the first major piled passenger pier.'[84]

Because of its closeness to Portsmouth, Ryde had long served as an entry point to the Isle of Wight. The major difficulty, however, was that at low tide passengers needed to cross a broad barrier of mud when journeying between terra firma and vessels anchored half a mile distant. People were typically moved between ship and shore by rowing boat or by horse and cart. A pier was an obvious and necessary solution to speed up the process of passengers travelling to and from the island.

The promoters of the venture turned to the engineer, John Rennie the elder, for advice. John Kent, a builder, architect and surveyor from nearby Southampton, was then commissioned to design a pier to traverse the mudflats revealed at low tide. The pier was largely constructed of timber, although a short section close to the shore was carried on brick arches. The still unfinished pier was opened on 26 July 1814. On completion in 1816, the pier's length was 1,740ft and the width just 12ft, except where there were wider passing places for carriages. Piles with a length of 24ft, far longer than was at first thought to be necessary, were driven deep into the seabed at the seaward end of the structure.

A decade later, a guide named *The Beauties of the Isle of Wight* proclaimed the romantic rather than functional appeal of the new pier:

One of the most attractive objects of a public kind is the pier. This ornament to the town forms a beautiful marine promenade … There is an iron railing on each side, which extends the length of the pier; and seats are placed in different parts for the accommodation of visitors. The upper part of this fine promenade is finished in a greater style of elegance than the lower … The descent to the water is very easy. A small flight of steps conducts to a lower basement, from which an arm stretching out on each side affords a very convenient landing. Those who delight to inhale the sea breeze will find this a most propitious spot in the neighbourhood. Here, hour after hour may be passed, without being sensible how rapidly time is gliding away. The vivacity which characterizes the company – the ocean spreading its fine blue waves in the front; the fishermen at the foot of the pier, occupied in their marine employments; the vessels sailing at short distances; the boats moving in each direction calmly and swiftly over the bosom of the deep – form a very beautiful scene.[85]

Even a severely abridged version of a long and intricate story reveals that, such was the success of the pier, it

The piers of Ryde in 1898. (Rijksmuseum, Amsterdam)

Ryde Pier in the late nineteenth century, although before the 1895 pier-head pavilion was constructed. (Rijksmuseum, Amsterdam)

was repeatedly developed further over the following decades. In 1833 it was lengthened to 2,250ft, thereby allowing it to be used by vessels whatever the tidal conditions. In the early 1860s a second pier, with a horse-drawn tramway, was constructed alongside the existing structure. By then fifty vessels a day were docking there. A third pier opened in 1880, again running parallel to the earlier structures and this time carrying a railway. The pier head, meanwhile, accrued not only improved landing stages and other facilities for the ships and passengers using it, but also entertainment buildings. In 1895 a pavilion opened designed by Richard St George Moore, the civil engineer responsible for a number of other piers including Brighton's Palace Pier and St Leonards Pier. The domed building included a concert hall seating 700 people, reading and refreshments rooms and, unusual for the time, a sun lounge. There was extensive work, carried out for well over a decade, replacing the old wooden piles with ones made of cast iron.

Ryde and its piers were in a unique situation. The only practical way of getting to the Isle of Wight was by boat and Ryde, at the narrowest crossing point with the mainland, was a magnet for passengers, particularly as the island became a popular holiday destination. Unlike the situation for resorts on the Thames estuary such as Herne Bay and Southend, the coming of the railways famously increased usage of Ryde Pier. It became the funnel through which vast numbers of holidaymakers passed on their way to or from the island.

With a substructure largely of timber, Harwich Ha'penny Pier dates from 1853. On the extreme right, the original ticket office once charged half an old penny toll to use the pier. June 2019. (Fred Gray)

PIONEER PIERS

Following the experiment at Ryde, the business of building seaside passenger piers developed relatively slowly. Timber rather than stone was the preferred construction material. Using timber piles – typically with an iron-shod tip – was cheaper and faster than building in stone, and a wooden pier was more amenable to use by vessels.

In the four decades to 1861 timber-piled seaside piers were built at Trinity, Edinburgh (1821), Brighton (1823), Southend and Walton-on-the-Naze (both 1830), Herne Bay (1832), Sheerness (1835), Deal (1838), Weymouth (1840), Great Yarmouth (1855 and 1858), Bournemouth and Southsea (both 1861): a total of twelve new timber piers in four decades, although

the number increases if timber jetties and landing places, such as those at Harwich, Yarmouth and Margate, are included.

Timber-piled passenger piers came in two forms. Most usually, as at Ryde, the uninterrupted open deck of a pier was carried on a wooden substructure that, in turn, was supported on regularly spaced timber piles driven into the seabed. An alternative and rarely used method was for the pier deck to be suspended from chains strung between pairs of towers supported on more widely spaced clusters of timber piles. Such suspension or chain piers were technically more complicated to engineer and construct than the relatively simple to design and build open-decked landing-stage piers.

A view of Herne Bay and the long timber pier. (*The Illustrated London News*, 13 July 1850)

Samuel Brown and piers of suspension

The two piers built in the early 1820s were both chain or suspension piers. Both were designed by Captain Samuel Brown (1774–1852). A retired Royal Navy officer who had seen action during the Napoleonic wars, Brown became an engineer and entrepreneur and was also a great inventor and experimenter.[86] He trialled, unsuccessfully, the use of wrought-iron rigging on a naval ship but then introduced, successfully, chain anchor cables to the Navy. Brown subsequently became a chain manufacturer and patented designs for both the improved manufacture of chains and for the construction of suspension bridges. He designed the Union Bridge, completed in 1820, spanning both the River Tweed and the border between Scotland and England. This bridge, the first to be able to carry vehicles, demonstrated the merits of his suspension bridge concept. In a short time, suspension bridges led to his proposals for suspension piers.

The first chain pier was built at Trinity, on Edinburgh's coastline on the Firth of Forth, to service passengers using the increasing number of steam ferries travelling around the ports on the estuary. Brown's pier, which was completed in 1821, was 700ft long but just 4ft wide. It was at best a two-by-two pier, although for Victorian women in hooped dresses it was a single-file

Trinity Chain Pier.
(Fred Gray collection)

The destruction of Trinity Chain Pier, 1898.
(Fred Gray collection)

cilities were included in the array of attractions on many later piers, with the exception of Ryde's Victoria Pier, the unique use of Trinity pier for the activity was never rivalled elsewhere.

Brighton's Chain Pier

The chain pier at Trinity was the prototype for Brown's far more spectacular and famous chain pier at Brighton. Although before construction started it was called the 'Royal Brighthelmstone Pier' and a 'pier of suspension', once completed in 1823 it quickly acquired the moniker of 'Chain Pier'. The pier was both the most iconic and the most peculiar of the new piled passenger piers, part landing stage and part select promenade.

The pier opened in the same year in which the remodelling of the Royal Pavilion, King George IV's marine palace, was completed. The pavilion, with its startling Indo-Islamic exterior designed by John Nash, was in view of and a short stroll from the equally idiosyncratic new pier. At the time Brighton's wealthy visitors were uniquely fashionable and numerous. The resort was Britain's – and the world's – greatest seaside

pier. Groups of wooden piles, driven into the bed of the estuary, supported three cast-iron standards, each with a central arch for people to walk through. These standards carried the wrought-iron chains from which the deck of the pier was suspended. Given that the deck swayed when walked upon, the provision of iron railings along the sides of the deck was a wise precaution.

Trinity Chain Pier at first prospered as a passenger ferry terminal. However, from the mid-1830s, improved harbour facilities close by led to a decline in the number of vessels using it. A new role then emerged, which lasted for half a century, with the pier used principally for sea bathing. While sea-bathing fa-

The startlingly innovative, exotic and regal architecture of Brighton in 1825: the Royal Chain Pier and, in the middle distance, the Prince Regent's Marine Palace. Print made by George Cooke, after Joseph Mallord William Turner. (Yale Center for British Art, Paul Mellon Collection)

resort. The town was also one end of an important cross-Channel route to continental Europe. The pier's enabling Act of Parliament emphasized the landing and shipping of people and goods function of the pier, but recognized too the 'Purpose of walking for Exercise [and] Pleasure'.[87] Indeed, the promoters of the enterprise anticipated that the revenue from promenaders would exceed that from passengers travelling to or from France.

In both architectural and engineering terms, too, the Chain Pier was an innovative structure. The deck of the pier was 1,134ft long and, at 13ft wide, three times the width of the pier at Trinity. The deck was hung from two sets of four extraordinary wrought-iron chains with links 10ft long, manufactured at Brown's London 'chain factory'. In turn, the sets of chains were suspended from four pairs of cast-iron towers fixed to and supported by four clumps of wooden piles. The iron-shod piles were driven 10ft into the chalk seabed and rose 14ft above the highwater mark. The chains were anchored into the root-end cliff face and, at the further end of the pier, into the seabed. The broader pier-head landing stage was paved with Purbeck stone. The pier edge was made safe with iron railings.

The pyramidal towers, 25ft high, were designed in the then fashionable Egyptian style and 'modelled on the pylon gateways of Karnak in Egypt'.[88] Egyptian-inspired seaside designs never became widespread. However, Brighton's pavilion and pier, both completed in 1823, were the two first examples of what was later described as seaside Orientalism. Such architecture helped transport visitors to the seaside to other, imaginary, lands. Later in the century, and often displayed on piers, Orientalism as an architectural style spread around the British coast and to seaside resorts further afield.

The architecture of the pier responded to the demands of aristocratic promenaders for a grand, imposing structure. *The Times* report of the opening of the pier, self-evidently written by a proponent of the structure, emphasized the national achievement it represented. The English iron forming the 'material part' of the structure had been 'brought to such perfection as to entirely supersede the necessity of going to a foreign market for it'. Of the pier overall, 'whether viewed as a national monument or as a novel invention [it] … is … gratifying evidence of the resources and intellect of our country'.[89]

The Chain Pier's chief attraction for promenaders

The innovative and idiosyncratic Chain Pier. Although considerable use was made of iron, the pier was supported by massive timber piles. (Rijksmuseum, Amsterdam)

The root end of the Chain Pier. The two groups of four chains passed through the building and were embedded deep in the chalk cliff. (Rijksmuseum, Amsterdam)

was to be able to walk over the sea. It was here, as Corbin argues, that aristocratic visitors to Brighton 'encountered the desire to see, feel, and experience the sea'.[90] *The Times* believed that 'to the man of pleasure and the valetudinarian, it offers a marine promenade unequalled'. Critically, however, this was a communal rather than solitary activity. The seekers after health, for example, were 'dragged to the farthest extremity of the chain pier, to inhale to the greatest advantage the invigorating sea breezes, and concentrated upon a single spot, they give a decided colour to the place, rendering it an open hospital'.[91] In the mid-1850s, Thackeray, the influential novelist, wrote admiringly of the structure running 'intrepidly into the sea' and how 'for the sum of twopence you can go out to sea and pace this vast deck without the need of a steward with a basin'.[92]

Apart from the pier itself and the promenade it provided, many of the initial attractions on the pier were to do with consuming nature in one way or another. The base of the iron towers contained small shops selling refreshments or souvenirs, in one case providing the home for a silhouette artist. There was a 'floating bath' at the pier head, a camera obscura, sundial, two small cannons and some benches under a large awning.[93] The pier experience was enhanced by musical performances from, amongst others, a Welsh harpist and regimental bands.[94] At the root end of the pier, a building housed a reading room and saloon offering traditional resort facilities, including a library, telescopes to view the coast and pier and musical entertainments. 'Meteorological results and prognostications were also posted daily for inspection'.[95]

Within a few years of its opening, both Turner and Constable were to feature the pier in their marine landscapes of Brighton. Over the following seven decades

Looking along the length of the Chain Pier from the entrance and toward the pier head. (Rijksmuseum, Amsterdam)

views of the pier were endlessly painted, drawn, engraved and photographed: there were over 150 different prints of the structure.[96] For a third of a century at least, the pier was the most important and popular attraction on the seafront. Although an idiosyncratic one-off, the product of a particular time and a particular place, the Chain Pier pointed, in embryonic form, toward the fully formed pleasure piers of the final decades of the century.

On the opening of the pier, the author of a *Times* report asserted the structure was 'of such beauty and accommodation, as stands unrivalled in the world'. The writer correctly noted that the future utility of the suspension pier was unknown, and then speculated that it was impossible to calculate 'the general and numerous purposes to which it [the chain pier] may be applied'. The speculation failed. Brown's solution to building in the sea was experimental and also peculiar. His chain pier ideas were not widely adopted.

The technology Brown promoted was still in its infancy and not fully understood. Unstiffened decks hung suspended from chains were liable to oscillate violently in particular wind conditions. The Chain Pier was severely damaged in this way in 1833 and again in 1836. The partial destruction of the pier, twice, must have limited the appeal of the chain pier concept. Such piers were really a series of linked-together suspension bridges, with the limitations that implies for how a pier might be designed. By the 1860s new ideas and technologies, and new uses for cast and wrought iron, transformed how seaside piers were designed and constructed, and how they looked and performed. The visitor market was changing anyway, away from many seaside towns being the resort of the elite and leisured to an increasingly broad and popular visitor population. In the process the Chain Pier was increasingly redundant, a relict from the past. From 1866, and just a stroll away, was the West Pier, a decidedly modern erection that looked to the future.

Just one other suspension pier at the seaside was completed, in 1881, at Seaview, a village on the northeast coast of the Isle of Wight. The cables, made of strands of galvanized steel wires, were supported on four pairs of pylon-shaped wooden towers and seamlessly joined to the timber piles beneath. The result was an elegant and graceful pier.[97]

As to Brighton's Chain Pier, already condemned as unsafe, it was 'swept completely away' by a storm late on Friday 4 December 1896. While 'huge timbers, including the enormous piles on which the pier stood, were tossed about on the waves', hundreds of people scavenged for the lighter wood strewn over the beach, carrying it home for firewood.[98] The pier at Trinity survived a little longer, but was destroyed in a storm on 17 October 1898. Seaview Pier fell into disrepair during the Second World War. In 1950 it was the first pier to be listed for its special architectural or historic interest; the designation was of little value and in the dying days of 1951 it was wrecked in a series of storms.[99]

Piers for passengers and promenades

Piers of suspension, despite the initial expectations, were a deviation. The timber-piled seaside piers built between 1830 and 1861 all adopted the simpler open-deck method. Driven piles supported a framework of wooden beams and joists on which the deck was laid. Each of these piers had their own complex life histories. The initial motivation behind most was to provide a convenient, safe and dry landing place for passengers travelling by steamer to the developing seaside resorts. At Southend, a resort on the north coast of the Thames estuary, a late nineteenth-century commentator explained that 'the great features of Southend are first the mud, and second the Pier that has been cunningly invented to get across it.'[100]

The first iteration of many of the new piers did not allow vessels to moor whatever the state of the tide. They were simply too short and many were subse-

Great Yarmouth's Britannia Pier, shortly before demolition and the construction of a new pier. (Library of Congress, Washington, D.C.)

quently extended, sometimes in a number of stages, into deeper water. The original wooden pier at Southend, opening in 1830, was just 600ft long. It was extended to 1,500ft three years later, and then, in 1846, to 1.25 miles in length, at last always allowing vessels to moor in sufficiently deep water. At Southend the immense extent of the mud revealed at low tide meant that the pier had to be very long: today it stretches for 1.38 miles into the Thames estuary. One benefit was that the resort was able to claim the prize of having the world's longest pier. The original wooden pier at Walton-on-the-Naze, also opened in 1830, was similarly successively extended. In contrast, the 3,633ft length of Herne Bay Pier was completed in one operation that lasted little more than a year; the first pile was driven in early July 1831 and the pier completed in September of the following year.

Apart from toll houses at the entrance, the earliest of these piers usually had open decks bereft of buildings except, perhaps, a shelter and restroom at the pier head. An exception was Southend Pier, which from its opening included the 'Octagon', most probably a marquee-like structure that was 'covered in and completely protected from the weather', used for musical perform-

ances and other events. At one stage a horse-drawn tramway, for conveying people and goods along the length of the pier, ran through the Octagon. Unfortunately, 'the noise made by the horses was very disturbing when performances were being given'.[101] Over the decades, the promenading and entertainment potential – and income-generating possibilities – of these timber piers was more obviously exploited. At Great Yarmouth, two timber-piled piers were built in the 1850s. The 1853 Wellington Pier was designed with a small concert pavilion at the pier head, while there were facilities for bands to play in the open air on the 1858 Britannia Pier.

In the event, many timber-piled seaside piers were simply not resilient enough. Most were a transitory architectural feature of the coast with a limited life expectancy. The two main challenges, seemingly often working in tandem despite the vast difference in scale, were storm and tiny marine borers. The consequences of the violence and fury of a coastal storm were clear to see. The more invidious problem of marine borers, such as shipworms and gribbles, feasting on timber piles, was typically hidden from view. These minute sea monsters could wreak havoc with the structure of a pier which, once weakened, might be finished off by a gale.

Two years after Trinity Chain Pier opened, the gribble worm *Limnoria terebrans*, a tiny marine crustacean, was found to have ravaged the structure's piling. Other piers were similarly attacked. In April 1839, just seven years after it had been completed, Herne Bay pier was declared unsafe because many of the piles had been eaten away, and extensive repair work was subsequently carried out.[102] The culprit at Jarvis's Landing Place in Margate and George Rennie's 1861 Bournemouth Pier was the marine worm, *Teredo navalis*. George's brother, the younger John Rennie (1794–1874), had designed the 1838 pier at Deal; never fully completed, within two decades the pier was similarly ruined both by worm and storm.

The response depended on the severity of the damage. Piles often needed to be replaced, with the new ones creosoted, 'nail-mailed' or sheathed in iron. Ultimately, however, most timber-piled piers proved not fit for purpose. Occasionally, as at Ryde, the timber piles were replaced with cast-iron ones. Sometimes, as at Deal and Bournemouth, piers were destroyed by storm. More often, after repeated damage, the structures were demolished: this happened, for example, at Margate in the early 1850s and Herne Bay in 1871.

Timber piling was never totally deleted from the palette of materials and methods used by pier designers, particularly once more durable timbers from abroad, such as jarrah and greenheart, became readily available. On the coast of East Anglia, the piers at Clacton-on-Sea and neighbouring Walton-on-the-Naze (both opening in 1871), Southwold (1900) and Felixstowe (1905) were all wooden structures. At Yarmouth, on the Isle of Wight, a simple wooden pier was completed in 1876; it survives today and is still made of wood, although the timber has been renewed on many occasions.

Such later wooden piers were, however, rarities. By 1860 timber piling was about to be swept away by piling with cast iron. The great wave of promenade and pleasure pier construction was beginning. Over the next four decades to 1901, seventy-seven new piers were built. This pier-building hysteria was accompanied by a mania for iron, both wrought and cast, and both structural and decorative. The age of the iron pier had arrived.

The pier head of the timber pier at Yarmouth, Isle of Wight, c.1993. (Wayne Walters)

Chapter Four

REVOLUTION: IRON TAKES OVER

THE COMING OF IRON

During the nineteenth century the seaside increasingly captured the British imagination. Entranced, ever more visitors from an increasingly broad cross-section of the population travelled to the coast to enjoy the natural and artificial delights of seaside resorts. The burgeoning resorts were bound up with a far-reaching leisure revolution. The railways, with capacity to carry large numbers of people speedily and relatively cheaply, facilitated the process.

The promenade pier concept developed. New materials and new technologies, the product of Britain's immense industrial ingenuity and strength, were put to new uses. Cast iron became the structural material of choice. Hollow tubes of cast iron were used for the piles and columns forming the substructure of a pier. In turn, atop the piles and columns, wrought iron was often used for the framework supporting the pier deck. When combined with innovative piling techniques, particularly screw piling, the increasing use of iron allowed piers to be built longer, wider and in more varied shapes than before. Iron was also put to architectural use to decorate piers and both accommo-

date and entertain visitors. Cast and sometimes wrought iron was the most critical element in an array of pier accessories including seats, railings, lamp standards and ornate weather screens.

Initially, however, the idea of the iron pier was slow to challenge and usurp that of the timber pier. The first iron pier was completed in 1834, the next in 1842 and the third, a decade and a half later, in 1857. Although the revolution was painfully slow to take hold, the first three iron piers demonstrated what might be possible. It all changed in the 1860s. A tidal wave of new iron piers swept all before it. Indeed, more iron piers – nineteen in total – were completed in that decade then in any other. Such revolutionary changes propelled the promenade pier concept onward.

The 1860s, or more accurately the decade from 1863 to 1872, was also the period when Eugenius Birch, the pier-building genius, was at his most productive and brilliant. During the last four decades of the nineteenth century many engineers were involved in pier work, often producing remarkable and innovative structures. However, much of what occurred was a consequence of Birch's intrepid engineering and design adventures in the 1860s and early 70s.

Left: The revolutionary Brighton West Pier, constructed using cast and wrought iron, shortly after the 1866 opening. (Rijksmuseum, Amsterdam)

It wasn't clear at first that iron piles and columns would be capable of carrying a heavy load. In any case, a central concept of promenade piers was that the promenade should be uninterrupted: they should be open-decked places to walk. For both reasons the first buildings on promenade piers – including the entrance toll houses, shelters and retiring rooms – were small and built of timber. During the 1860s buildings became larger and with more iron being used, far heavier. The eventual conclusion, in the 1870s, was the birth of the first pleasure piers with large entertainment buildings, usually at the pier head.

It is also worth noting that piers, like the established toll roads, were privatized spaces. It was unsurprising, then, that 'toll house' became the term to denote the buildings designed to guard the entrance of a pier and extract a fee from pier promenaders.

First experiments at Gravesend

Gravesend, on the south bank of the River Thames to the east of London, is located at the section of the river where water conditions become fully marine. Early nineteenth-century visitors could enjoy bathing in seawater from bathing machines and other attractions including purpose-built bath houses and public gardens and esplanades. Although nowadays Gravesend is not considered to be a seaside town, two centuries ago proponents could lay claim to it being the seaside resort closest to the metropolis. It is also the place where both the first two cast-iron piers were built.

Visitors to Gravesend mostly came from London. Travelling by water, the journey was usually quick and economical. However, the major barrier to fulfilling the increasing popularity of the resort was the inability of the large vessels to use the Town Quay at low tides.[103] Instead, wherries – light boats rowed by watermen – needed to be employed to take passengers between ship and shore. Although short, the journey by wherry was time consuming, expensive and some-

Gravesend Town Pier, April 2010. (Fred Gray)

times disagreeable and unsafe. A pier was needed 'that might be approached by Steam-packets at all times of the tide'.[104]

A temporary wooden pier, stretching from the Town Quay further out into the Thames, was constructed in the early 1830s. Their livelihoods threatened, the watermen were furious. During the night of 22 June 1833, they attacked the new pier and 'the toll-house on the quay was much damaged, the iron railing by which the quay was enclosed, was destroyed, many of the piles of the jetty were cut through, and part of the platform was torn up'.[105] The watermen were offered compensation, in the form of employment on the new pier, and the opposition lessened. The new permanent structure, the Town Pier, opened on 29 July 1834.

The pier was designed by William Tierney Clark (1783–1852), a civil engineer specializing in bridges. Clark was responsible for two suspension bridges over the Thames, another at Shoreham near Brighton, which he worked on with Samuel Brown, and a cast-iron bridge in Bath. He is most famous for the Széchenyi Chain Bridge over the River Danube at Budapest.

Clark's expertise was readily transferable to pier design. The Gravesend pier was built with stone, timber and iron. The use of iron, the principal construc-

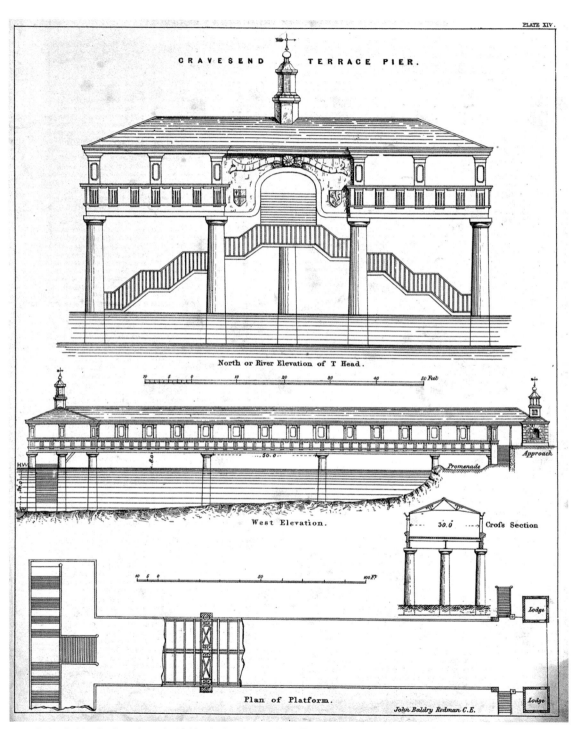

John Baldry Redman's early 1840s design for the iron Terrace Pier at Gravesend. (Wellcome Collection)

tion material, was ground breaking. The most revolutionary feature of the pier was the use, for the first time, of hollow cast-iron piles and columns. The T-shaped pier head, the business end of the structure, was like the neck of the pier supported by cast-iron columns, each 18ft in length and 2ft 9in in diameter. Each of the eighteen columns at the pier head stood on an iron plate with, in turn, each plate resting on three cast-iron piles, 14ft long and 15in in diameter, driven deep into the river bed.

The completed pier reached 157ft into the river and was 40ft wide except at the pier head, which measured 76ft by 30ft. The neck of the pier, forming the bridge between the shore and the pier head, was carried by three wide and shallow iron arches typical of those used in bridge design. The broader pier head carried two shelter pavilions, each with a small turret, one housing a clock and the other a bell to announce boat departures. A 35ft hollow cast-iron column, with a large gas lantern at the top, acted as a lighthouse for shipping using the pier.

The new pier was proclaimed as 'not only a noble place of embarkation and debarkation, but a fashionable and much-frequented promenade.'[106] The iron pier had arrived. Although made real at Gravesend, more important was the setting free of the notion that seaside piers could and should be made of iron. It was an idea that over the coming decades was to be examined, pursued and developed by other pier designers.

The success of the Town Pier was so great and the demand for passengers to journey to and from Gravesend so considerable that in 1835 a second pier, built of timber, opened. That, in turn, was replaced with an iron structure, the Terrace Pier (a Royal prefix was added in 1865) in 1842. The new iron pier was designed by John Baldry Redman (1816–1899), an engineer specializing in river and coastal engineering, particularly relating to the Thames.

Redman gave an account of the construction of his new pier on 8 April 1845 at a meeting of the Institution of Civil Engineers. Redman's use of iron would have been a revelation to the gathering, which was chaired by Sir John Rennie, President of the ICE and the son of one of the engineers of Margate Pier. The younger Rennie had gained his knighthood in 1831 for the building, in stone and to the designs of his father, of

Gravesend Royal Terrace Pier in April 2010. (Fred Gray)

the famous London Bridge. He was also responsible for the 1838 wooden pier at Deal, a project that was ultimately unsuccessful.

Redman's pier, 250ft long by 30ft wide, again made use of hollow cast-iron columns to carry the structure. The twenty-two 'bold and massive' columns were 26ft long, with the diameter tapering from 4ft at the bottom to 3ft at the top. Unlike the method used by Clark in the construction of the Town Pier, the columns were fixed to 'brick piers capped with stone, on a substratum of solid chalk'.[107] The deck of the pier was enclosed by corrugated-iron walls with windows and a wrought-iron and slate roof 'to afford protection from the weather, both for passengers and for the persons frequenting it as a promenade'.[108] The space was sufficiently flexible and attractive to be used for musical performances and balls on summer evenings. This was, most probably, the first reasonably large interior performance space on a pier.

The Town Pier was completely restored in 2000. It is the world's oldest iron pier and the first built using hollow cast-iron piles and columns. The Royal Terrace Pier nowadays functions as a Port of London Authority pilot station in continuous daily use. Both piers are architecturally listed as Grade II structures.

The two iron piers at Gravesend demonstrated some of the possibilities of the material and the technology. However, both piers were short in length and both were in a river rather than a fully coastal setting. It wasn't until the mid-1850s that a more substantial and much longer iron pier was constructed at the seaside proper. The designer was Eugenius Birch.

EUGENIUS BIRCH

The greatest and most prolific of British pier designers was Eugenius Birch (1818–1884). A professional civil engineer, Birch was multi-talented, combining the skills of engineer, architect and designer, inventor, promoter and entrepreneur. Although nowadays there is increasing appreciation of Birch's work, he remains an elusive figure.[109] No image of him has been located to portray his physical appearance. Nor do we have much sense of what he believed and thought about his extraordinary pier-building endeavours. Instead, we have the resources of plans, photographs, paintings and written descriptions and in addition, of course, the physical remains – albeit usually much changed – of his surviving piers.

Birch was responsible for fourteen of the fifty-one pleasure piers constructed between 1855, the year his first pier was realized, and 1884, the year his final completed pier opened and of his death. He also designed the 1865 pier at Netley on Southampton Water, built as a landing stage for the Royal Victoria Military Hospital.[110] There were designs for piers in Britain and France that remained unexecuted. He sometimes illustrated how his completed piers would look, using his skills as an accomplished water-colourist. Apart from seaside piers much of his other professional work involved engineering for water. He designed aquaria, waterworks, docks and harbours and bridges over rivers and canals. Like many of the eminent engineers in the age of steam he was also involved in the engineering for railways in Britain and, early in his career, in India. On the subcontinent, and working with his older brother, he designed bridges and viaducts for a railway between Calcutta and Delhi.

Birch's success as a pier engineer and designer coincided with Britain's pier-building mania. Armed with the innovative designs, he was in the right place at the right time to become Britain's most famous and hard-working pier designer. His most frenzied, productive and innovative period of design activity was in the ten years to 1872. Over this decade he was responsible for ten of the twenty-four piers that were completed. Averaging a pier a year, he was able to transform the pier design and building business almost single-handed.

His overall body of pier work was an impressive oeuvre. What was deemed a successful or attractive innovation on one pier was frequently repeated on subsequent ones. Sometimes he returned to his earlier piers to embellish them with his later innovations. But some ideas were unsuccessful when made real, and subsequently required substantial changes. Birch's designs were also contingent on an array of factors including the nature of the resort and site, the wishes of the pier promoters and the funding available. Even late on in his career he would design an open-decked promenade rather than a pleasure pier, if that was what the circumstances required.

Birch's influential innovations changed the way piers were built, what they looked like and the very idea of the seaside pier. His peculiar skill was to be able to take techniques, materials and design ideas from other contexts and to apply them to piers. More than any other designer he was responsible for both the initial development of the open-decked promenade pier and its subsequent transformation into the pleasure pier equipped to amuse and entertain visitors indoors and out. Four of his most revolutionary and seminal pier designs were for, in chronological order, the confusingly named Margate Jetty, Blackpool Pier (now the North Pier), Brighton's West Pier and Hastings Pier.

Birch's creativity and vision allowed him to imagine how piers might be in the future and to explore 'what if' questions. He understood the new freedoms provided by the technology of cast-iron piling and columns. Rather than the monotony of long, straight structures, piers could be designed in a startling array of shapes. Birch was the first pier designer to realize that an iron pier, suitably engineered, could carry not just a wooden promenade deck and wooden shelters but far heavier and more substantial structures. He also realized that decorating a pier would help create

the sense of it being a different, separate and exclusive place. He appreciated that decorative cast iron, a product of Britain's industrial and creative genius and commonly in use in buildings on *terra firma*, might be put to good use on piers.

Margate Jetty

Birch's designs for his first pier, at Margate, were ground breaking. The word 'jetty' rather than pier was used to distinguish the new structure from the adjacent and older stone harbour pier. Work on the Jetty began in 1853 and, while it opened two years later, the 1,240ft long structure wasn't fully completed until 1857. The new pier, jutting out from the exposed northeast Kent coast, was eight times longer than Gravesend's Town Pier of two decades earlier.

Margate Jetty was the earliest substantial seaside pier with the substructure built almost entirely of iron and the earliest to make use of iron screw piling to fix the pier into the seabed. Whether cast or wrought, iron was far more durable and stronger than wood and could be used to build a pier high above the sea. Except where the seabed and immediate surface geology was inhospitable, the screw pile, invented by the Irish engineer Mitchell, allowed piers to be built quickly and in a variety of shapes. Combining cast and wrought iron as construction materials with screw piling as an engineering technique was a giant leap forward. It allowed for an unlimited array of possibilities in the shaping and making of seaside piers, possibilities that were to be exploited by Birch and other pier designers.

The wooden Jarvis's Landing Place, which Birch's Margate pier eventually replaced, was covered by water at high tide. Sometimes formally and revealingly called the 'high water landing pier', the new pier featured a deck 14ft above the high water of ordinary spring tides. People no longer risked being drenched by seawater in going between the land and a passenger vessel.

Birch turned to the technology used to make cast-

Margate Jetty. (*The Builder*, 22 September 1855)

iron pipes for the majority of the Jetty's piles. The 20ft-wide timber deck of the pier was carried on wrought-iron girders that, in turn, were supported by fourteen regularly spaced clusters of five cast-iron columns. Each of the clusters was secured with wrought-iron ties and braces. The component columns were 16in in diameter and piled 10ft into the chalk seabed. The result was that the 950ft long neck of the pier resembled a series of joined-together bridges. Birch had put his bridge design work in India to good use at the English seaside!

The broader pier head, which was added later, was designed in anticipation of the stresses and strains on the structure coming from the passenger vessels using the three integral landing stages. Wrought iron, with its greater tensile strength, was the primary material used. The pier head was supported on fifty-seven screw piles. While the actual screw piercing the chalk was 30in in diameter and made of cast iron, the pile to which it was attached was solid wrought iron, 5.5in in

Birch's 'cluster of piles'. (*The Builder,* 22 September 1855)

Margate Jetty after the 1870s extensions. (Library of Congress, Washington, D.C.)

diameter and 20ft long.

Birch's Margate Jetty design was a bold engineering statement. The Jetty, however, lacked the refinements, intricate engineering and architectural embellishments of Birch's subsequent pier designs. The innovative Margate design divided opinion. One contemporary commentator thought that 'whatever may be its mechanical sufficiency, the ugliness of the new pier is unquestionable'.[111] The issue perhaps was that iron, with all its industrial and associated connotations, seemed out of place when used so boldly and baldly at the romantic and pleasurable seaside.

Eight years later Margate Jetty was acclaimed as a 'handsome and substantial landing and promenade pier, which was the first sea structure of the kind composed of iron-work resting upon iron-screw piles ever erected, and which … is as sound in its iron-work as it ever was'.[112] The point about the longevity of the pier at Margate, proving that iron piers worked and lasted,

was key to ensuring that Birch was offered more pier work. Iron and the screw pile became the basic building blocks used for many other Victorian piers.

IRON TAKES HOLD

Birch was not the only pier designer. Other engineers, many of them with notable careers, also applied their skills and expertise to iron seaside piers. Indeed, after Margate, the next two iron piers were designed not by Birch, but by two other prominent Victorian engineers.

Southport and the first promenade pier

Designed by James Brunlees, Southport Pier was the second seaside pier to be built largely of iron. With considerable local celebrations and press coverage in such important national publications as *The Illustrated*

London News, the pier opened in August 1860.

Southport was the first seaside pier designed principally for promenading, for leisure, pleasure and health, rather than for passengers. Railways had already connected Southport to the rapidly expanding urban centres of the north of England, from port cities such as Liverpool to the industrial and commercial metropolis of Manchester. Although steamers did call at the pier when the tide was in, the pier-head stairs were also designed 'for descending to the sands at low water … [which] … will prove a great acquisition to visitors wishing to encounter the breeze at the elevation of the pier, or the milder air at the lower level of the sands.'[113]

The pier was a select promenade for wealthy residents and visitors to the town. Guarded by iron gates, turnstiles and gatekeepers, the high entrance toll of sixpence was another significant barrier to the pier being accessible to all. The prototype promenade pier was soon criticized for its plainness and inconvenience. In appearance the simple structure was narrow, very long and architecturally unadorned. The edge of the wooden deck was guarded by unembellished iron railings. The walk to the end of the pier, unrelieved by shelters or retiring rooms, or even the provision of seating until the pier head was reached, could be wearisome. There were complaints about the difficulty that women, in their voluminous Victorian dresses,

The opening of Southport Pier. (*The Illustrated London News*, 18 August 1860)

had in navigating the turnstiles.

As discussed in Chapter 2, the pier at Southport was where jetting was first employed as a piling technique.

Worthing Iron Pier

The third iron pier at the seaside, and the second to use screw piles, opened at Worthing, Sussex, in 1862. The structure was designed by Robert Rawlinson, an engineer and sanitarian noted for his success in public health engineering and improving water supply, drainage and the disposal of sewerage. The simple pier was 15ft wide and 960ft long with a small toll house guarding the entrance to the promenade deck. One innovation, subsequently copied by other pier engineers, was the use of shallow-angle raked piles in addition to the more usual vertical ones. Two years after it opened, one commentator described how 'Worthing Iron Pier' 'is supported on many thin iron legs, and it looks for all the world like a gigantic centipede taking a saltwater bath'.[114]

BIRCH BREAKS FREE

By the 1860s Margate Jetty was seen to have survived and prospered. Birch began to acquire a reputation as the nation's most esteemed pier engineer. By the time his second pier at Blackpool opened in 1863, Birch had commissions to design at least four others. Some design ideas were carried from one pier to another, although it is also possible to identify progression and evolution in Birch's finished work.

The pier at Blackpool

The pier at Blackpool, although essentially an open-decked promenade, was resplendent with new ideas. Birch used the versatility of screw piling to vary its shape. Piers no longer needed to be long, thin, functional and unadorned. Blackpool illustrated that they could accommodate an array of buildings. The landward end included four square ones for collecting tolls and use as shops. For the first time the long neck of a pier carried buildings; in this case six identical small

Worthing Pier after the 1880s addition of pavilion and entrance kiosks. (Library of Congress, Washington, D.C.)

Detail of watercolour by Birch portraying the root end of Blackpool Pier and the entrance buildings. (Leisure Parc archive)

octagonal structures. Another remarkable innovation was that the edge of the pier was not only a railing and safety barrier, but was also used to provide seating for potentially thousands of people. In addition, Birch was concerned to decorate and ornament his innovations. Unlike Margate Jetty, at Blackpool Birch confirmed that piers should not simply be a bridge between land and sea but had far more potential as places of pleasure and profit.

Although at the pier head the engineer used both cast- and wrought-iron piles, the main body used cast iron filled with concrete for additional stability. The clusters of piles, each 60ft apart and tied together with rods and braces, carried the main girders of wrought iron.

The tops of the girders had the additional novel role of being used as the basis of 'continuous and most comfortable sitting accommodation for between 3,000 and 4,000 people, who will thus have an excellent view

of the promenaders, without at all interfering with the width of the pier as a promenade.'[115] The backs of these pier-edge seats were made of an 'ornamental casting' of an open lattice design fixed to the top of the main girders. This seemingly insignificant development fundamentally changed the pier experience. If they wished, people could exit the promenade throng and sit, facing inwards, on the edge of the promenade and watch the crowd strolling along the deck of a pier. Observing other people on a pier was as fascinating, perhaps even more so, as looking out to sea. Birch used the idea in his subsequent pier work, and it was taken up by other pier engineers.

The ease and versatility of screw piling was also put to good use in the shaping of the pier. Three pairs of 'side projections' along the neck of the pier acted to destroy 'the stiff and monotonous appearance which the long straight outline of the pier would otherwise make.'[116] Each of these 'embayed' recesses carried a

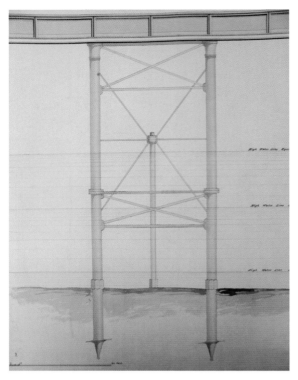

Blackpool Pier: extracts from the Birch drawings. The arrangement of iron piles and columns. (Leisure Parc archive)

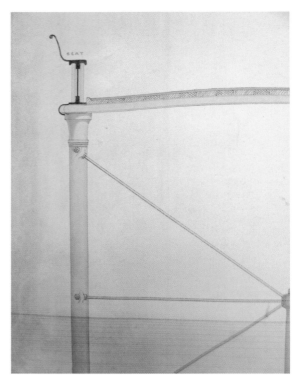

Birch's innovative proposals for pier seating. (Leisure Parc archive)

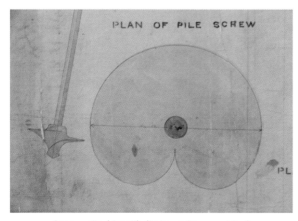

Screw pile (detail). (Leisure Parc archive)

small wooden shelter or 'refreshment house'. These structures really performed as belvederes designed to take advantage of the maritime views. The pier-edge seating and belvederes greatly enhanced the promenade experience.

At Blackpool, Birch began searching for an appropriate style for seaside pier buildings. Those both at the entrance and on the neck of the pier were simple wooden structures. Although only really posh seaside sheds, there were discernible Italianate stylistic characteristics. The shallow-pitched roofs, topped by decorative finials, had projecting eaves supported on wooden brackets. For the timber-clad walls, Birch made extensive use of narrow, extended, half-round windows with horizontal glazing bars. The windows

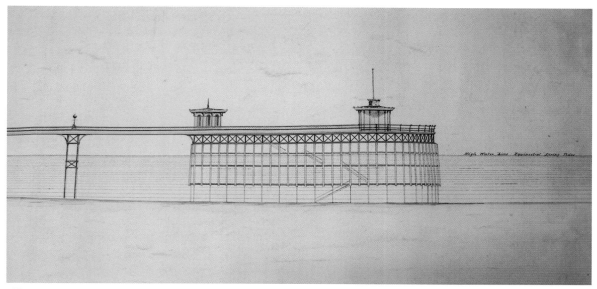

The pier head rested on solid wrought-iron piles. The flights of steps leading to the landing stages are also indicated.
(Leisure Parc archive)

The wonders of Birch's Blackpool Pier. (Marlinova Collection)

helped determine the applied decoration and detailing, highlighted in different colours, of the overall building. Birch returned to a similar window design for many of his later piers.

Birch also innovated with the pier decking, using two layers, one laid on top of and at right angles to the other. This meant there were 'no open spaces to admit the wind or spray blowing up, and thus inconveniencing the promenaders'. Birch subsequently tried other forms of pier decking. For example, on Brighton's West Pier gravel and bitumen covered close planking while at New Brighton he experimented with a concrete deck 'to render it comfortable for walking in wet weather'.[117]

A particularly difficult aspect of pier design concerned the berthing of passenger-carrying vessels at the pier head. Steamers needed to arrive or depart whatever the state of the tide or size of the seas. In the case of Blackpool Pier, at its most extreme there was a 35ft height difference between high and low tides. Birch responded to the challenge with an intricate design making much use of wrought-iron piles and 'fender piles' of wood. In addition, 'ample landing stages, with noble flights of steps, 10 feet wide, and of an easy incline, are provided … so that passengers will be able to land and embark with great readiness and comfort at all stages of the tide'.[118] Despite Birch's best endeavours, at Blackpool and elsewhere, integrated landing stages forming part of the pier head created many problems, often causing damage to both vessels and pier. The ultimate solution, arrived at by engineers after Birch had died, was for the landing stage to be an essentially separate structure from the pier head, accessed by a bridge from one to the other.

Next steps: Deal, Aberystwyth and Lytham

Birch's next three piers showed the evolution of his ideas, particularly about the pier design above the substructure. The unfinished Deal Pier opened in July 1864 and can be read as a simplified version of Black-

pool. It included continuous pier-edge seating and two root-end buildings identical to those designed for his pier at Blackpool.

Aberystwyth Pier opened on Good Friday 1865. Although once again in an incomplete state, such was the enthusiasm to experience the pier that 7,000 people visited on the opening day. The major design innovation at Aberystwyth concerned the four elegant buildings at the entrance. The concave tented roofs suggested an exotic playfulness and are the first indication that Birch believed that Oriental design motifs might be just what he (and piers) needed. The inspiration may have been the two graceful tent roofs designed by John Nash as part of the remodelling, between 1817 and 1820, of the Prince Regent's Brighton Pavilion.

The visual evidence indicates that, at Aberystwyth, Birch also began to turn to ornamental iron for the structural components of pier buildings. The projecting eaves appear to have been supported by ornate iron – not wooden – brackets. The seaward pair of buildings made exceptional use of glass walls: on sunny days the interiors would have been flooded with natural light. Turning to the substructure, for the first time Birch, perhaps drawing on the design of Worthing Pier, used raked columns and piles. These were 'mounted on concrete bases tied to the bed rock'.[119] The design of the substructure proved grossly inadequate. In January 1866, just five months after the opening, violent waves destroyed 100ft of the end of the pier. A few years later a sarcastic commentator described how the pier 'or rather a fragment of one … [was] … deserted and incomplete, the sea having washed away a great part of it soon after its erection'.[120]

Three days after the festivities marking the opening of Aberystwyth Pier, similar celebrations took place in Lytham, Lancashire, 100 miles to the northeast. People promenading on Lytham Pier on its 17 April 1865 opening experienced what by then were all the hall-

The elegance of the new pier at Aberystwyth. (Marlinova Collection)

The mature and much truncated and altered Aberystwyth Pier in 2013.
(Wayne Walters)

Aberystwyth Pier entrance in 2013. (Wayne Walters)

THE NEW PIER AT LYTHAM, LANCASHIRE.—SEE PRECEDING PAGE.

'The New Pier At Lytham, Lancashire'. (*The Illustrated London News*, 29 April 1865)

marks of a typical Birch pier. However, the two octagonal toll houses and the similar-shaped waiting room at the pier head reveal that the designer's thoughts about pier buildings had continued to develop. The decoration was more obviously ornate and the Oriental allusions more explicit. The roof was topped by a domed and minaret-like skylight. The window and door designs were more elaborate. Most significantly,

One of the two octagonal toll houses on the 1865 Lytham Pier. (Marlinova Collection)

the visual evidence indicates that Birch made a substantial breakthrough in the use of cast iron to provide the building's structural frames.

The pier transformed: Brighton's West Pier

Birch's most outstanding and original pier was the West Pier at Brighton. Opening on 6 October 1866 the pier drew on and further developed the structural and decorative ideas revealed in his earlier designs. However, he also introduced a number of major innovations that had lasting impact on pier design into the next century.

The West Pier was architecture and engineering designed to use, consume and dominate nature, allowing society to access a separate, distinctive and exotic world above the sea. It represented a remarkable leap forward in pier design. The outrageously innovative new structure, so startlingly different from earlier piers, also provided a visual feast for promenaders walking along the seafront or venturing onto the pier itself.

The grandeur and originality of the new pier re-

The October 1866 opening ceremony for the West Pier, Brighton. (*The Illustrated London News*, 13 October 1866)

An early photograph of the West Pier with Birch's architectural innovations on display. The band dais was soon replaced by a more substantial structure. (Brighton West Pier Trust)

flected Brighton's continuing status as the leading British resort. It revealed the transitional state of pier technology, style and function, which was still being attempted, tested and searched for rather than taken for granted and assumed. The pier was at once ambitious, innovative but also somewhat uncertain on matters of engineering, architecture, decoration and purpose.[121]

The West Pier Company's object, announced in 1863, was 'to erect a handsome, commodious, and substantial Iron Promenade Pier ... in the centre of that portion of the Esplanade which, at all seasons of the year, is the most thronged by residents and visitors.'[122]

Speakers at the opening events were caught up with the idea that the pier was exceptional. One speaker poetically described the pier as 'a kind of butterfly upon the ocean to carry visitors upon its wings and waft them amongst the zephyrs and balmy breezes of Brighton.'[123] The Mayor of Brighton looked to the future, trusting 'that the Pier would ever remain a benefit to the town,

that the elements above and below it would be propitious; and that the healthy and sick, the rich and the humble, might alike enjoy the health-inspiring breezes to be obtained upon it; and that the weak might be restored to robust health. He hoped that the Pier might remain to future ages to prove what speculation had done.'[124] The press agreed with such sentiments, *The Brighton Examiner,* for instance, arguing 'we now look upon the structure as artistic and elegant, outrivalling everything of the kind in this country, and perhaps the world…'[125] Grand claims indeed!

Although much the same length, the long, narrow neck of the West Pier, at 55ft wide, was four times the width of the older Chain Pier. Commentators admired the design strengths of the overall structure with its columns and piles 'braced and tied in such a manner as to ensure the greatest amount of stiffness to the Pier, and least amount of resistance to the sea.'[126] Contemporary reporters marvelled at the expanse of the open deck, providing 'altogether over 100,000 superficial feet of promenade'. Simulating a promenade on land, the deck of the pier was of close planking covered by 'gravel laid upon bitumen'.

The unwanted were kept off the pier by money, architecture and social convention. Turnstiles, ornamental iron gates and two imposing identical square toll houses guarded the entrance and marked it out as a separate place. The toll houses were the most contentious feature of the new pier, nearby residents arguing they were so large 'the whole vista of the sea was cut asunder',[127] and one press critic agreeing that 'no beauty of structure can compensate for the loss of sea view'.[128]

The pier had other innovative and distinctive architectural features designed to capitalize on the nature of promenading and the mid-Victorian seaside holiday. Following the innovations on Blackpool Pier, there was 'ample and continuous sea-accommodation', including curved cast-iron bench seating along the edge of the pier, 'for 2,000 to 3,000 persons'.[129] The seating, facing inwards rather than outwards over the sea, allowed visitors to rest, talk and spectate. For the first time, the seat backs were cast in an ornate pierced geometric design. The idea was copied on many other piers and the original open lattice seat design at Blackpool was replaced with one that followed the West Pier template. The railing, running along the edge of the pier, was partly formed by the seats and by a cast-iron tubular handrail. It was embellished by regularly spaced cast-iron gas lamp standards decorated with two entwined serpents.

Another major West Pier innovation addressed the Victorian preoccupation with health and the common mid-century conviction that the most beneficial aspects of the seaside came from breathing sea air. In response Birch provided innovative ornamental weather screens on the pier head, forming a horseshoe shape around a small open platform for band performances. The distinctive architecture of the screens – made of cast iron, plate glass and timber, roofed over but open at the sides, with a 'line of double raised seats' either side of the screens – represented design for health, comfort and social mixing:

On a sunny winter's day invalids can enjoy the mild temperature and life-prolonging air with perfect freedom from chilling blasts … In summer the screens will shade the visitors from the sun without putting up an awning, which gives closeness and an air of confinement. It might be thought that with all this shelter the head of the pier would be confined in appearance. Nothing, however, could be more open. The manner in which Mr Birch has obtained the maximum of accommodation and weather protection with the minimum of air-stoppage and light-obstruction, is a charming specimen of engineering skill … As a sanatorium, this part of the Pier must be productive of the most beneficial effects to invalids and persons of delicate constitution.[130]

The screens, in one contemporary view 'a novelty in pier architecture', also provided an opportunity to observe the power of nature in relative comfort. As the same commentator pointed out, 'in rough weather the visitor will have the opportunity of viewing the ocean in its angriest moments without being exposed to the fury of the wind.'[131] The sanatorium function of the innovative weather screens was rather quickly forgotten. However, the screen idea was copied and adapted on many subsequent piers, with weather screens providing protection for visitors seeking sheltered seating or walking the length of a pier in bad weather.

Another feature of the pier's architecture proved to have a lasting reflection in pier design elsewhere. There were six 'ornamental houses', occasionally described as 'ornamental towers', integral to the deck of the pier, used when individuals wanted to leave the promenade crowd. Of these 'octagonal-shaped erections', two were 'retiring rooms', one for women and one for men, two were refreshment rooms, and two were shops for 'toy or fancy businesses'.[132] The structures, which were eventually called kiosks, provided the first instance of substantial buildings on the body of a pier above the sea. They were an embryonic form of the larger pavilions subsequently characteristic of fully fledged pleasure piers.

The weather screens and kiosks were unique. The like of either of the structures had not been seen before. But with them, and the toll houses, Birch demonstrated that reasonably large and heavy cast-iron-framed structures could be safely erected on a pier.

For the first time on the West Pier, Birch inten-

Islamic-inspired cast iron decoration on a 1866 West Pier kiosk, photographed late 1990s. (Fred Gray)

sively used decorative or ornamental cast iron for pier buildings and fittings. As the name implies, the 'ornamental houses' weren't simply minimally adorned sheds above the waves. The roof of each kiosk was held up by a complex system of cast-iron brackets, ornamented with pierced geometric patterns. The brackets, in turn, were carried on eight pairs of decorated columns fixed to waist-high rectangular bases. A squat minaret (an idea Birch trialled at Lytham) surrounded by ornate railings topped each kiosk roof. Many of the same decorative ideas were used on the two square toll houses at the pier's entrance.

The kiosks, the extraordinary weather screens, together with the lamp standards entwined with serpents and the ornate seat backs ringing the edge of the pier, created an astonishing architectural environment that had not been seen before. Birch had taken the daring step of using architecture and design in an attempt to evoke an exotic and other-worldly mood for the pier's visitors.

Birch also resorted to colour to heighten the impact of the pier. Modern analysis of the twenty layers of paint covering the pier's kiosks reveals that the original colour scheme was 'Light Cream with picking out in Red-Brown'.[133] This scheme extended over the whole pier. The cream and red-brown of the new pier, surrounded by the blues and greys, light and shadow, of the sea and sky, would have created a compelling visual feast.

Design influences

Where did Birch's extraordinary design ideas come from? The West Pier provides a useful case study, allowing us to explore a number of the processes at work. Some of Birch's ideas, for example, for toll houses and for pier-edge railings and seating, evolved as he developed his own approach to pier work. Those commissioning Birch would have had perhaps strong opinions on what they wanted to see built; for Brighton the demand was for opulence, innovation, modernity and uniqueness. Birch was also working in a particular professional context. His work would have been informed by the engineering and design milieus of mid-nineteenth century Britain, and its associated set of possibilities, constrictions and attitudes.

Birch's West Pier designs are difficult to classify stylistically. He adopted an eclectic range of designs, motifs and symbols, searching for styles and decorations that for him represented seaside pleasure and leisure. Birch seems to have looked to the east and the Orient for his design inspiration. Although not to the extent seen on later piers, such as Hastings, it is on the West Pier that seaside Orientalism initially took root as a design motif as suitable for use above the waves as on the land.

Birch may have drawn upon the architectural sights seen while he worked in India. Brighton's Royal Pavilion had, almost half a century earlier, established that Orientalism was a suitable style for the seaside. However, by the 1860s the pavilion, abandoned by royalty, stripped of its interior decoration and in municipal ownership, was sometimes reviled as ridiculous and absurd.[134] Living and working in London with of-fices in Westminster, Birch, as an increasingly successful engineer and designer, would have been open to an array of contemporary ideas. The available evidence indicates that, most probably, Birch was strongly influenced by Owen Jones (1809–1874), one of the most significant design theorists of the nineteenth century. Jones had a particular interest in Islamic decoration and architecture.

As an architect and designer, Jones was able to put into practice his theories. He controversially decorated the interior of the Crystal Palace, housing the Great Exhibition of 1851, using only the primary colours of blue, red and yellow. He also designed the Oriental Courts – there was an Indian Court and a combined Chinese and Japanese Court – completed in 1863, for the South Kensington Museum. (In May 1899, on her final official public appearance, Queen Victoria renamed the museum the Victoria and Albert Museum.) Jones's design inspiration for the new galleries was the Alhambra in Spain. In the 1830s, at the conclusion of a tour of Mediterranean countries, Jones had made a detailed study of 'Moorish' decoration in the magnificent Islamic palace.

Jones was the author of the seminal design book,

An early idea of the Brighton West Pier envisaged by Birch the watercolourist in February 1863. The toll booths and the pier head integrated landing stages were built much as portrayed. By 1866 the substructure (here reminiscent of his pier at Margate) was radically different and the revolutionary pier included Oriental kiosks and ornate weather screens. The sketch of the pier-head pavilion was added later. (Private collection)

The Grammar of Ornament, published in 1856. Richly illustrated, the book explored the designs, styles and colours used in the 'Ornamental Art' of twenty different societies, past and present. Jones advocated thirty-seven 'general principles in the arrangement of form and colour in architecture and the decorative arts.' For example, proposition fourteen stated that 'Colour is used to assist in the development of form, and to distinguish objects or parts of objects one from another.'

Birch would have been fully aware of Jones, as a writer about ornamental art and a proponent of Islamic designs. Working in cast iron, it would have been impossible for Birch to directly transfer Islamic designs to the West Pier. However, the use of columns, arches and brackets, and the geometric patterns decorating the seat backs, weather screens, kiosks and toll houses, suggest that he was very sympathetic to Islamic stylistic ideas such as those from the Alhambra Palace. Islamic style, in cast iron, decorating an English seaside pier.

In his use of colour, too, and again in the context of the constraints imposed in painting a pier, Birch appears to have implemented many of Jones' proposals. Jones' twenty-third proposition stated, 'No composition can ever be perfect in which any one of the three primary colours [red, yellow and blue] is wanting, either in its natural state or in combination.' The West Pier fulfilled the proposition, with the red-brown and cream (a muted yellow) paint being complemented by the shades of blue found in the sea and sky. As Jones also proposed, the two contrasting colours were used to highlight and emphasize different elements of the pier's architecture. In June 1867 *The Penny Illustrated Paper* described the West Pier, which had opened the previous autumn, as 'the most magnificent specimen of the kind in the world … painted after the principle adopted by Owen Jones, and of which the new buildings at the South Kensington Museum form such splendid examples.'[135]

Pier engineers and designers, such as Birch, would have been delighted that Jones, unlike Ruskin, was progressive when it came to modern materials. He questioned: 'Could the Medieval architect have ever dreamed that his airy vaults could be surpassed, and that gulfs could be crossed by hollow tubes of iron?' It was even more extraordinary that, at the seaside, the hollow tubes crossed gulfs that sometimes raged with turbulent seas.

The journey continued

Birch's remarkable pier work continued apace. In 1867, the year following the completion of the West Pier, two more Birch piers opened.

The new pier at Weston-super-Mare, Somerset, was unique in forming a 1,040ft bridge between the island of Birnbeck, after which the pier was named, and a point on the foreshore known as Anchor Head. Unusually, a contemporary newspaper report was explicit about the colour scheme used on the pier:

The general appearance of the bridge, looking at it from the main land is exceedingly effective. The principle tint is a dark chocolate, which is relieved occasionally by the introduction of a fawn colour which affords a very pleasing contrast. The facial [sic] boards are thus lightened in effect, and the cast girders – those immediately surmounting the piers – are bordered in the same way. An appearance of elegance, united with great stability, is given to the work, and it may fairly be said to be quite ornamental as well as useful.[136]

Three months later, in September 1867, Birch's pier at New Brighton Pier opened. 'A kind of marine suburb to the town of Liverpool', New Brighton was a ferry ride across the River Mersey. A peculiar pier, until 1900 it was effectively an island, accessible only by stairs from a functional ferry landing stage. Birch copied and adapted many of the innovations from his

New Brighton Pier on opening. (*The Illustrated London News,* 7 September 1867)

pier at the old Brighton. It included octagonal ornamental houses with minarets, continuous pier-edge seating and 'weather-screens similar to those erected at Brighton New Pier for the first time, which have been highly appreciated.' [137]

The most important New Brighton innovation, not finished until the following year, was a large covered 'saloon', 130ft in length and 28 to 34ft wide, with a central tower another three stories high. A report in the *Liverpool Mercury* described how:

This magnificent apartment will be fitted with glass folding doors, and will form a fine promenade in itself during unfavourable weather. It is also intended to make this saloon available for a variety of purposes, such as refreshment rooms, bazaars, flower shows, concerts, &c. Over the saloon there will be a promenade of the same dimensions, with a magnificent tower built in the Byzantine style of architecture, which will give the whole structure a handsome and striking appearance.[138]

Birch was developing both his stylistic reference points

The 'saloon' constructed on New Brighton Pier used many of the architectural elements Birch first employed for his Brighton West Pier. (Marlinova Collection)

and his views of the appropriate size and use for a pier building. As the report makes clear, it was uncertain just how the saloon with its tower would function, but entertainment would be part of its role. It was also the largest building to date to have been erected on a pier. It was a harbinger of things to come. With hindsight, and although it is often neglected, the saloon was a noteworthy if tentative statement about the future of piers and pier architecture. A year later Birch designed a pier and huge and exotic pier-head pavilion for the French Mediterranean resort of Nice; the plans were unrealized.

Although two simpler piers were to follow, they still bore many of the Birch pier hallmarks, including deck recesses, continuous seating, cast-iron decorative work, toll houses and kiosks. In July 1869 the pier opened at the eminently respectable Yorkshire resort of Scarborough. In June the following year, visitors to aristocratic Eastbourne on the Sussex coast could promenade on a Birch pier, although one that was not completed until two years later.

Then, in 1872 and fifteen miles to the east of Eastbourne, the pier at Hastings opened. The event marked a further milestone in Birch's adventurous journey in pier design. The leap forward was that for the first time the designs featured a large pavilion on the wide pier head. Although open-decked promenade piers continued to be built, the significance of Hastings Pier was

New Brighton Pier and the adjacent landing stage for ferries to and from Liverpool.
(Library of Congress, Washington, D.C.)

that it heralded the arrival of the pleasure pier. That story is told in the next chapter.

COMPETITION

During the 1860s and 70s iron piers became an increasingly common feature of British seaside resorts. Birch's piers at Brighton, New Brighton and Hastings apart, most were open-decked and designed for promenading and as landing stages for pleasure boats. Buildings were mostly relatively small and ranged from toll houses, restrooms and waiting rooms to shops and refreshment kiosks.

By 1880, several dozen iron promenade piers could be found around the coast. The following list, although not comprehensive, gives a sense of the variety of places becoming pier resorts. There were new Welsh piers at Rhyl and Llandudno and, in the Irish Sea, there was one at Douglas on the Isle of Man. Exceptionally, there was another Scottish pier built at Portobello, just a few miles away from the earlier chain pier at Trinity. In the Bristol Channel there was a spectacular pier at Clevedon and a troublesome one at the tiny Devon resort of Westward Ho! The up-and-coming Lancashire resort of Morecambe gained a pier. A second one opened at booming Blackpool. Originally called a jetty (and today known as Central Pier) it was designed for 'promenading and steamer and pleasure-boat traffic during all times of the tide'.[139]

On the Yorkshire coast piers ranged from those at Hornsea and Withernsea in the south, to the trio of neighbouring piers in the north at Redcar, Coatham and Saltburn. The Lincolnshire and East Anglia resorts of Hunstanton and Cleethorpes shared in the building spree. Financial difficulties meant that the pier planned for Aldeburgh was begun but never completed; perhaps the resort was too small to support the enterprise. In the Southeast, the old timber pier at Herne Bay was replaced by an iron structure and Ramsgate gained a new promenade pier. The string of south coast resorts to obtain iron promenade piers by 1880 included Bognor and Teignmouth and, on the Isle of Wight, Ventnor, Totland Bay and Sandown.

No pier designer was as prolific as Birch. However, Joseph William Wilson (1829–1898) was responsible for the four relatively simple piers at Bognor, Teignmouth, Hunstanton and Westward Ho! The narrowness of the 1,000ft long pier at Bognor, which opened in May 1865, led one commentator to remark that its value was in the 'encouragement of sociability, as it was impossible to avoid rubbing shoulders with fellow promenaders in such a confined space'.[140] Following his 1860 pier at Southport, James Brunlees was to be intermittently involved in designing piers, including one in France, for another three decades.

Blackpool's second pier, initially called the Jetty, featured another attempt to cope with the tidal range in the resort – a low-level landing stage extending further into the sea. (*The Engineer,* 23 April 1869)

Of all the promenade piers constructed during the period, the most unique and most elegant was at Clevedon. Formally opened on Easter Monday 1869, the pier was designed by John William Grover (1836–1892) and Richard James Ward (1817–1881). Speaking

Ventnor Pier, built in stages between 1872 and 1876, became an important feature of the small resort described as 'The English Madeira'. (Rijksmuseum, Amsterdam)

Withernsea Pier existed for barely more than a quarter of a century. It was completed in 1877 and had disappeared by 1903. The entrance building, supposedly modelled on Conway Castle, survives and is pictured here in September 2017. (Fred Gray)

to the Institution of Civil Engineers in 1871, Grover reported that the pier had 'withstood very severe storms without injury', and this despite the huge 45ft rise and fall of average spring tides and the great speed of the water in the Bristol Channel at that point.[141] Unusually, the designers used wrought iron for the neck of the pier, purchasing redundant and unused rails originally made for the South Wales Railway. Two curved V-shaped rails, of a type invented by William Henry Barlow, were rivetted together back-to-back to make girders. These, because they were of wrought iron, could be made into the arches forming the eight 100ft spans. Cast iron was used for the pier head and the 2ft in diameter screw piles.[142] Below the pier head, five 'landing-decks' at ever lower levels allowed steamer access to the pier, whatever the state of the tide.

The open-decked iron piers served their purpose of providing promenades and steamer landing stages. As business enterprises, the financial model was simple. Most income came from promenade tolls and landing fees, supplemented by secondary sources such as revenue from kiosk and shop rentals and advertising. However, seaside resorts were growing and changing. There were new ways to profit from the business of seaside pleasure. In order to capitalize on the possibilities, piers needed another revolution; a pleasure revolution. With his pier at Hastings, Eugenius Birch had chartered the direction of travel. Although it took some time for many other pier promoters and designers to follow, the eventual architectural consequences were captivating.

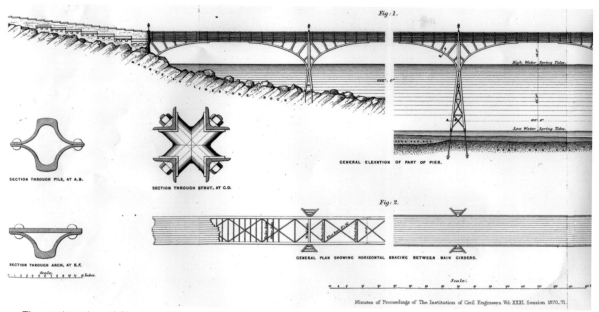

Minutes of Proceedings of The Institution of Civil Engineers. Vol. XXXI. Session 1870_71.

The engineering of Clevedon Pier, including the innovative use of wrought-iron Barlow rails. (Proceedings of the Institution of Civil Engineers, 1870-71)

The 1869 opening of the unique Clevedon Pier. (*The Illustrated London News*, 10 April 1869)

Chapter Five

THE GOLDEN AGE OF SEASIDE PIERS

PEOPLE'S PALACES

The most exuberant and fantastic architectural expression of British seaside piers emerged late on in the nineteenth century. Unlike relatively unadorned promenade piers, the finest of the new pleasure piers were to develop as visually remarkable multi-entertainment complexes with at least one large pleasure building. At their most splendid, pleasure piers gave purpose and meaning to individual coastal resorts. For the holidaymaker, to walk on to a pleasure pier and over the sea below was to enter a new world of make-believe. Apart from the extraordinary location, seemingly soaring in the air and above the waves, and the varied pleasures available for the delectation of pier goers, there was the distinctive and often outlandish design of pier entertainment buildings, and the fantastic ornamental decoration of pier seating, railings, lamp standards and the like.

Once again, the great originator and innovator, Eugenius Birch, played an early major role. Building on his designs for Brighton and New Brighton, his next audacious leap forward was his 1872 pier at Hastings. The pier was the first to be designed with an integral and large pier-head entertainment building and was

the first in an explicit Oriental design. The architectural and commercial possibilities of seaside piers were revolutionized. In the same year, 1872, Coatham Pier on the Yorkshire coast opened with a glass-fronted saloon located halfway along and to one side of the main pier deck.[143] Far less spectacular than the Hastings building, the Coatham saloon also functioned as a reading room and refreshment house.

There were two ways a pleasure pier could come into being. Like the pier at Hastings it could be designed from scratch. Or it could be a promenade pier transformed, with the structure strengthened, decks widened, and new buildings designed for pleasure added. With the magnificent Indian Pavilion, completed in 1877, on the head of Blackpool's North Pier, Birch was responsible too for the first promenade structure metamorphosed into a pleasure pier.

Hastings and the first pleasure pier

The official opening of Hastings Pier took place on the wet and windy Monday of 5 August 1872. The day was symbolically important as the country's second-ever August Bank Holiday, a public holiday that subsequently helped represent both the British summertime seaside and the growing flow of excursionists to the

Left: The magnificent and Oriental-styled Blackpool North Pier, in c.1900. (Leisure Parc archive)

The opening ceremony for Hastings Pier.
(Steve Peak collection)

coast. The pier was remarkable as the culmination of Eugenius Birch's pier-building adventures. It was the first to be designed with a large entertainment building on the pier head of a size to rival or exceed the pleasure palaces and halls on the shore. With onion domes, finials, verandas with sheltering lattice screens and many other decorative elements, it was the first large pier building with a fully fledged Oriental exterior. The exotic design themes were carried over into the rich interior décor.

The 1869 prospectus for the pier explained Birch's intentions:

The principal and novel feature of the design will consist of a Crystal Saloon or Pavilion of extensive dimensions and ornamental character, to be constructed mainly of iron and glass at the head of the Pier. Whilst permitting a free circulation of air, it will be arranged so as to afford complete shelter and protection as well from the heat of the summer, as from cold winds and vicissitudes of other seasons. Its equable temperature will, it is anticipated, render it most attractive at all times to the general public, as well as beneficial to the class of invalids who so largely resort to Hastings for purposes of health.[144]

Birch was maintaining his preoccupation with designing a pier with health benefits to the fore. However, the building was to also include: 'Reading-rooms, Stalls for the Sale of Refreshments, Fancy Goods, etc, Orchestra, Seat accommodation for upwards of 2,000 persons.'

Once the pier was completed, the national press praised the new building. *The London Journal*, for example, believed:

The Oriental Pavilion in 1872. (Steve Peak collection)

The interior of Hastings Pier Pavilion in 1902 following improvements made in 1899. (Steve Peak collection)

The great feature of the pier is a large square saloon built on the end ... already christened 'The Palace on the Sea', and destined to form undoubtedly one of the great local institutions. Externally, it presents an Oriental type of construction, its walls and roof, mostly of glass, being upheld by iron pillars, and surmounted in the centre by a cupola, and at each corner by a miniature dome. Internally, it is a large room fitted for public dinners, concerts and assemblies, capable of holding 2,000 people at a time, and affording to many hundreds a grateful shelter from sun or storm, and a splendid prospect of land and sea.[145]

Another London-based paper, the *Morning Post*, highlighted the distinctiveness of Birch's achievement, arguing 'The pavilion, or saloon, out in the sea, is unique in its way. It is in the Alhambra style of architecture, and is handsomely decorated.'[146] The mention of the Alhambra style references contemporary design ideas and suggests, once again, the influence of Owen Jones on Birch's thinking.

The entertainment potential of the fantastic building, which provided the largest room in Hastings, proved to be the foundation of the pier's success. Within the year, 'the pier had become established as the best music, theatre and variety venue in the borough, offering a continuous round of entertainment for visitors and townsfolk alike.'[147] The pier attracted huge numbers of visitors: 482,000 in the first twelve months and 584,000 in the second.

The Indian Pavilion on Blackpool's North Pier

Hastings Pier was the crescendo to Birch's pier-building frenzy. There was then an interlude until the end of the decade. In the winter of 1874–75 he enjoyed a well-deserved holiday – a painting tour of Italy, Egypt and Nubia. Professionally Birch pursued other aspects of his 'provision for the delectation of visitors to the sea-side' including the 1877 People's Palace and Aquarium at Scarborough.[148] He was also kept busy as consulting engineer for his portfolio of existing piers.

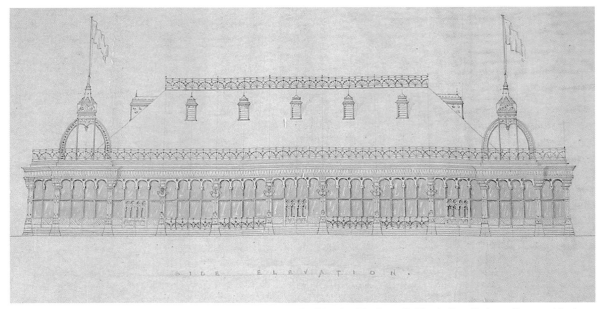

Birch's 1876 drawing of the side elevation of his Indian Pavilion for Blackpool's North Pier. (Leisure Parc archive)

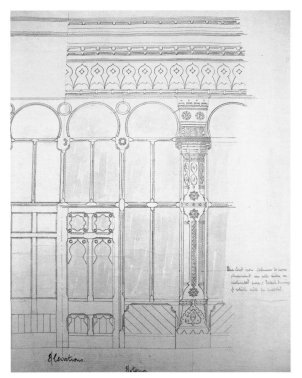

Drawing detailing the decoration of the pavilion's cast-iron column. (Leisure Parc archive)

Illustration of Birch's concern with detailed ornamentation of the pavilion. (Leisure Parc archive)

In the mid-1870s Birch was called back to Blackpool to transform his promenade pier into one fit for pleasure-pier purposes. The North Pier, as it was by then called, faced increasing competition from a host of new entertainment and amusement buildings in the rapidly expanding resort. These included theatres, gardens, aquarium and baths, with the huge Winter Gardens complex due to open in 1878.

The often-repeated story is that the new chairman of the pier company, H. C. McCrea, wanted a different design to the Italianate one originally proposed by Birch. Seeking inspiration, and no doubt having regard for the Hastings building, the two men visited the Indian Office in London and agreed that one of the many temples of Binderabund (present-day Mathura-Vrindavan) provided an ideal exemplar.[149] Despite adopting some design motifs from whichever religious building inspired them, the primary purpose of the Indian Pavilion at the end of the pier was to entice and entertain the most select of Blackpool's holidaymaking visitors.[150] The result, opened in 1877, was Birch's finest pier building, a magnificent Oriental 1,500-seat pavilion on the extended pier head.

The porcupine's quills

Despite the exemplars of Hastings and Blackpool, the pleasure pier model was surprisingly slow to be taken up. Perhaps there were better and easier investment opportunities elsewhere in seaside towns and inland. Even so, in the last two decades of the nineteenth century over thirty new piers were constructed; another dozen followed in the 1900s. One 1890s commentator remarked that, if the speed of pier development continued, 'it will be necessary to alter the map of England, and represent it as a huge creature of the porcupine type, with gigantic piers instead of quills'.[151] Wales, too, should have been added to complete the geographical coverage.

Particularly in the 1880s these new piers usually began life with open promenade decks and small-scale and simple buildings such as shelters, toll houses and perhaps a few shops or a refreshment room. Taking a clockwise journey round the coast, in the two decades to the end of the century new promenade piers included those at Herne Bay (1899), Ramsgate (1881), Dover (1893), Lee-on-Solent (1888), Southampton (1892), Hythe (1881), Seaview (1881), Shanklin (1890), Alum Bay (1887), Totland Bay (1880), Boscombe (1889), Southbourne (1888), Swanage (1896), Torquay (1895), Penarth (1895), Mumbles (1898), Bangor (1896), Rhos-on-Sea (1895) and finally, on the Isle of Man, the 1886 pier at Ramsey.

Despite the absence of a substantial entertainment building, some of these piers – examples include Dover, Penarth and Bangor – were delightfully ornate, with delicate kiosks and much use made of decorative cast iron; the promenade over the sea would have been a glorious experience.

Birch bows out

Eugenius Birch returned to designing new piers – at Hornsea, Bournemouth and Plymouth – in the late 1870s. However, despite his triumphs at Hastings and Blackpool, he was to have no further success with pier pavilions.

His pier at Hornsea on the Yorkshire coast was to be over 1,000ft long and feature a saloon on the pier head. Construction was nearly finished when, in October 1880, over 200ft of the pier, including the pier head and saloon, was destroyed after being hit by a vessel adrift in a violent storm. The shortened structure, opened to visitors the following year, only survived as a functioning pier until 1897.[152]

Birch's initial plans for Bournemouth Pier included a large pavilion, but the local commissioning board were not in favour. Apart from a large, multi-pinnacled and Gothic-styled entrance building, the pier that opened in 1880 was open-decked.[153] In the mid-1890s

The distinctive Gothic entrance to Bournemouth Pier. In 1894 the pier was lengthened and the pier-head bandstand added. (Fred Gray collection)

the pier was lengthened and a pagoda bandstand and other structures added to the enlarged pier head.

The original plan for Birch's pier at Plymouth included 'a handsome and commodious pavilion ... [to] ... be erected upon the pierhead capable of holding 2,500 persons, and the whole design ... [to] ... be of a graceful character, due regard being paid to solidity and strength.'[154] Because of difficulties in raising the necessary capital, the pier was much delayed and when opened on 29 May 1884, was without the planned pavilion. The new pier was, though, architecturally distinctive, with extensive use made of decorative cast

The pagoda bandstand added to Bournemouth Pier in the 1890s. The canvas awning was designed to provide shade from the sun. (Marlinova Collection)

97 BOURNEMOUTH. — On the Pier. — LL.

Plymouth Hoe's promenade pier. The unusually shaped structure was encircled by a graduated landing stage. (Rijksmuseum, Amsterdam)

The pier after the completion of the 2,000-seat pavilion in 1891. (Rijksmuseum, Amsterdam)

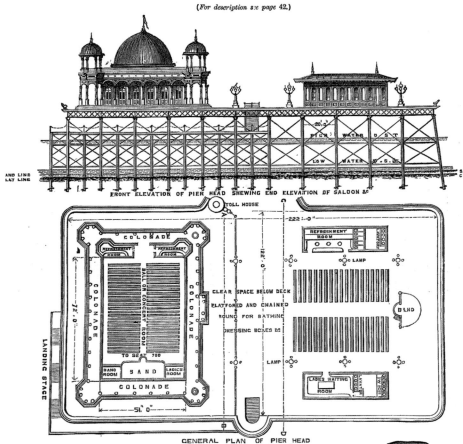

IRON PROMENADE PIER AND BUILDINGS, SKEGNESS.

MESSRS. CLARKE AND PICKWELL, HULL, ENGINEERS.

(For description see page 42.)

FRONT ELEVATION OF PIER HEAD SHEWING END ELEVATION OF SALOON &c

GENERAL PLAN OF PIER HEAD

The pier head at Skegness as planned. The basic structure survived until it was demolished in the mid-1980s. (*The Engineer*, 16 June 1880)

iron. A suite of entrance buildings included a tall and visually dominating ornamental clock. The short neck of the pier led to a huge pear-shaped pier head. There a large bandstand was encircled by weather-screened seating – reminiscent of his West Pier work – and there were kiosks and other buildings, some housing a post office, reading room and a refreshment room. Birch did not live to see the opening of the pier, having died in early January 1884.

Pleasure pier developments

After the 1872 Hastings Pier, the next purpose-designed and successfully executed new pleasure pier was probably the 1879 pier at Paignton, with a large seaward-end pavilion, used for varied musical performances and, added just two years later, a billiard room. Skegness Pier, opening in 1881, also featured a 700-seat pier-head saloon with external ornamental ironwork and with visitor access to the flat roof.[155] Architecturally confused, it included two pairs of Italianate kiosks along the neck and three brick buildings at the entrance in a heavy Gothic style. Paignton and Skegness were up-and-coming late nineteenth-century resorts. So too was Folkestone, and it acquired a carefully designed pleasure pier with ornate pier-head pavilion in 1888.

The early pleasure piers typically had one flexibly used entertainment building, usually located at the pier head although sometimes at the shore end or even midway along the neck of a pier. Externally, the new pavilions included covered verandas and colonnades, and spaces to promenade or sit. A multi-purpose hall might be the venue for an orchestral concert, a theatrical play, concert party, magician's performance, celebratory dinner, magic-lantern show, an exhibition or, cleared of seating, a place for music and dancing, roller-skating or even a dog show.

Lynn Pearson has calculated that seven pier pavilions were built in the 1870s, thirteen in the 1880s, twenty-three in the 1890s and twenty in the first decade of the new century. Once established as a pleasure pier, a typical pattern was for additional entertainment buildings to be added along its length. Pleasure piers evolved and developed over time, responding to new demands and fashions and the resultant business possibilities.

As entertainment fashions and profitability changed more substantially, pier buildings might be more fundamentally transformed. A multi-purpose pavilion might be transformed into a more specialized

The new pier, Southend-on-Sea, c.1890s. (Fred Gray collection)

Clacton Pier with its new 1890s pier-head pavilion. (Library of Congress, Washington, D.C.)

Southampton's Royal Pier was designed for pleasure and as a transport interchange. (Rijksmuseum, Amsterdam)

theatre. What was originally a concert hall might be converted to house a roller-skating rink or a rifle range and then an amusement arcade.

Into the 1890s, the flow of new purpose-built pleasure piers increased. Southend-on-Sea reinvented itself and its pier. The new iron pier of 1890 included a large barrel-roofed pavilion close to the pier's entrance and sited across its narrower neck: the pier company clearly did not expect the pavilion's patrons to walk to the end of the world's longest pier for their pleasures. Then came St Leonards (1891), Blackpool Victoria (now South) (1893), Morecambe West End (1896, although the huge pavilion opened the following Easter), Brighton Palace (1899, with the Oriental pier-head theatre finally completed two years later), the Victoria Pier, Colwyn Bay (1900), Great Yarmouth Britannia (1901), Weston-super-Mare Grand (1904) and, in 1908, the last pleasure pier of the golden age, Southsea South Parade.

As the following examples illustrate, many promenade piers also subsequently metamorphosed into piers for pleasure. The pier at Clacton-on-Sea was lengthened and enlarged during the early 1890s; apart from the indispensable landing stages the new pier head featured an unusual two-storey pavilion, opened in 1893, with an exterior balcony. A sparkling Oriental pavilion and accompanying bandstand topped by an onion dome opened on Southampton's Royal Pier in 1894, just two years after the pier had been completed. Because of funding difficulties Dover, in contrast, had to wait eight years before its shallow-domed pavilion opened on the pier head in 1901. For Shanklin Pier the transformation took almost two decades: the pavilion halfway along the pier was completed in 1909. In many smaller and quieter resorts, such as Cromer and Hunstanton, the transition from promenade to pleasure pier had a muted architectural expression. In such seaside towns, pier buildings, like the resorts they were in, tended to be architecturally understated rather than outrageous, at best pleasant and at worst plain.

Although it never mutated into a fully fledged pleasure pier – the structure was too precise to be radically changed – in 1894 Clevedon Pier acquired a light and fanciful Japanese-style pagoda and two shelters at

Shanklin Pier after its transformation into a pleasure pier. (Fred Gray collection)

Morecambe's Central Pier and its enormous and exotic 1898 pavilion photographed in the early twentieth century. Ethel Cadman was a music hall star. (Fred Gray collection)

the pier head. It was an unusual and specific form of seaside Orientalism.

In some resorts a new pleasure pier was in competition with an existing pier enterprise. In this situation rival piers might enter into a glorious architectural race to provide the most lavish, opulent and modern entertainment buildings. At Morecambe, the huge and imposing five-domed pavilion, accommodating more than 2,000 people, opened in 1897 on the new West End Pier. The older Morecambe pier, renamed Central Pier, had the perfect response, opening its own magnificent 'Taj Mahal of the North' pavilion in July 1898. The pavilion (really a People's Palace): 'could hold 3,000 people and featured a concert hall with private boxes supported by nude figures, refreshment rooms, baths, an aquarium, sun decks [an early date for such

facilities], promenades and an observatory with telescopes.'[156]

DESIGNS FOR OTHER WORLDS

Western seaside resorts have always sought to provide out-of-the-ordinary experiences. Particularly from the mid-nineteenth century, architecture was used to intimate other exotic and pleasurable places and times. Visiting the seaside came to mean not only journeying to the edge of the land and, transported on piers, beyond (in itself a unique experience), but also encountering a fantasy architecture designed to transport users to alternative worlds.

During the great period of pleasure-pier construction no single architectural style dominated. There was a continual jostling of alternative ideas and visions. However, seaside Orientalism, a protean style, and related exotic motifs, became an important architectural theme. It was a pastiche of architectural and design ideas abstracted, often at several removes, from varied Eastern cultures.

Many pier buildings boasted exotic, vaguely Eastern and often sizeable domes, minarets and associated embellishments. Cast iron decorated in exotic and imprecise Oriental styles was also endlessly used for smaller architectural elements including seating, railings, lamp standards, brackets and screens. It was as though the Taj Mahal's architectural symbolism had been seized from India, repatriated to Britain and re-shaped to meet the needs of the burgeoning seaside resorts. Hugely eclectic in the range of architectural elements and ideas and usually remote from the real thing, seaside Orientalism became endlessly adaptable.

The formative building in the birth of seaside Orientalism was Brighton's Royal Pavilion, designed by John Nash for the Prince Regent (later George IV). It was not for another four decades, however, as the seaside market broadened and demanded new leisure buildings, that seaside Orientalism began to take hold, subsequently spreading around the coast and being exported overseas. Whereas the Orientalism of the Royal Pavilion was architecture for a privileged royal and aristocratic elite, its later use was an altogether different project. This 'demotic Orientalism' was a popular, spectacular, mood-forming and modern architecture for a widening mass of holidaymakers.[157]

The experience of Orientalism

Oriental seaside architecture could be applauded as magnificent or reviled as silly by contemporary architectural and other commentators. However, what of its consequences for the holidaymaking users of the architecture? Answering the sedate question is to be drawn into the debate about the nature and role of Orientalism in the West more generally. In Edward Said's influential view, Orientalism was 'a Western style for dominating, restructuring, and having authority over the Orient', so promoting Western imperialism and

The exotic Hastings Pier. (Library of Congress, Washington, D.C.)

colonialism.[158] 'The Orient' also became another characterized and abstracted place, stereotypically distinguished from the West on the basis, for example, of excessive leisure and heightened sexual promise and sensuality. Viewed this way, the Orientalism of seaside architecture presented the illusion of being another place apart from the West, but in doing so helped perpetuate a complicated myth of Eastern inferiority or threat.

Others contend it was just not like that. David Cannadine, for example, has argued that in Britain gradations of class were more important and that empire was often disregarded or taken for granted.[159] John MacKenzie addresses the Orientalism of seaside architecture directly, arguing it was nothing to do with belittling or subjugating the East but was a significant new style, 'grand, mysterious, fantastic and opulent all at once', removed from any reference to a specific culture, in any case often mixed with or butting onto other architectural styles, and bound up with the development of the important seaside holiday business.[160]

Architects, of course, worked in the context of the dominant societal and political perspectives of the times. These included views about Britain's imperial power and subjugation of other parts of the world. And yet the primary design purpose of architects was simply to build spectacular, fashionable and competitive leisure buildings for the seaside. For holidaymakers, thronging the astonishing piers and pavilions, seaside Orientalism must have helped generate a sense of excitement, confirming that the seaside, with its devotion to pleasure and health, was different from ordinary and everyday inland places. Commenting on Llandudno Pier in 1886 a local reporter thought the visitor, strolling along the pier to the sound of the 'siren-like' musical entertainment, was transported 'from the world and its cares' to a 'fairy-land'; the pier promenader 'could not fail to drink health and pleasure with buoyancy of spirit that [proved] a real recre-

The geometric design of the pier railings, Llandudno, 2013. (Fred Gray)

ation to both body and mind.'[161] Kenneth Lindley probably judged it correctly when, in the early 1970s, he wrote: 'Restraint or good taste have never been the characteristics of pier design. It is doubtful if many people take much notice of strange details or exotic forms used as motifs. It is the overall effect of freedom from normal restraints and standards which is so important.'[162]

There was also the association between an architecture suggestive of other places and worlds looking onto, and, in the case of piers, built over, the very seas and oceans that led to foreign lands. In whatever way holidaymakers, as individuals and members of social groups, mediated buildings in Oriental style, the British seaside was a place where signs of empire and the nation's military might were continually on display.[163] The seaside was island Britain's front to other places and peoples, the pier, promenade and cliff-top conjuring images of what lay over the horizon. The coastal waters, over which the piers strode so boldly, were a 'protective barrier' as well as the primary resource for the seaside resort.[164]

There are also links to be made between the British seaside and ideas of empire and racial superiority. In one well-developed late nineteenth and early twentieth

The Oriental pier-head theatre, Palace Pier, Brighton, shortly after the 1901 opening. (Fred Gray collection)

century perspective it was 'the invigorating temperate climate which stimulated enterprise and spawned civilization'.[165] It was at the seaside, and particularly on the pier or promenade, where the climate was at its best and most readily consumed. Unsurprisingly, perhaps, many seaside resorts became the preferred locations both for private boarding schools for the children of those serving overseas, and the retirement homes for the returning servants of empire.

Whether despised or acclaimed in the past, in Britain the surviving vestiges of nineteenth-century Oriental architecture at the seaside have been increasingly represented as valuable architectural heritage, its eclecticism fashionable in the modern world.

A LANGUAGE FOR PLEASURE PIERS

Exotic buildings deserved exotic names. A new vocabulary was needed to describe the growing accumula-tions of entertainment and associated buildings on the new pleasure piers. There was initial uncertainty about what to call these new multi-purpose pier entertainment buildings. A variety of names were tried out before a more standardized vocabulary was agreed by the end of the nineteenth century.

Two words in particular, 'kiosk' and 'pavilion', emerged to denote the buildings designed to provide pleasure seekers with exotic and out-of-this-world experiences above the waves. Pavilion was the English word closest in meaning to kiosk and sometimes the two words were used interchangeably. Although, even in the late nineteenth century, both might be applied to seaside entertainment and leisure buildings whatever the size, by the twentieth century kiosk was increasingly reserved for describing smaller structures and pavilion applied to larger ones. This linguistic consensus only developed, however, following a long and complex etymological journey.

Etymological roots

During the early modern period Western travellers venturing beyond Europe encountered the Turkish word *kiūshk* and the Persian word *kūskh*. The former word was taken to mean a Turkish version of a European pavilion, while in Persia (historically the common Western name for Iran) the word meant palace or portico. It entered French as *kiosque* and Italian as *chiosco* and then into English, although it took time for the 'kiosk' spelling to become standard. The word rarely appeared in print in English before 1800.

Some kiosks far from Europe were large and elaborate structures. An early nineteenth-century traveller to distant lands recounts a kiosk 'as the Sultan's summer residence. It is situated on the sea shore, and commands one of the finest views the eye ever beheld … The kiosk itself [is] fashioned after the airy fantastic style of Eastern architecture.'[166]

By the mid-nineteenth century a kiosk was often used to describe 'an open pavilion or summerhouse of light construction, often supported by pillars and surrounded with a balustrade'. Such buildings were common in Turkey and Persia and imitated in Western gardens and parks. The word also began to be used to describe buildings designed and constructed in Britain, albeit inspired by Oriental styles. One example is a report on the huge 'bathing kiosk' in Oriental style (materials included cast iron and glass) constructed on the banks of the Thames in 1858 for the Viceroy of Egypt and designed to be shipped in pieces and re-erected in the Nile.[167] A related although distinct use of the word developed from the 1860s when kiosk was increasingly used to describe 'a light ornamental structure' used for band performances or the sale of refreshments and items such as newspapers or tobacco.

In contrast to kiosk, 'pavilion' has a longer history as a word in European languages. The English usage is a borrowing from French and was first used in the thirteenth century to describe 'a large, stately, or ornamental tent' for use by royalty, nobility or military leaders. Its meaning was subsequently extended to include structures, especially opulent or ornamental ones, resembling a tent. From the early seventeenth century the word also came to mean an ornamental building, typically of a light construction and designed for shelter, refreshment, rest, entertainment or recreation. The first use of the word to describe a seaside building was when Henry Holland, the architect of the Prince Regent's new Brighton residence built in 1787, named it 'the Marine Pavilion'.

Words for piers

The emergence of 'pavilion' as the agreed word to describe a multi-purpose pier entertainment building most probably originates with Hastings Pier. On the pier's opening, commentators were unsure what term to use. The word 'pavilion' jostled for acceptability with 'saloon', 'crystal saloon' and 'palace on the sea', with other terms being tried including concert hall, promenade hall and even 'crystal music room'.[168] Quite quickly, however, pavilion became the accepted term for the building on Hastings Pier. Perhaps the comparison was made with the older Royal Pavilion along the coast at Brighton. From Hastings, the word was increasingly applied to buildings on other piers.

However, the use of 'pavilion' was not initially restricted to large pier buildings. Although they are now recognized as kiosks, the six octagonal buildings erected on Brighton's 1866 West Pier were originally described by Birch as 'ornamental houses'. The term was mundane and, recognizing that pier promenaders needed a more enticing and exotic name, the West Pier Company began to use 'pavilion' to publicize those houses used as performance spaces. In July 1889, Miss Louie Webb performed in one of the ornamental houses by then called the 'No. 2 Pavilion': submerged in 3ft of water in a glass tank she portrayed the 'Model Undine'. However, some independent commentators

Gladys Powsey, one of the Brighton West Pier aquatic entertainers, early twentieth century. One of the pier's ornamental kiosks is seen in the background. (Fred Gray collection)

thought 'kiosk' was a better descriptive word: in 1885 *The Builder*, an influential professional magazine, described the West Pier 'with all its paraphernalia of bazaars and kiosks'.[169] Etymological confusion reigned!

In October 1893 the West Pier's enormous new pier-head pavilion opened, transforming the character and fortunes of the pier. A *Daily Telegraph* report of the opening acclaimed the 'admirable pavilion', which 'surpasses all its rivals'. The *Telegraph* correspondent was less enthusiastic about the six ornamental houses:

There still remain upon the pier, sublet to shopkeepers and showmen, half a dozen kiosks, sadly in need of paint. It may be understood that hitherto these buildings have produced a certain rent revenue … [providing] … houseroom for such played-out wonders as a 'strange lady' and performing fleas … Surely with a little ingenuity and perseverance, picturesque and bright little entertainments could be arranged, of a description which would aid rather than run counter to the success of the more ambitious programmes in the pavilion.[170]

The 1890s became the West Pier's etymological tipping point. 'Ornamental house' and 'pavilion' were aban-

doned in favour of 'kiosk' to describe the six identical 1866 buildings on the pier, and the large new pier head entertainment structure assumed its title of 'Pavilion'. Ironically, the West Pier's new flexible entertainment pavilion did not survive for long. Just three years into the new century, and following substantial internal changes, it was transformed into the permanent West Pier Theatre.

Consensus achieved

Other piers followed the nomenclatural conventions established for the West Pier and Hastings Pier. The new breed of large multi-purpose entertainment buildings, typically located on the pier head, were most often called pavilions. Kiosk, in contrast, had increasing currency to describe a relatively small pier building. Stylistically, many although not all pier kiosks and pavilions provided a very British seaside interpretation of a 'fantastic style of Eastern architecture'.

EXTRAORDINARY PIERS

Apart from the entertainment buildings, piers hosted an extraordinary range of vernacular architectural structures designed for the pleasure of pier goers and often specifically for individual piers.

All at sea

The exteriors of seaside piers developed idiosyncratic architectural edifices designed for the use and enjoyment of the sea.

A major part of the business of seaside piers, pleasure steamers took passengers on watery excursions from pier head to pier head. In the larger resorts, as pleasure boat traffic increased, piers needed to accommodate more passengers and, whatever the state of the tide, more vessels. Landing stages, which in the early promenade piers had often been an integral part of the

The paddle steamer *Seagull* leaving Hastings Pier, early 1890s. (Steve Peak collection)

A jump into the unknown? Aquatic entertainment continued on the Brighton West Pier into the 1960s. Here the Great Omani (Ron Cunningham) performs his Houdini act. (Brighton West Pier Trust)

pier head, increased in size and complexity. At their most developed, landing stages were separate structures, linked to the pier proper by broad flights of steps, usually stretching out from and encompassing the pier head on three sides, and allowing vessels to be embarked or disembarked whatever the state of the tide.

Bathing stations allowed the public, on payment of a fee and agreement to precise bathing regulations, to bathe, swim and play in the deeper water at the end of

'Rinking' on the American Palace Pier, St Leonards, c.1909. (Steve Peak collection)

the pier. In the more bustling resorts swimming clubs organized nautical regattas with swimming races and even aquatic tea parties viewed by throngs of pier promenaders. Some piers also developed a specialist functional architecture, including precariously flimsy high-diving boards, from which the aquatic entertainers and high divers provided extraordinary displays of skill and bravery.

The amusing pier

In the busiest and most popular resorts piers became palaces of fun and sites of active participation and spectacle; watching was almost as much fun as enjoying a ride. Technology had a part to play, producing new artificial attractions and amusements. A significant development, with specific and sometimes dramatic architectural manifestations, was the emergence of pier-based funfair attractions and similar entertainments. A related change on popular piers was an increasing profusion of mechanical and later electromechanical 'penny-in-the-slot' amusement machines.

Funfair

As early as 1888 the deck of Ramsgate Promenade Pier was used for a switchback railway. The undulating journey over the waves on a gravity-powered roller-coaster was a feature of the pier for three years; the rather shaky ride was then dismantled and removed.[171] In 1894 the pavilion on St Leonards Pier was put to part-time use for the then hugely popular pastime of roller-skating. In the first decade of the new century the island forming part of Weston-super-Mare's Birnbeck Pier acquired a flying machine, water chute and switchback railway.[172] At the same time, the new Britannia Pier at Great Yarmouth quickly gained a helter-skelter. As the Edwardian period ended, Blackpool's Central Pier featured attractions such as an Electric Grotto Railway, a 'joy wheel' (a circular ride that when rotated at increasing speed threw riders into cushioned side walls) and an open-air skating rink.

By 1911 Hastings Pier's funfair attractions included a joy wheel, bowling alley and shooting range housed in three new buildings. Two of the structures were located along the previously open neck of the pier

By August 1911 Hastings Pier had accrued new funfair buildings. (Fred Gray collection)

while the joy wheel was accommodated in a large new circular building at the pier's entrance.[173] Other piers conformed to the pattern of an increasing proliferation of structures for rides and amusements on previously unencumbered decks. Hastings' joy wheel was swept away just four years after it had been installed and the site purchased by the council, enlarged and used for a new bandstand and band enclosure. Elsewhere such Edwardian pier funfairs became an established feature, pointing the way to future developments later in the century.

Amusements

Mechanical and later electromechanical amusement machines also began to appear on piers. The first solitary machines on pedestals were placed next to pier-edge railings. Then clusters of external wall-mounted machines emerged in sheltered locations. As the profit-generating potential of amusement machines became apparent the logical next step was the provision of amusement arcades.

Coin-operated slot machines came to offer a great range of artificial entertainments. Mutoscopes, or 'What the Butler Saw' machines, were invented in New York State in the 1890s. What the butler and the viewer saw were seemingly moving pictures of often risqué scenes. But the mechanical feasts were magnificently varied. Punchball and gripper machines tested a user's strength. Working models showed miniature animated tableaux with violent or scary themes including 'The Haunted Churchyard' and 'The Guillotine'. A fortune would be told on a pre-printed card delivered for a penny. Electricity helped provide some shockingly entertaining games. Then there were machines for competing mechanical horses, cyclists and football or ice-hockey teams; prize-giving cranes; gambling in various guises; testing love or sex appeal; pistol shooting; and spinning metal balls hurtling around circular mazes and spirals, ending up in a winning or, more likely, losing cup. More mundanely but similarly money making, chocolate, cigarettes and other essential items were dispensed from machines. The mechanisms were contained in cases decorated as eclectically as many of the companion pier pavilions although, by

Amusement machines on St Leonards Pier, c.1910. (Steve Peak collection)

The Palace Pier 1911 Winter Gardens laid out for a concert. (Fred Gray collection)

The original use of the Winter Gardens was abandoned in the 1920s and the building converted into an amusement arcade – a role that continues to the present day. (Fred Gray)

the 1930s, more streamlined casing reflected contemporary decorative ideas.[174]

The Brighton Marine Palace and Pier Company was quick to catch on to the possibilities. The first stand-alone machines appeared as the pier opened in 1899. By 1906 the exterior of the Oriental pier-head pavilion accommodated groups of wall-mounted slot machines. Then, in the 1920s, the Winter Gardens, a splendidly decorated music and dance venue that had opened near the entrance of the pier in 1911, was refashioned as a dedicated amusement arcade and renamed the Palace of Fun.[175]

Even the West Pier, the more respectable of Brighton's two piers, succumbed to the lure of funfair rides and amusement machines.[176] 'Skee Ball', an American arcade game, was introduced in 1923. Four years later, the broad shore end of the pier was used as an 'auto-motor track'. A contemporary commentator disparaged the development, arguing the 'toy motor track … is anything but an ornament to the pier … the writer sincerely hopes that another fashion may soon lead to this disfigurement being replaced by something more pleasing to the eye'. The hopes were unrealized. By 1937 the pier featured a large amusement arcade in a low building hung under the reconstructed root end of the pier. New attractions included gaming machines, Flash O Ball, Auto Golf and a mirror maze. There was also a Phono Disk, a recording device similar to the one featured in the haunting closing scene – set on the nearby Palace Pier – of the 1947 film *Brighton Rock*.

There were dissenting voices about the appropriateness of amusements and rides. At Bognor in 1909, the new pier company prohibited mutoscopes and similar machines which were of an 'objectionable nature or contain or display obscene photographs or pictures.'[177] Bournemouth Corporation banned slot machines – far too vulgar for such a proper resort – from the pier until the 1960s.

The musical and dancing pier
Live music had long featured as an important accompaniment to the seaside promenade experience. In the early nineteenth century, musical facilities were often provided on the stone harbour arms and the first timber landing stages that quickly took on an additional promenade role. Musicians played in the open air, on a raised dais or platform, and sometimes without the protection of even a rudimentary shelter. Later in the century, seaside piers became vehicles for listening to music. Although there was usually competition from similar amenities on dry land, the musical experience was arguably more intense above the sea.

Bandstands
Music, played in the open air, was quickly established as an essential feature of promenade piers. Respectable seaside holidaymakers expected to be provided with rational, ordered – and largely passive – recreations such as listening to music. Bandstands were one of the first structures (along with toll houses and shelters) to

Bandstands were occasionally used for other types of performance. Here Pierrots perform on St Leonards Palace Pier, c.1909. (Steve Peak collection)

be installed on the early iron promenade piers and the concept developed further with the birth of fully fledged pleasure piers. By the end of the Victorian period, a bandstand and band enclosure were necessities for a pleasure pier: a common pattern was a substantial circular raised bandstand with open sides, although perhaps with moveable glass screens, facing or surrounded by an open area of seating, itself sometimes enclosed by temporary or permanent screens. Stackable, moveable and easy to increase or decrease in number, deckchairs provided the archetypal band enclosure seating from the 1900s.

Music lovers who arrived early for a performance were often able to seek the comfort of sheltered seating. The 1908 Southsea South Parade Pier band enclosure included two projecting wings of weather screens. The 1916 shore-end 'parade extension' to Hastings Pier – another First World War pier development – followed a similar pattern. When in use, the neo-Classical styled bandstand was surrounded by rows of deckchairs in the open air, although some audience members were shielded from adverse weather by two curved and open-fronted wooden shelters, echoing the design of the bandstand. Although long functioning for other

The bandstand and enclosure, Hastings Pier, c.1930.
(Steve Peak collection)

An artist's impression of the stylish delights of listening to music on Southend Pier in the mid-1930s.
(Fred Gray collection)

purposes, and despite the devastation visited on the pier in the conflagration of October 2010, one section of the curved bandstand shelter survived to 2019. On some piers adjustable canvas screens and awnings provided additional protection from sun or rain.

Circular bandstands were essentially designs from the nineteenth century and by the inter-war years proscenium stages, albeit in sometimes simple form, became a more common architectural open-air feature for band performances on piers. Such facilities also offered the possibility of staging other types of performance including dancing, with holidaymakers assuming a more active, participatory role in the musical entertainments provided. The idea was taken to its logical, delightful, Modernist and unexpected conclusion with Weymouth's 1939 Bandstand Pier.

The problem with band enclosures however was that they were, at least in part, in the open air; adverse weather put a real dampener on the enjoyment of listening to music and the commercial potential of a performance. The obvious solution was to bring the outdoor inside and this began to occur during the Edwardian period. The 1911 bandstand on Brighton's Palace Pier was accompanied by a substantial enclosure with a permanent roof and glass and wooden slid-

ing wall screens: when required these allowed for a completely weatherproof environment. Over time the walls were permanently fixed in place and then, as band music became unfashionable, the building was eventually put to new uses. By 2019 it was the Palm Court restaurant and bar with, unexpectedly and surprisingly, the skeleton of the 1911 bandstand still surviving in the centre of the building. Purpose-built concert halls were to become an increasingly common pleasure pier feature.

Boisterous dancing on Blackpool's Central Pier. (Leisure Parc archive)

Open-air dancing

An early record of open-air dancing on a pier is for Blackpool's South Jetty (re-named Central Pier in the 1890s) in July 1870, just two years after the pier opened. The entrepreneurial and innovative Robert Bickerstaffe, then the newly appointed manager of the pier, needed to increase its business. Bickerstaffe organized a half-price afternoon steamer excursion from the pier to Southport and, while the ship was away, went 'looking for a band of some sort'. Bickerstaffe was later to recount that when the ship returned 'the band was playing … [and] … instead of going off the pier the passengers set to and had a dance, most of them stayed on the pier all evening'.[178] Open-air dancing was the making of what became known as the 'People's Pier' with the dancing platform often in continual use from daybreak to 10pm.

It was during the inter-war years of the twentieth century that open-air dancing became a requisite participatory entertainment on many piers in larger re-

sorts – including Morecambe and Blackpool on the northwest coast, Great Yarmouth on the east coast and Hastings, Brighton and Bournemouth in the south. In some resorts the activity continued into the 1960s and 70s.

A PIER MAKER

Many professionals were involved in designing and making piers during the golden age explored in this chapter. The long career of pier engineer-cum-architect Martyn Noel Ridley (1860–1937) spanned six decades. His work illustrates many of the themes and issues pier architects and engineers grappled with from the 1880s to the inter-war years.

M. Noel Ridley, as he was professionally known, trained under Eugenius Birch and was involved in drawing the plans for Plymouth Pier. His first complete pier, designed when he was just twenty-six and clearly showing the influence of his mentor, was the Victoria Pier, Folkestone. Opening in July 1888 the pier's name commemorated the Golden Jubilee of the Queen's accession to the throne. The open promenade deck led to a pier-head pavilion, which included a concert hall and, on the roof, seating for 'a large number of people … on regatta days and other special occasions.'[179] The floating pier-head landing stage was of 'unique construction', allowing passengers to access steamers and pleasure boats at all states of the tide (although it proved unsuccessful).

Ridley often worked with other engineers and architects and, later in his career, focussed especially on the substructure of piers and on landing stages rather than on the design of pier buildings. Ridley, and a fellow engineer F. C. Dixon, designed the promenade-orientated open-decked Shanklin Pier on the Isle of Wight, which opened in August 1890. Not all of Ridley's schemes were realized. In the late 1880s and early

NEW PROMENADE PIER, FOLKESTONE.

MR. M. N. RIDLEY, A.M.I.C.E., WESTMINSTER, ENGINEER.

(For description see page 418.)

GENERAL ELEVATION.

GENERAL PLAN.

LOWER SANDGATE ROAD

TOTAL LENGTH 682'·0"

SECTION C.D.

END ELEVATION OF PAVILION

SECTION A.B.

ELEVATION OF TOLL HOUSES

Folkestone Pier plans. (*The Engineer*, 27 May 1887)

90s, and now working with W. M. Duxbury, his plans for a pier for Hove, less than a mile away from the Brighton West Pier to the east, came to nothing. Although bankrupted in 1893, Ridley was a resilient professional who developed a diverse portfolio of work in the early decades of the new century.

In collaboration with architect Robert J. Beale he designed the 1901 pier-head pavilion on Dover's Promenade Pier. It included a concert hall with accommodation for 950 people, refreshment bars, a shop and pier master's office. A distinctive part of the design, which also featured in at least one of Ridley's subsequent pier buildings, was the open concert hall space, unencumbered by supporting pillars. A contemporary account described how: 'The hall is roofed in one span, with semi-circular steel trusses carried down to the pier girders, and there are no columns to obstruct the view of the platform, which is of ample size for an or-

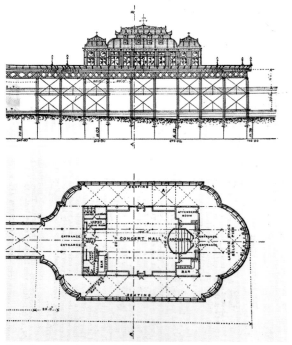

Detail of the pier head, Folkestone Pier. (*The Engineer*, 27 May 1887)

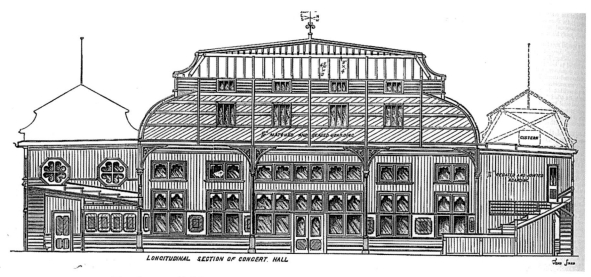

The Concert Hall in section, Folkestone Pier. (*The Engineer*, 27 May 1887)

chestral chorus.'[180]

As a consulting engineer Ridley designed new buildings, extensions and landing stages for a number of existing piers originally the work of his old mentor, Birch. On Eastbourne Pier Ridley was responsible for the large seaward pavilion theatre of 1901. The building, which in keeping with the fashion of the time was originally named the Kursaal, was a critical step in modernizing Birch's promenade pier and providing pleasure-pier entertainments fit for the new century. Apart from the theatre, with seating for 1,350 people and standing room for another 200, the structure included a camera obscura, two games pavilions, a licensed 'American Bar', 'two cosy tea-rooms' and two refreshment buffets. At its opening the exterior of the building was said to be 'of an Oriental appearance, a minaret rising from each of the four corners of the roof'.[181] In the auditorium 'the most striking feature … is the turtle backed ceiling, the ten roof trusses being supported on special piles screwed ten feet into the solid rock beneath the bed of the sea.' The prosce-

nium arch was decorated with plaster work featuring a golden shield supported by two cupids bearing a floral festoon of gold. The racked floor of the theatre was fitted out with red-plush tipping seats with ornamental iron frames.

On the West Pier in Brighton, a new 1,400-seat concert hall opened in 1916. The architects were Clayton & Black, a local firm of architects and surveyors. As engineer, Ridley was responsible for the essential structural work of widening and strengthening the central section of the pier where the building was to be located and also designed the 'light and graceful' steel girders and roof trusses necessary to ensure the interior of the hall was unbroken by supporting pillars and columns. The interior roof trusses were said to resemble 'the delicate fan lines of a Late Gothic roof'. Despite the size of the new concert hall, the broad and sheltered new deck allowed promenaders to walk around both sides of the building's exterior. Although it seems remarkable that a pleasure palace should be built, and opened, while the horrors of the First World

War were taking place across the Channel, the first conflict was not as disruptive to the pier and seaside business as the second. The contract for the concert hall had been entered into in 1914 and the work was carried out at pre-war prices. However, away from Brighton, Ridley's essential war service work was designing jetties and wharves in England and France.

Ridley's career increasingly focussed on the use of 'dovetail corrugated sheeting' in making reinforced concrete for use in civil engineering projects. He argued the material could and should be used for reinforced concrete walls, floors and roofs in a great diversity of buildings, in the construction of jetties and wharves and even in making concrete ships.[182] Dovetail corrugated sheeting was also used in his most notable design – not for a British pier but for an Irish bridge. He designed the startling modern and dramatically located Mizen Head Bridge of 1909. The single-arch reinforced concrete footbridge provided access to the coastal signal station on Cloghan Island in County Cork in the extreme south west of what is now the Republic of Ireland. A very early use of reinforced concrete in the country, the National Inventory of Architectural Heritage nowadays proclaims the bridge as 'one of the most innovative engineering structures to be found in Ireland'.

Ridley's fascination with reinforced concrete was prescient. Along with steel it became one of the defining materials used in the transformation of British seaside resorts in the first four decades of the twentieth century. In the mid-1930s, Ridley continued to lecture and write about making piers.[183]

THE NEW CENTURY

New piers

A dozen new piers were completed between 1900 and 1910.[184] Some were designed as unpretentious landing stages. For example, the 700ft-long Minehead Pier, completed in 1901, was constructed largely to service the flourishing pleasure-boat business in the Bristol Channel. Two new piers, both opening in 1905, had similar roles despite quite different lengths. The pier at Felixstowe was an anachronism from the past. Built to service steamer traffic along the East Anglia coast it was constructed of timber and at 2,640ft, like the early piers in the Thames estuary, it was very long. In contrast, in the same year the very short – just 510ft – Prince of Wales Pier opened in the Cornish port of Falmouth.

Other new piers in the first decade of the century were grand structures designed for pleasure. One was Great Yarmouth's 1902 Britannia Pier with its ostenta-

The new Southsea South Parade Pier in 1911. (Geoffrey Mead collection)

tious pavilion. The last fully fledged and completely new pleasure pier, Weston-super-Mare's Grand Pier of 1904, was resplendent with a 2,000-seat pier-head pavilion theatre. Both piers were erected by Mayoh and Haley, and given the design similarities between the Great Yarmouth and Weston pavilions, both in a Gothic-cum-Baroque rather than Oriental style, Lynn Pearson may be correct to suggest that they came from the same source.[185]

Southsea South Parade Pier was completed in 1908 to replace the one destroyed by fire four years earlier. In recognition of the earlier disastrous conflagration, the deck of the new pier was made of concrete (a harbinger of things to come). This pier featured a bandstand at the octagonal pier head and a large shore-end pavilion housing a theatre and a combined café and dance hall. Two years later, in 1910, the low-key and unprepossessing Fleetwood Pier was completed; it gained a plain pavilion at the root end the following year.

And new pavilions

Although during the 1900s the rate of new pier building slowed, 'pavilions continued to be erected apace.'[186] Two dozen significantly sized pleasure buildings were added to existing piers between 1900 and 1916. Stylistically they continued some Victorian trends but began to point in new and unexpected directions.

On the larger piers with a myriad of entertainments, pleasure buildings also tended to become more dedicated. General-purpose pavilions could not easily accommodate specialized requirements. Some late nineteenth-century pavilions were converted into dedicated theatres with both seating and stage raked. Rather than being described as a pavilion, a new pier building was more likely to be named as a theatre or concert hall or, in later years, a dance hall.

Brighton Palace Pier

Pier connoisseurs debate the apotheosis of Victorian piers. One contender is Brighton's Palace Pier. The pier's gestation was laboured. The revealingly titled 'Brighton Marine Palace and Pier Company' – the marine palace was as important as the pier itself – was incorporated in 1888. Although construction began in 1891, the opening ceremony – of the still unfinished structure – didn't take place until 1899. The intent was to produce a forward-looking and modern pier. Innovative use was made of electric lights on a series of delicate triple arches along its neck: as a night-time spectacle the new Palace Pier was far superior to the neighbouring West Pier. The final step in completing the pier as originally planned was the opening of a magnificent and ornate pier-head theatre on 3 April 1901, just ten weeks after the death of Queen Victoria. The exterior of the theatre was indeed akin to a palace and was the apogee of Victorian seaside Orientalism.

In July 1901 an editorial in the theatrical newspaper *The Stage* commented approvingly on the emergence of new pavilions and theatres at the seaside, particularly on pleasure piers. Noting that the summer 'holiday exodus has begun. The pleasure resorts are filling up'; the comment continued that in the past 'the simple marine enterprise that put up a pier and squeaked and blared a dubious music upon it did not grapple with the zeit-geist precisely in the right way.' There were handsome new pavilions on the piers at Dover and Eastbourne, while at Brighton 'The Palace Pier, with its spacious and beautiful pavilion and all its excellent arrangements, is a striking example of the new spirit that has come over the dream – and drone – of the old marine order.'[187]

St Annes Pier

The turn-of-the-century success of St Annes as a resort led to considerable embellishment of the town's pier. Most notable were two buildings on the enlarged head

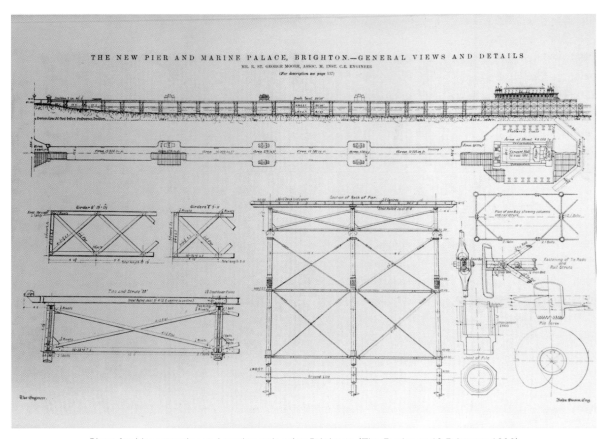

THE NEW PIER AND MARINE PALACE, BRIGHTON.—GENERAL VIEWS AND DETAILS

MR. R. ST. GEORGE MOORE, ASSOC. M. INST. C.E. ENGINEER

(For description see page 137)

Plans for 'the new pier and marine palace' at Brighton. (*The Engineer*, 12 February 1892)

of the pier. A gloriously ornate Moorish pavilion was completed on one side of the pier head in 1904. It featured two large and conspicuous domes and, in the centre of the roof, a lantern light topped by another smaller dome. The exterior was painted 'a bluish-green with yellow tints'.[188] Inside there was seating for 920 people. The intention was to create an exclusive space, costing extra to enter, and iron railings, a box office and turnstiles fenced the building off from the remainder of the pier.

Six years later, and on the other side of the pier head, an existing open-air stage and enclosure were converted into a much more substantial building called the Floral Hall. The hall was to be the home of the pier's orchestra (most of the musicians were women) for almost six decades.

The last hurrah of Orientalism

The Palace Pier theatre and St Annes Moorish pavilion were splendid evocations of seaside Orientalism. But despite the brilliance of the two buildings, seaside Orientalism as an architectural style for pier buildings faded as the Edwardian period began. Never totally dominant as a design motif for piers, it was not really for the twentieth century, perhaps because it seemed to represent the past rather than the future.

The intricate decorative detail of the sheltered arcade around the pier-head theatre, Palace Pier, c.1960s. (Fred Gray collection)

Some architectural motifs did hark back to classical architectural themes, although many commentators were at a loss to classify and categorize a pier entertainment building as of a particular style. For example, despite some classical references, one observer thought it was best to describe the 1916 concert hall on Brighton's West Pier as 'architecture in holiday mood'.

Cleethorpes, Cromer and Bognor

Architectural responses might also be more functional, with the main purpose of a design to house as efficiently as possible new fashions in seaside entertainment, or to provide a replacement for a building destroyed by fire or storm. For example, the pier-head concert hall on Cleethorpes Pier burnt down in 1903 with the site subsequently used for shops and a café. Two years later, a new dancing and entertainments pavilion was erected on a side extension close to the entrance to the pier. The new Cleethorpes pavilion was an example of the 'barrel-vaulted halls with little decoration' typical of piers in smaller Edwardian resorts.[189]

Cleethorpes Pier showing the short-lived concert hall on the pier head. (Rijksmuseum, Amsterdam)

Construction of Cromer Pier. (HOP Consulting Ltd)

A tale of two piers: Great Yarmouth

The peculiarities and specifics of these trends in pier and pavilion building are illustrated by Britannia Pier and Wellington Pier at Great Yarmouth.[192] At the turn of the century there was intense competition between the organizations responsible for the two piers.

The company owning the Britannia Pier demolished the mid-1850s pier at the end of 1900 – it simply could not be adapted for modern seaside entertainment purposes – and set about building a new structure. Pride of place was a large pier-head pavilion with seating for 2,000 people. With a central dome and four corner turrets – by then a common pattern – the building was in an Anglicized Second Empire style.[193] The pavilion was prefabricated by the firm of Boulton & Paul at its manufacturing works in nearby Norwich. The company specialized in designing horticultural buildings, conservatories, plant houses and 'portable iron buildings', and was ideally suited to providing an entertainment building that could be quickly erected over the waves.[194]

Witnessing the rebirth of Britannia Pier just to the north, the Wellington Pier Company conceded that the existing pier would not survive in its ownership. Aware of the need to invest in the entertainment facilities of the growing resort, Yarmouth Corporation took over the pier and began transforming it. The middle section was strengthened and broadened, becoming the site of a new (1903) pavilion of revolutionary design. The pavilion, constructed in just two months, was designed by John William Cockrill (1849–1924), the locally born Borough Surveyor. 'Concrete Cockrill', as he was nicknamed, was clearly familiar with contemporary international developments in architecture and design (the stylistically influential Exposition Universelle had been held in Paris in 1900).[195]

Influenced by the growing fashion for Art Nouveau, the style of the pavilion was startlingly original. Compared with other pier buildings of the same pe-

The pier at Cromer opened in 1901 as a delightful late promenade pier, 500ft long and varying in width from 40ft at the narrowest point to 112ft at the pier head. The structure, a classic of its type, showed off all the advantages of structural and decorative cast iron, although the piles were made of wrought iron and the trusses of steel. There were ornamental entrance kiosks with cupola roofs, cast-iron gates, embayed shelters on the neck, eight decorative gas lamp standards running down the centre of the pier, and a pier-head bandstand and encompassing enclosure. The success of the pier in attracting visitors pointed to the value of a more solid and weatherproof entertainment building. The bandstand was roofed over in 1905, a new floor laid in 1907 (and roller-skating introduced) and then 'from 1912 to 1921 the building was gradually transformed into a fully fledged theatre'.[190]

In 1908 the pier at Bognor, which had been owned by various local government bodies for the previous thirty years, was sold to a private company.[191] The new owners set about redeveloping the shore end of the pier. The result was a huge, dominating and stylistically unclassifiable structure, built in 1910–11, including a 1,180-seat theatre with a roof garden, a cinema with a capacity of 528 people, a dozen shops and a restaurant.

The pavilion was the central element on the 1902 new Britannia Pier, Great Yarmouth. (Fred Gray collection)

riod, the exterior, with its domes, towers and decorative finials, was unfussy and clean: 'On the front elevation the roof curved between tapering towers topped with copper mob-cap domes. The tympanum was split into three glazed segments, thin projecting finials rising upwards between them. Similar finials rose above the roof line on either side, as well as the projecting side arcades.'[196]

The pavilion was most likely the inspiration for subsequent pier buildings elsewhere, including the 1908 pavilion on Southsea's South Parade Pier and the similar structure, built two decades later, on Penarth Pier. Cockrill's design was a remarkable forerunner of the Modernist seaside buildings of the 1930s.

Another innovative development was the build-

ing's steel (rather than iron) frame. The structure was covered in ceramic panels clad in Uralite, a patented fireproof material which, according to the British Uralite Company in 1903, was 'the invention of a Russian Colonel of artillery … [and] … a substance composed of asbestos fibre cemented with glue'.[197]

As Kathryn Ferry has demonstrated, Cockrill had a major role in the transformation of Great Yarmouth into a modern seaside resort.[198] He improved the town's sea defences and infrastructure. One of his Great Yarmouth buildings, erected in 1900, was what was described at the time as a combined 'pumping station, urinal and shelter built of concrete tile and terracotta'. Designed to provide for public health and public comfort, the building was clad in tiles patented by

The metamorphosis of a pier pavilion. The Wellington Pier pavilion before the original architectural detailing was lost in the 1950s recladding. (Fred Gray collection)

Cockrill himself and Doulton, the ceramics company.[199] Cockrill designed a number of other iconic buildings in the resort including the Hippodrome, also of 1903, just a short walk away from the pier, an outstanding example of British Art Nouveau and rare purpose-built seaside circus. Another substantial addition to the resort's entertainment buildings secured by Cockrill was a cast-off 1881 cast-iron and glass Winter Garden that had been languishing in Torquay. The building was dismantled, transported to Great Yarmouth and re-erected in 1904 at the entrance to Wellington Pier, where it became the home of the Wellington Pier Orchestra.[200]

And then ...

The Uralite cladding Wellington Pier's pavilion was removed and replaced with another material in the 1950s, with much of the architectural detail lost in the process. Early this century the pavilion was demol-

ished, the steel frame briefly revealed as a stark skeleton. The 2008 'Wellington Bowl' building was a reproduction of Cockrill's pavilion, constructed with modern materials although also incorporating some of the restored original structural elements. In 2019 the interior space was used for a tenpin bowling alley and other amusements. After a century of varied use for seaside entertainments, the adjacent Winter Garden was closed as unsafe in 2010. Architecturally listed as Grade II*, the at-risk building stood forlornly empty in 2019. Described as the UK's last surviving Victorian Winter Garden, the elegant structure awaited renewal and reinvention for twenty-first century purposes.

The entertainment buildings on Britannia Pier repeatedly changed. The huge pier-head pavilion was destroyed by fire in December 1909, just seven years after its opening. The 1910 replacement with a 'towered Baroque façade' also burned down in April 1914 and remarkably another pavilion opened by the end of

The Wellington Pier pavilion, still functioning but increasingly decrepit, 1993. (Fred Gray)

The closed pavilion, June 2000. The Jetty and Britannia Pier can be glimpsed in the distance. (Fred Gray)

July.[201]   Reflecting changing demands and seaside pleasure, the large Floral Hall Ballroom was added to the pier in 1927; that building was destroyed in another blaze in 1932 and replaced, in 1933, by the Grand or Ocean Ballroom.[202] The accursed history of fire on Britannia Pier was not finished and in 1954 a further conflagration removed both the third pavilion and the ballroom. While the ballroom was not replaced, in 1958 the Britannia Theatre opened on the site of the pavilion. Although one of Great Yarmouth's major entertainment venues, the functional structure has been described as 'a giant shed which must be the ugliest pier pavilion in England'.[203] The authors of the pre-eminent architectural guide to Norfolk were slightly less judgmental, believing the pavilion was dull, but 'better inside than out'.[204]

The reconstructed Wellington Pier pavilion, August 2010. (Fred Gray)

Artificial palms add an exotic touch to the view of Britannia Pier and its barn-like theatre, June 2000. (Fred Gray)

'Summer Madness' on Britannia Pier, 1993. (Fred Gray)

The golden age concluded

Although it was not evident in 1900, when it must have seemed pier-building business as usual, within a few years the building of new piers dramatically slowed and, by 1911, had ground to a halt.

By 1900, piers had been built in most of the suitable and receptive resorts. Despite a proliferation of proposals for new piers around the coast of seaside Britain many fizzled out where a resort was already adequately supplied with piers, where the municipal authorities or residents were resistant or where the proposed pier was intended for a smaller and more marginal seaside place.

Only the largest and most vibrant of resorts could sustain more than one pier. On the Yorkshire coast, the twin settlements of Coatham and Redcar could not sustain the two 1870s pleasure piers. Repeatedly storm damaged and commercially unsuccessful, Coatham's pier 'had a very chequered and disastrous career' and was eventually demolished in 1899.[205] By 1900 Blackpool had three working piers and Bournemouth had two functioning ones and another – Southbourne – by then closed. Hastings and St Leonards, Lowestoft, Morecambe, and Southsea each had two piers. Although Brighton's Chain Pier was no longer a feature of the seafront, having been destroyed in a storm in 1896, the West Pier was going strong and, to the east of it, the Palace Pier had just opened. Great Yarmouth's two old piers were about to be transformed, and in 1904 Weston-super-Mare gained a second pier.

Bexhill-on-Sea in Sussex illustrates the difficulties in successfully executing a pier proposal at the turn of the century. Between 1895 and 1907 eleven pier schemes were formulated for the emerging resort. Although one early proposal led to the opening in 1896 of a concert hall, the Kursaal, built on iron piles on the beach, the remainder of the envisioned pier never materialized. The ten other proposals also came to nothing. The resort was too small to make a pier viable and, in some cases, council and resident opposition too great.[206] In any event, by 1907 the national pier-building frenzy was a thing of the past.

It became clear that a pier was not a milch cow providing easy and limitless income and profit. There were various issues. Not all piers were as popular or as profitable as anticipated. Specific pier companies were under-capitalized from the outset. Still more discovered that, once capital had been consumed in the construction of the new pier, income fell short of what was subsequently required for necessary although sometimes unanticipated expenditure on the structure of the pier. Conflagration, storm and collision represented significant risks threatening the financial viability of pier companies.

As it turned out, Fleetwood Pier was the somewhat unremarkable Edwardian conclusion to fifty years of

Southsea Clarence Pier, 1900s. (Library of Congress, Washington, D.C.)

pier building. That was it! The sun set on the golden age of pier building. With the exception of just four other piers – two constructed at Weymouth in the 1930s, and two post-war piers replacing structures destroyed in the Second World War – no new piers were built during the remainder of the twentieth century.

Bournemouth Pier shortly after the 1894 enlargement of the pier head and the addition of a pagoda bandstand, long linear shelters and kiosks. (Rijksmuseum, Amsterdam)

Chapter Six

PIERS AND THE SUNNY SEASIDE

THE NEW AGE

This chapter explores the architecture of seaside piers in the interlude between the two World Wars. Radical changes in seaside holidaymaking and the number and diversity of people visiting coastal resorts were bound up with fundamental changes in what people thought about and wanted from seaside nature. Although the antecedents may be traced back to the late nineteenth century, it was during the inter-war years that the appreciation of the joys of the sun came fully to the fore. And the coming of the sun was related to the emergence and flowering of seaside Modernism. The two combined had profound consequences for the architecture of at least some piers with, where the opportunity arose, radically different pier buildings designed for seaside sun and fun.

One aftermath of the immense loss and disruption of the First World War was to strengthen the popularity of seaside resorts and seaside piers. It was as though the nation needed a seaside holiday to recuperate from the tragedy of war.

The state, in its various guises, was newly emboldened by the war to intervene at the seaside in radical ways. Alarmed at the poor condition and fitness of working people drafted into the forces, the post-war British government became increasingly concerned with the importance of improving the nation's health. There was a national campaign, for example, to build a 'Fitter Britain'. Municipal authorities wishing to enhance the entertainment and leisure facilities provided for public use were, from 1928, able to fund appropriate infrastructure projects with money borrowed from central government.

In response to a period of intense competition between resorts and new powers granted by central government, seaside councils became increasingly interventionist in the physical infrastructure of their resorts. Between the two World Wars seaside local authorities provided many new pavilions and entertainment venues, parks and gardens and remodelled promenades. There were also new indoor swimming pools and baths and, most symbolic of all, open-air pools and lidos: exercise, according to one government spokesman in 1937, took 'no better form than swimming in clean sea-water open to the sun and air'.[207] Following sustained trade union lobbying, in 1938 there was legislation to secure holidays with pay for all workers.

The new sunny seaside also increasingly became a

Left: The Modernist Worthing Pier in 1999. (Fred Gray)

place of display, performance and spectating. Holiday-makers, their costumes for beach, sea and pool, and their bodies, were on show with the new seaside architecture the stage. The beauty contest was one manifestation of such developments, and by the mid-1930s the more popular piers were hosting 'bathing belle' parades and competitions.[208]

Architecture for the sun

Underlying such developments was a growing love affair with the sun.[209] The Victorian preoccupations with sea bathing, seawater, sea air and ozone became things of the past. Instead a broadly based social movement including holidaymakers themselves, designers and architects, the medical professions, social reformers and the government, became obsessed with the benefits of the sun and sun bathing. The movement reached maturity in the 1930s.

Victorian mediocrity and mean parodies

The coming of the sun led many architectural and planning critics to condemn much of what had gone before while heaping praise on the modern designs and materials. Writing in 1935, the influential architect and town planner Wesley Dougill (1893–1943) argued contemporary resorts demonstrated 'lack of imagination in both architecture and planning; shoddy buildings steeped in Victorian mediocrity; designs of bandstands, ornamental railings and seats taken direct from old catalogues.'[210] Dougill loathed how fine early seaside architecture was 'almost submerged in a sea of later mediocrity' dominated by 'mean parodies' – for example, of Brighton's Royal Pavilion – and pastiche.

Piers provided pastiche *par excellence*. Writing in 1934 the journalist and satirist Malcolm Muggeridge (1903–1990) argued 'A pier can be a sterile promontory. It can be just planks reaching into the sea. It can also be, and usually is, a kind of pasteboard Taj Mahal. For some reason or other the designers of piers have always looked for inspiration to the East.'[211] A year later, the journalist and commentator Ivor Brown (1891–1974) expressed a more sympathetic although nostalgic view of the significance of piers:

The seaside town must have its pier. The pier, used for fun, is an oddity of English taste which has found ex-

'Sunday Parade' on the respectable Blackpool North Pier, c.1920s. The pier's nineteenth-century architecture appeared increasingly old fashioned. The big wheel was demolished in 1928. (Fred Gray collection)

pression in a weird splendour of Oriental knobs and garish expression. … One wonders how the thin metal legs of those strange centipedes can withstand the winter storms; but endure they do. … On the pier age slumbers in the sun, youth dances or dallies in a gallery of cunning slot-machines, and children patiently pursue the small fry of the sea with line and sinker. Piers, architecturally absurd excrescences from the Marine Parade, are happy places; their lamp-lit platforms end in lovers' meeting.[212]

As much by omission as by explicit comment, 1930s architectural commentators thought little of the pleasure piers arranged around the coast. The concern, instead, was building for the future seaside using Modernist design, modern materials including concrete and sheet glass and modern construction techniques such as the steel frame. For Dougill, resorts needed to take advantage of the new opportunities to forge a new conception, with new buildings showing 'that beauty, economy and fitness for purpose and environment are not irreconcilable'.[213] The following year the *Architectural Review* set out 'the programme the architect has to follow in planning for leisure spent at the seaside', arguing that the 'newly appreciated' virtues of light and air provided architects with the maximum opportunity of 'achieving a characteristic modern expression'.[214] Seaside designers were particularly beguiled by the symbolism of Nautical Moderne with its references to ocean liners, brave new modern engineering and construction, and to other distant places.

MODERNISM AND PIERS

Pleasure piers were mostly removed from the Modernist architectural discourse. Most appeared ill equipped to respond to society's love affair with the sunny seaside. Surely not much could be done to fundamentally modernize the existing built infrastructure of piers.

Some superficial changes could, however, be made. At night decorative lighting could hide assorted design sins from earlier eras. Deckchairs – a seemingly insignificant piece of beach furniture that came to represent the idling away of time in the sunshine –

Photographed in the early 1920s, Bournemouth Pier was ill equipped to cope with the coming of the sunny seaside. (Fred Gray collection)

ON THE PIER, BOURNEMOUTH

The 1930s Modernist makeover to St Leonards Pier, postcard sent summer 1934. (Steve Peak collection)

became *de rigueur* on piers. In addition, with minimal modification to existing piers – perhaps simply an area of deck enclosed by glass screens – new sun lounges and sun terraces were added in the hope of tempting sun lovers away from beaches and the new open-air pools. However, beyond such measures unless radical action was taken it was awkward for piers, built in the past for earlier pleasures and entertainments, to be readily adapted to entice and attract modern sun-seeking holidaymakers.

Storm and fire also sometimes acted as agents of change, sweeping away – often in just an hour or two – existing buildings and large sections of a pier. Within a period of just over four years Eugenius Birch's two revolutionary Oriental pavilions were both destroyed by fire: the one on Hastings Pier on 15 July 1917 and Blackpool's North Pier Indian fantasy on 11 September 1921. The destruction wreaked by fire and storm provided the opportunity – indeed the necessity – to re-mould and reshape a pier. Except for the most successful resorts and piers, such elemental forces created financial challenges for pier companies. Following

significant damage some piers did, indeed, disappear. Sometimes the private enterprise owning a badly damaged structure was wound up and the assets transferred to another company. On occasion, however, the private sector was unwilling or unable to provide adequate funding to sustain a pier. Local authorities often took a different view, intervening to take control of a struggling enterprise because of a pier's importance in the local seaside economy. From this perspective a pier was a key asset, critical in sustaining the prosperity of a seaside resort. At Southport, for example, the corporation purchased the pier in 1936 following a ruinous fire three years earlier and implemented an improvement scheme. It included a 'magnificent Café at the seaward end of the Pier, and the modernizing of the rolling stock of the Pier Tramway'.[215] Other developments included glazed windscreens, decorative lighting the length of the pier and a new entrance.[216]

Clacton Pier

In other circumstances the private sector was perfectly capable of acting as a catalyst for change. For private

Clacton Pier in the 1920s. (Marlinova Collection)

pier owners, the task was to find additional ways to lure visitors onto piers, enhance income and generate profit. Developing and enhancing existing structures, particularly with new pavilions, theatres, concert halls and dance halls, was the obvious way forward, especially in the context of the continual radical changes in seaside holidaymaking expectations.

Occasionally the transformation was immense. An extreme example is Clacton Pier. When purchased by Ernest Kingsman in 1922, 'the useless old jetty' contained 'a few rusty slot machines' and employed nine people during the holiday season. 'The King of Clacton Pier' set about revolutionizing the purpose of the pier, turning it into 'a self-contained holiday town over the sea'.[217] By 1934 Kingsman boasted that the pier business employed 400 people, with 40,000 visitors often going through the turnstiles in one day.

The physical structure and architecture of the pier was remade. That part of the pier closest to the shore was massively enlarged and the substructure, and much of the deck, rebuilt in immensely strong reinforced concrete. The huge six-and-a-half acres deck

area was redeveloped with new pleasure structures including theatres, a zoo, the exotically named Blue Lagoon Dance Hall – 'The Beautiful Dance Hall Over the Sea' – and the Crystal Casino – 'The Hall of Fun'. The cavernous entertainment sheds presented entertaining Modernist fronts at the entrance of the pier. There was even an Olympic-size open-air swimming pool suspended above the waves – proclaimed as the 'wonder swimming pool' with 'sea bathing in perfect safety

Clacton's funfair and amusement pier fully developed in the late 1930s. (Marlinova Collection)

under ideal conditions'. The deck was extended further, and the massive Steel Stella rollercoaster – 'the longest ocean run in Great Britain' – was added in 1937. By then the pier was 'the gayest of gay piers' and 'Britain's pleasure ground over the sea!'[218]

The remaking of the pier was a major part of the transformation of Clacton-on-Sea as 'the modern holiday resort for modern holidays'. Another key element was the opening of Butlin's holiday camp in 1938. In the summer of 1939, the resort was advertised as 'Britain's Happiest Holiday Town "For Everything Under the Sun"'.[219]

The story of the piers in other two resorts, Worthing and Colwyn Bay, illustrate how Modernism might arrive on piers in municipal ownership.

Worthing

Storm, fire and a change of ownership from public pier company to local authority enterprise – all in the context of the broader societal developments outlined above – were involved in the metamorphosis of Worthing pier in less than a quarter of a century. In March 1913 a storm on the night of Easter Monday destroyed the neck of the pier, severing and leaving stranded as an offshore island the 1889 pier-head pavilion; it was nicknamed 'Easter Island'. Although within fourteen months the pier was repaired and reopened, the cost of

the work fatally wounded the pier company, and in 1920 the pier was acquired by Worthing Corporation: it was too important for Worthing as a seaside resort to be left to the whims and vagaries of the private market.

Adshead & Ramsey

Eager to modernize Worthing seafront and in particular develop the resort's musical entertainment facilities, the council employed the architectural and town planning practice run by Stanley Davenport Adshead (1868–1946) and Stanley Churchill Ramsey (1882–1968) to design a seafront renewal scheme. The dysfunctional Oriental entrance kiosks to the pier and nearby Victorian cast-iron birdcage bandstand were swept away. A short distance from the pier the new horseshoe-shaped and whitewashed band enclosure projected beyond the tidal line on piles and columns and was 'half-way to being a pier'.[220] However, Adshead & Ramsey's most significant new building, constructed at the widened root end of the pier and opened in June 1926, was a large concert venue named the Pier Pavilion.

An anonymous architectural reporter writing in the professional journal, *The Architect and Building News*, lauded the pavilion to such a degree that one suspects the architects themselves must have had a role in the review. The commentator believed the design was 'distinguished by the spirit of urbanity which

The 1913 damage to Worthing Pier. (Fred Gray collection)

Construction of the Pier Pavilion, Worthing, c.1925. (West Sussex Library Service)

marked the best work of the eighteenth and early nineteenth centuries, yet strikes a note of modernity'. The 'suave composition' included a roof design that:

… symbolizes an intellectual victory and marks, as it were, the end of the epoch, for it implies that the industrial age has passed, or is on the very verge of passing, through its first phase when in the flush of triumph in its new found scientific and inventive ability it took pleasure in displaying constructional forms which had no other merit than that derived from mechanical efficiency. The time has now come to civilize these constructional forms and, while doing full justice to the scientific skill of those who first showed us how to create them, to make the engineer subservient to the artist.[221]

The epoch-changing symbolism of the construction was apparently particularly evident in how 'Messrs Adshead & Ramsey … scorned … concealing their roof trusses behind a shell of lath and plaster, but have decided upon the bolder and more original course of exposing the steel trusses in all their nakedness.' The architects had solved 'one of the most important problems of modern design' – that of 'how to make a pattern of the framework composing the steel truss'.

Such claims were preposterous. The large functional structure dominated the seafront. The voluminous roof resembled the oval lid of a gigantic Victorian serving dish or a gargantuan blancmange mould. Although formally part of the pier it was not of the pier, the intrusive structure forming a major visual barrier, separating the pier from the resort. Rather than being revolutionary, the design of the pavilion was derivative and unoriginal. The building's lineage reached back to the past. From the outside the roof looked remarkably similar to Adshead's own 1903 Ramsgate Royal Victoria Pavilion, a building based on the style of a Robert Adam orangery. The new pavilion deliberately echoed the design of the pier's earlier Southern Pavilion. The

The interior of the new Worthing Pier Pavilion shortly after the 1925 opening. Members of an orchestra are on the stage. (West Sussex Library Service)

exterior was also embellished with Baroque motifs – including garlands, vases laden with flowers and bewigged heads – reminiscent to those used on many earlier seaside pavilions. Even the supposedly innovative and outstanding open truss work had been used a decade before in Brighton's West Pier 1916 concert hall.

Although a building for the future of Worthing as a seaside resort, in design terms the Pier Pavilion was rooted firmly in the past. It was, though, functionally successful and according to a guide of 1927–28, 'a commodious Pavilion with adequate seating accommodation for the large audiences attracted by the various concert parties, orchestras and other entertainers who come here.'[222] The pavilion, the interior 'elaborately decorated in blue and gold', quickly became the focus of the resort's musical life and by 1930 the home of Worthing's municipal orchestra.[223]

The council architect and borough engineer

But the radical changes afoot in what holidaymakers

wanted from the British seaside were, within just a few years, to have a profound impact on the subsequent development of Worthing pier.

In September 1933 the old Southern Pavilion was destroyed by fire in just half an hour. The replacement, formally opened on 29 July 1935, was unashamedly futuristic and in complete contrast to the Adshead & Ramsey landward pavilion of less than a decade earlier. This most Modernist of 1930s pier buildings was in the fashionable Nautical Moderne style and associated with transatlantic travel in streamlined ocean liners. The commentator in *The Municipal Review* – the trade magazine for local authorities – described how 'The new building is somewhat novel in design in that externally and internally it has been based on the atmosphere of a ship, but with the maximum use of glass in order that extensive views of the sea and coast can be seen in every direction.'[224] Designed by the council's chief architect, C. H. Wallis, and overseen by the borough engineer, P. E. Harvey, the new larger replacement pavilion used lightweight materials since 'it was not desired to increase the weight of it on the pier substructure beyond that of the old building.' The exterior of the building, for example, was 'covered in a metal-cased plywood, secured by teak bands'. There was an understandable awareness of the danger from fire: the building rested on a fireproof concrete deck and the interior walls were covered with fireproof fibre board.

Technical details aside, the pavilion was designed for sun-loving and modern holidaymakers. The building included sun lounges and sun decks, a dance hall and a tea room. The ground-floor sun lounge, accommodating fifty people, was 'fitted with ultra-violet ray lamps … so that the maximum benefit of natural or artificial sunlight can be enjoyed.' The first floor included another sun lounge and outside decks that could seat 200 sun-seekers. The dance hall included a polished maple dance floor, a band stage floored in Siberian ash and surrounding 'sitting-out' promenades for eighty couples. Green and pink shades and decorative lighting added mood and the dance-hall pendants were shaped as moons and stars. On the pavilion's opening the *Daily Mirror* eulogized it as 'the sun trap of the South Coast'. A late 1930s guide to Worthing described 'the Sun Pavilion, with vita-glass sun lounges, and a café and a good dance floor.'[225]

The Modernist transformation of the pier was completed in 1937 with the opening of the central amusement pavilion, in a similar style to the Sun Pavilion, and a windshield running the length of the pier. Worthing Pier and its array of inter-war pier entertainment buildings survived the ensuing eight decades remarkably intact.

Colwyn Bay

The Victoria Pier, Colwyn Bay, opened in 1900, the final pier to be built on the north Wales coast. Its major attraction was a huge wooden five-domed 'Moorish' pavilion constructed on a platform offset from and at right angles to the promenading deck of the pier. Used for dramatic and musical entertainments, the pavilion could seat 2,500 patrons. The key source of revenue for the fragile finances of the pier, it was destroyed in a conflagration in 1922; with the cost of reconstruction unaffordable, the blaze also ended the Victoria Pier

The Nautical Moderne style of the Southern Pavilion, Worthing Pier, 1999. (Fred Gray)

The 1900 pavilion on the Victoria Pier, Colwyn Bay.
(Marlinova Collection)

The Victoria Pier's second pavilion of 1923.
(Marlinova Collection)

Modernism takes hold – the pier's pavilion of 1934.
(Marlinova Collection)

Company's ownership of the pier. Now in council hands, a smaller and plainer pavilion, built of timber on a steel frame with four corner towers and a central dome, opened the following year. A decade later that too burnt down.[226]

Following the 1933 fire, the council commissioned a third pavilion. On this occasion the designer was the borough surveyor, W. J. Dunning, working in collaboration with the architect and urban planner Stanley Davenport Adshead. Professor Adshead's seaside design pedigree reached back thirty years and included the Worthing Pier pavilion described above. At Colwyn Bay the collaboration between the two men resulted in a decidedly forward-looking and modern leisure building. A report in *The Architect and Building News* commended the 'stimulating gaiety about exterior and interior' and concluded that the building, which opened on 8 May 1934, struck 'exactly the right note in the architecture of pleasure'.[227]

In tune with the times, modern materials and construction techniques were used to create the new pavilion. The building was designed to be weatherproof and – using a variety of materials including asbestos sheeting and reinforced steel decking – fireproof but also lightweight. It had at its core 'a light steel structure, rigidly framed and latticed'. In addition:

Great care has been exercised in the choice and application of materials so as to compensate in some measure for expansion and contraction. The outside cavity walls are finished on the weather side with coloured cement; on the inner side expanded metal lathing and expansion rods are finished with pumice-stone concrete, the lightness of pumice in comparison with more customary aggregates having weighed with the designers.[228]

The internal decoration was in tune with the Modernist aesthetics of the 1930s. The programme for the pavilion's opening recorded that the tea room murals

The Victoria Pier, Colwyn Bay with the Modernist 1933 pavilion, a year before the start of the Second World War. (Geoffrey Mead collection)

by Eric Ravilious (1903–1942) struck 'an original note':

The theme represents a scene on the bed of the ocean. Pink and green seaweeds float through the ruins of a submerged palace. A bright red anchor suggests a connection to the world above. The white and brown arches of the palace are in strong contrast with a golden background. This decorative scheme is in the manner of an eighteenth century scenic wallpaper. The curtains of the Tea Room are shell pink, and the doors and windows grey.[229]

The year before his Colwyn Bay work, Ravilious, an important inter-war English artist, had designed and painted murals for the Midland Hotel, Morecambe, one of Britain's most outstanding Modernist seaside buildings.

The pavilion's multi-purpose auditorium – it could be used for concerts, 'light theatrical programmes' and dancing – was decorated by the painter, illustrator and muralist Mary Adshead (1904–1995), the daughter of Stanley Adshead. A contemporary commentator described how her murals suggested 'a tent or marquee

supported by ornamental poles and ropes, and decorated with a number of abstract motifs derived from musical instruments and nautical emblems. The colour scheme is grey and white, with some scarlet and yellow, the dado being vivid emerald green in a scarlet and yellow reticulation.'[230]

In his only comment on piers, the fierce architectural commentator Wesley Dougill believed the new Pier Pavilion at Colwyn Bay was an outstanding addition to seaside architecture.

DEVELOPMENTS ELSEWHERE

Almost a Modernist pier

The most complete architectural expression of Modernism and the cult of the sun was the 1935 De La Warr Pavilion at Bexhill-on-Sea, the resort where several decades earlier varied pier proposals had foundered. The influential pavilion was much in the news because of its radical purpose, design and construction, the cost, the process of deciding on the design (an architectural competition), the standing of the winning architects and ferocious opposition to the proposals.

The Bexhill authorities looked to the future to rejuvenate the young but unfashionable resort. The winning competition entry, by the German/Russian architectural partnership of Erich Mendelsohn (1887–1953) and Serge Chermayeff (1900–1996) became the first public building in Britain to be designed and built on International Style principles.

With the southern side presenting large expanses of sheet glass to the sea and sun, the building made use of nautical symbolism. The Pavilion included a large, flexible theatre, restaurant, library, conference room and lounge. Outside there were terraces for sunbathing and listening to music and a rooftop sun deck for sports and games reminiscent of those on ocean liners.

Behind this startling appearance lay some innovative construction techniques. For example, it was the first large building in Britain with a welded steel frame.

Earl De La Warr, the aristocratic but socialist mayor of the town, was the driving force behind the Pavilion. The Earl believed that the architecture of recreation should be a significant force in local and national regeneration, with the building at Bexhill intended to perform as a centre for entertainment and the means of achieving a new form of cultural and social provision. The old-fashioned 1896 entertainment pavilion, the start of the pier that was never completed, was demolished in the year following the opening of the De La Warr Pavilion.

The Pavilion as built – today acclaimed as one of Britain's greatest Modernist buildings – was part of an unrealized larger and more ambitious scheme by Mendelsohn and Chermayeff. The Pavilion was to face a large, circular open-air pool partly built over the beach. From the pool a slender two-level promenade pier was to soar out above the sea. The end of the pier featured a slim and tall pylon. Some of Mendelsohn's designs appear to show the pylon as a statue of a diver. The architects' musings suggest a prelude to subsequent landscape-defining iconic figures such as Antony Gormley's 1998 *Angel of the North* and Damien Hirst's 2012 statue, *Verity*, which stands on Ilfracombe Pier (the harbour arm). Although the completed Pavilion opened in December 1935, intense opposition from the ratepayers' association to the necessary additional borrowing had led Bexhill council to abandon the pier and pool scheme less than two months earlier.[232]

Modernism takes hold

The Modernist pier pavilions at Colwyn Bay and Worthing demonstrated that, in appropriate circumstances, piers could be remade to meet the requirements of holidaymakers seeking the new sunny seaside.

Elsewhere there were other examples, some superficial, some substantial, of Modernism on seaside piers. Between the wars at Hastings on the Channel coast

The huge 1933 pavilion, Grand Pier, Weston-super-Mare, c.1990s. (Wayne Walters)

A dramatic fire in 2008 destroyed much of the Grand Pier, Weston-super-Mare. A new, even larger pavilion opened two years later. (Author: mattbuck. This file is licensed under the Creative Commons Attribution-Share Alike 2.0 Generic license)

there were continual developments to the pier including a 1933 Art Deco façade added to a 1920s pavilion at the landward end of the pier.[233] At Penarth in South Wales the pier was taken into council ownership in 1924 and a large Art Deco ferro-concrete pavilion opened in 1929. The new pavilion, although visually reminiscent of the 1903 Wellington Pier pavilion at Great Yarmouth, was also a decidedly Indian-styled version of Art Deco.[234] A simple, unadorned and startlingly modern two-storey entrance building, dating from 1936, replaced the old wooden structure at the front of Southwold Pier. At Skegness, the original three early 1880s Gothic entrance buildings to the pier were replaced by a much larger structure in 1937. The Art Deco building included an extensive two-storey covered entrance and side-wings housing shops and a café.

At Weston-super-Mare, between the wars a booming resort, the pavilion at the seaward end of the Grand Pier burned down in 1930. The opportunity was taken to considerably increase the size of the pier head and to construct a vast pavilion – larger than any other British pier building – which opened in 1933. Designed by a Weston architect, Nicholas Darby, the structure maintained the four-corner tower idea but was relatively plain and unadorned: three cavernous side-by-side sheds with an Art Deco façade, 'a Wembley Empire Stadium-type pavilion'.[235] From the outset, the building was designed for use as a funfair and for amusements and, during the day, copious windows and the glass roof would have flooded the interior with natural light.[236]

The sunny seaside even had an impact on the Blackpool pier most resplendent in Victoriana, the North Pier. In the early 1930s one side of the pier head was transformed into a sheltered sun lounge with a stage for musical performances. Then, later in the decade and on the other side of the pier head, the 1924 pavilion burnt down and was replaced, in 1939, by an Art Deco theatre.

The destruction of the 'Taj Mahal of the North' pavilion on Morecambe's Central Pier, 31 July 1933. (Fred Gray collection)

Morecambe

The wonderful 'Taj Mahal of the North' pavilion on Morecambe's Central Pier was destroyed in just an hour in an intense blaze on 31 July 1933. The conflagration financially ruined the existing private owners and the pier was sold to a new company. A large new Art Deco pavilion, primarily used for dancing, opened in July 1936 with other new additions on the pier including an open-air dance floor, the Floral Hall and the Modernist two-storey and double-bayed 'Don Café' close to the entrance.[237] The unplanned renewal of the pier became part of Morecambe's Modernist transformation. The resort's much applauded and iconic seafront Midland Hotel had opened in the same month that the old pier pavilion had been destroyed. Three years later, and just eleven days after the refurbished pier fully reopened, the resort also celebrated the opening of the massive Super Swimming Stadium. Morecambe, it seemed, was being remade into a sunny modern seaside place equipped for holidaymakers as both participants and spectators.

Lee-on-Solent Pier

A huge and multifaceted leisure building was constructed on the land at the root end of Lee-on-Solent Pier in 1935. The developers, a syndicate of local business people who owned the pier, clearly believed that Lee-on-Solent was about to boom. The designers of the Lee Tower complex, the architectural practice of Yates, Cook & Derbyshire, took Modern Movement design to heart. Although the building hinted at the influence of the graceful contemporary De La Warr Pavilion, the heavy bulk of the pavilion dominated the seafront. With hindsight, it was a strange architectural foreshadowing of the concrete coastal defences built a few years later by the German occupying forces on the other side of the Channel.

The set of buildings (there were really three distinct structures) respected 1930s construction methods and included steel frames, reinforced concrete elements, and stuccoed brick walls. The symmetrical structure was composed of two similarly shaped leisure buildings, at right angles to each other, and linked by a slender but stark 120ft observation tower soaring above the main entrance. The complex included a 900-seat cinema, dance hall, restaurant, cafés and bars, as well as sun terraces and a viewing platform, accessed by a lift, at the tower's peak. Facing south, the white-painted building gleaming on sunny

Building of the Lee Tower complex at the root end of the pier, Lee-on-Solent, c.1935. (Fred Gray collection)

Queuing to enter Weymouth's new Bandstand Pier. (Marlinova Collection)

days, it appeared to offer many of the attractions a 1930s seaside holidaymaker might wish for.[238]

Weymouth Bandstand Pier

In its last gasp, inter-war seaside Modernism did finally produce a completely new pier at Weymouth on England's south coast. Opening on 25 May 1939 the pier performed as a huge Modernist bandstand and enclosure (although it was also curiously reminiscent of the pier-head seating arrangement and open bandstand on Brighton's West Pier in 1866). The result of another architectural competition, 3,000 tons of reinforced concrete were used in its construction. A two-storey streamlined and curvilinear promenade entrance building over the beach – with the by now essential nautical design references – led to a square platform extending 200ft into the sea. Although called a bandstand, musicians actually performed on a rectangular proscenium stage, the focal point for the enclosure accommodating 2,400 patrons (cover was provided for only 800 seats) and a perimeter prome-

nade deck.[239]

In the early post-war years the Bandstand Pier prospered, providing 'entertainment in sunshine'. The venue hosted nationally famous dance bands such as Ted Heath and His Music, weekly bathing beauty contests and wrestling shows. As fashions changed, in the 1970s the pier became 'Fun World', an entertainment venue with rides and amusements. Structurally un-

The remnants of Weymouth Bandstand Pier. (Wayne Walters)

sound, explosives were used in 1986 to assist in the demolition of three-quarters of the pier, although the shore-end remnants survive today.

PIERS AT WAR

The United Kingdom and France declared war on Germany on 3 September 1939. The event stopped the pier modernization process in its tracks. The war years proved to be a period of great trials and tribulations for many piers, from which some never recovered. Modernism on sea was to resurface after the war but never with the vitality and purpose of the 1930s.

Despite the commencement of hostilities, it was relatively quiet on the Western Front during the eight-month 'Phoney War' from September 1939. For Britain's seaside piers there were actions to take, such

as blackout precautions, but otherwise it was the business of pleasure as usual. The situation changed in May 1940 when German forces reached the Channel coast. The seaside piers on the south and east coasts of England were, suddenly and literally, on the frontline. The invasion threat was formidable. The British military fear was that, since the Germans lacked shallow-draft landing craft to go ashore on beaches, piers (and harbours) jutting out into deeper water could be used to land enemy troops and their equipment.

As a defensive measure, many piers were requisitioned by the military authorities, closed to the public and action was taken to disable their use as landing stages by enemy forces. Using explosives, most piers within invasion distance of mainland Europe were then severed into two or three sections and the stairs and gangways between the landing stage and pier proper removed. Large areas of pier decking were also

Boscombe Pier in the late 1930s. Bubbles, a show in the new pier-head pavilion, was 'A Super Concert Party with a Super Cast'. By the end of the Second World War what remained of the pier was derelict. (Fred Gray collection)

The partially dismantled Worthing Pier, c.1944. The café and dancing advertised on the pavilion's roof-top sign were both unavailable to visitors until the pier reopened in 1949. (West Sussex Library Service)

taken up. At Clacton-on-Sea the 1932 Crystal Casino was demolished as part of sectioning the pier in 1940. As John Walton has observed, 'why Hitler's army should have wanted to invade Britain along Clacton Pier is a mystery to those of us who are not military strategists'.[240] The long pier at Herne Bay, on the Thames estuary, was breached in two places, including one 80ft gap near the pier head. At the neighbouring resort of Margate, the Jetty played a vital role in the Dunkirk rescue, being used to land almost 47,000 troops in the early summer of 1940. In a symbolic raising of the castle drawbridge a section of the Jetty's decking was removed a short while later. As a further defensive act the isolated piers, islands off the shore of many south and east coast resorts, were then booby-trapped. Even the pier in the fictional *Dad's Army* resort of Walmington-on-Sea was cut in two with, on one occasion, Captain Mainwaring's platoon stranded overnight on the isolated pier head.

On the Thames estuary, Southend Pier played a critical war role. Requisitioned for the Royal Navy and renamed HMS *Leigh*, its major function was as the control and marshalling point for convoys to and from London and its docks. Between September 1939 and June 1945 3,367 convoys formed from 84,297 ships were organized from the pier. The pier's strong defences included anti-aircraft guns in large concrete emplacements. The 'sunny Pier Head built for nothing but pleasure' was transformed into 'an armed colony or island, thinking of nothing but war'.[241] The Solarium became the venue for the essential convoy conferences: 'Here among the painted cut-outs, the cardboard palms and banana trees, under the blue Oriental sky and the tropical jungle blossoms, the cold and anxious, but undaunted masters met the Navy and received their orders.'

Wartime damage and destruction

Further away from mainland Europe some piers, including the three in Blackpool, remained partially or fully open during the conflict. Elsewhere in the north-west of England, other piers were requisitioned by the

War Office. New Brighton and Southport piers were both used for searchlight batteries as part of the defence against the air attack of Liverpool. In the southwest, the pier at Minehead in Somerset made the ultimate sacrifice. It was demolished in 1940 to ensure a clear line of sight for nearby batteries of guns. Another Bristol Channel pier, Birnbeck at Weston-super-Mare, was requisitioned by the military authorities, renamed HMS *Birnbeck*, and used as a naval experimental weapon station. By the end of the war the pier was in a decrepit state, not least because of the major damage caused when a Lancaster bomber accidently dropped a large concrete block on the engineering shed on Birnbeck Island.

The fabric of many other piers was also harmed significantly during the war. In some cases, the cause of the damage was apparent. Brighton's West Pier and those at Clacton and Eastbourne suffered from the explosion of drifting mines. Structural damage frequently resulted from the use of a pier for gun emplacements and other military purposes. Margate Jetty's camera obscura was destroyed in an air raid. Worse still, in January 1940 an abandoned motor vessel, mortally damaged by a mine, repeatedly smashed into Deal Pier, wrecking a 200ft section. The broken pier was later demolished to improve the firing line of the guns defending England's coastal frontline. Just the pair of Eugenius Birch's toll houses remained on the promenade. In January 1941 Southsea Clarence Pier, so close to the Portsmouth naval base and dockyards, was destroyed in a bombing raid. Another Birch pier, on Plymouth Hoe, was also a casualty of the conflict. Wrecked in a night-bombing raid in March 1941, the derelict ruin was eventually removed in 1953.

The devastating fire on St Leonards Pier, March 1944. (Steve Peak collection)

St Leonards Palace Pier, Sussex, was another war victim. Breaching and damage from an air raid in 1940, and from severe gales in 1943, had left the pier semi-derelict. Then, in March 1944, the shore-end pavilion was destroyed in a brief but devastating conflagration. The reputed cause of the blaze was a flare that had been fired into the sea by a Canadian soldier and then drifted under the pier.[242] The forlorn ruins were eventually cleared away in the early 1950s.

The pleasure pier closest to France, at Folkestone, survived five years of the town being under constant attack from 'bombs, parachute mines, shells from across the Channel, flying bombs and machine gunning.'[243] With the ending of the war in Europe on 8 May 1945, the Victoria Pier was surely safe. But ignominy awaited and less than two weeks later, the pier-head pavilion was destroyed in a homemade arson attack. The last remains of the pier were finally blown up in November 1954.

Even where traumatic events were absent, there was another significant problem for all the inaccessible and sealed piers. The years of closure were years without maintenance. The outcome was sometimes severe weathering and corrosion. By 1945 many closed piers presented a sorry architectural sight, with paint blistered and flaking, timber rotting and metal rusting.

The decay was so bad in the case of the Royal Victoria Pier, Tenby, and council dithering and reluctance to commit funding so great, that the structure – a landing-stage pier – never reopened after the war. The eventual fate, finally completed in 1954, was demolition. Lytham Pier was also closed during the war years. However, in this case its fortunes had declined to such an extent in the decade before the Second World War that, by 1938, the decrepit pier was open to anglers alone. The pier remained closed after the war and the

Folkestone Pier shortly after the end of the Second World War. (Marlinova Collection)

remaining structure was eventually removed in 1960.[244]

Although only in part, the war was also a factor in the protracted death of Lee-on-Solent Pier and the associated Lee Tower. The hoped-for financial success of the tower facility was an illusion and within two years of the mid-1930s opening, the company owning it was liquidated. Late in the decade negotiations were underway with Gosport Council to assume ownership of the pier. During the Second World War the Lee Tower complex was requisitioned and the tall tower, a tempting navigation aid for enemy planes, was camouflaged. The pier itself was breached and the shore-end suffered major storm damage. Post war, the council did buy the pier and received compensation from the War Office. The money was not spent on repairing the structure and the landward section was never reinstated. The relics of the pier were removed in 1958. After the war, Lee Tower continued to struggle financially and that, too, was taken into council ownership. The cinema closed in 1958.[245] New entertainments, including wrestling and tenpin bowling, were insufficient to save the complex. Demolition awaited in 1971.[246]

The end-of-life stories of the piers at Tenby, Lytham and Lee-on-Solent piers illustrate that, on occasion, pre- and post-war events were as important as wartime travails in determining the fate of a pier.

Chapter Seven

THE ROLLERCOASTER YEARS

Although many British seaside resorts were traumatized by the Second World War the vast majority of piers survived the conflict, battle scarred but alive. Then came a period of national recuperation and pier restoration. By the mid-1950s there was a sense that the seaside and piers would join with a revitalized nation to 'have never had it so good'. The sentiment was a chimera. From the 1960s the continuing British love affair with the sun combined with rising living standards, changing transport technologies and the development of seaside places on foreign shores, led to an increasing holidaymaking exodus to the sunny seaside overseas.

All resorts struggled to confront the whirlwind of change, but for some the unfolding circumstances had dire results, with the resort infrastructure hollowed out and holidaymakers leaving, never to return, except perhaps as infrequent or nostalgic day trippers.[247] Piers, too, often began a spiral of decline: fewer visitors, falling income, reduced expenditure, and the structure and its architecture a pale and decrepit shadow of its former self. At times aided and abetted by storm or fire, some crumbled into the sea and were lost. Time and nature – and economic reality and financial necessity – were relentless challenges.

Elsewhere, however, the resilience was remarkable. The determination to save a pier, while not always successful, could be tenacious and resolute. The idea of seaside piers could be re-evaluated and sometimes reinvented. At best some piers not only survived but also prospered. There were wonderful engineering and architectural restorations and innovative designs for new pier buildings.

RESTORATION AND REJUVENTATION

With the end of the war the requisitioned piers were returned to their owners. Making them fit for pleasure purposes was a demanding and daunting task. However, as holidaymakers and day trippers flocked to the seaside after the war, the reopened piers were greeted with great acclaim and thronged with visitors. There was also, sometimes, an accompanying transformation in the purpose and use of a pier, with former theatres and concert halls, for example, converted into cafés, restaurants and amusement arcades.

In 1945 Richard Sheppard sketched out his ideas for a post-war pier 'at a popular seaside resort'. His intention was to 'cater for traditional requirements, while

Left: Herne Bay Pier, May 2010. The 1976 sport pavilion was demolished in 2012. Although disintegrating, the 1899 pier-head structure still survived in 2019. (Fred Gray)

Post-war hope and promise. Cleethorpes shortly after the end of hostilities. (Marlinova Collection)

adapting the structure to contemporary form'. The result was a massive and architecturally futuristic structure that included a tall tower topped by an observatory, huge 'landing floats' and a sea aquarium. But the proposed uses, including a restaurant, concert hall, amusements, promenade and 'open-air dance hall', were backward rather than forward-looking. Sheppard's ideas were not realized in Britain, although the post-war pier at Scheveningen, in the Netherlands, provides an architectural approximation.

However, Modernism did reappear, in new piers and new pier buildings, although never with quite the confidence that characterized the years immediately before the war.

Making good

At Southend, HMS *Leigh* was decommissioned from active service, and the pier, which had been well maintained throughout the war years, reopened to the public on 17 May 1945. It was neither as easy nor as quick for the piers that had been closed and sectioned. The defensive gaps made by the military authorities needed

to be reinstated, decking re-laid, buildings refurbished, the structure once again made whole and fit for seaside pleasure and promenading over the waves. There was some government funding available for the restoration task. Pier owners made significant claims for financial recompense to the War Office, although such claims were rarely if ever met in full. Building materials were scarce because of the great reconstruction project underway in towns and cities throughout Britain. As a result it was years before some piers reopened.

As revealed by this postcard sent in the summer of 1946, Clacton Pier was largely reopened the year after the war ended. (Fred Gray collection)

Worthing Pier portrayed on a postcard sent in July 1948. The neck of the pier remained closed and work was being undertaken to reunite the pier head with the remainder of the structure. (Fred Gray collection)

At Clacton the owner of the pier was cautiously hopeful that it would be fully functioning for the 1947 season. Holidaymakers reading the official guide to the resort were told:

The [pier's] recovery from the ravages of war is proceeding apace and every effort is being made to restore all the attractions and amenities which were so popular. The Swimming Pool with its up to date Café and Sun Deck and the Children's Theatre will, in all probability, be re-opened.[248]

Further north, at Cromer, the pier did not formally reopen until June 1951. By then the entrance had been replaced by a much larger concrete structure, in Modernist guise, of shops and shelters. The two matching circular buildings fronting the pier echoed the original Edwardian kiosks with their cupola roofs. The deck, too, was partly remade in concrete.

In Hastings work bridging the gap between pier and promenade began in March 1946. Three months later, on Victory Day, 8 June, the landward pier theatre and restaurant both reopened. Over the following months the central breach was also bridged. The seaward end of the pier opened to visitors in the summer of 1947 and pleasure steamer and speedboat trips resumed from the landing stages. However, a shortage of imported hardwood delayed the restoration of the root end of the pier butting onto the seafront parade until May 1948.[249]

By the end of hostilities Saltburn Pier was derelict, having been sectioned, stripped of its decking and damaged in wartime gales. By September 1946 some restorative work had been undertaken but it was incomplete. An inspection of the pier in April 1949 showed the decay, corrosion and dilapidation was severe and the structure dangerous. It was another two years before the steel became available to rebuild the section that had been breached. At Easter 1952 the pier reopened: a dozen years after it had closed visitors could once again enjoy a promenade on its decks.[250]

The restoration project for Mumbles Pier was even more drawn out. It was not fully reopened until June 1956. A pleasure steamer service began at the same time, making use of a new landing stage of reinforced concrete and steel piles.

In Brighton the owners of the West Pier took the opportunity to transform the attractions offered to visitors. The principal pleasure buildings were put to new uses. The former theatre was divided in two, with the

The West Pier's island pier head photographed at the end of the war. (Brighton West Pier Trust)

The early post-war transformation into a funfair of the root end of Brighton West Pier. (Brighton West Pier Trust)

rant, advertised with the slogan 'lunch and tea over the sea', provided glorious views. The concert hall was converted into a café with small-scale musical entertainments. The root end of the pier was transformed into a funfair with helter-skelter, dodgems, a ghost train and amusement arcade.

By the end of the 1940s, the West Pier's metamorphosis from pleasure pier to funfair and amusement pier was complete. Curiously, though, the exterior of the pier buildings – the original toll houses and kiosks, the pier-head pavilion and the concert hall – were remarkably unchanged. All that could be done to modernize them was to abandon earlier colour schemes and paint the structures white. The use of white paint as a tactic to superficially disguise old buildings was employed on a number of other piers in the second half of the twentieth century.

interior Victorian decoration removed or hidden behind panels. The ground floor became the Games Pavilion, later renamed 'Laughterland', housing an indoor funfair. The upstairs space was turned into a restaurant and given a plain makeover in what a short time later could be called a 'Festival of Britain' style. The simple decoration of the dining room was, however, enlivened by a ceiling mural. The nautical theme included Neptune, dolphins and mermaids, and was reminiscent of the murals in Colwyn Bay's mid-1930s pier pavilion. On sunny days the new Ocean Restau-

Brighton West Pier Concert Hall remodelled as a café with accompanying musical entertainment. (Brighton West Pier Trust)

The pier as another world, as portrayed on the cover of the entertainment programme for Blackpool North Pier, 7 September 1950. (Geoffrey Mead collection)

The phoenix piers

Just two of the piers completely destroyed during the war were to reappear, phoenix like. Deal Pier, a promenade pier built of reinforced concrete, opened in 1957 and Southsea Clarence Pier, a large amusement and funfair complex, was completed in 1961. Although often recognized as the only two piers to be built in Britain between the end of the war and the end of the century, the situation is more nuanced. Other piers were so extensively remodelled and remade that they were unrecognizable from how they once appeared.

Deal Pier

After the war only the toll booths remained from the old Birch pier. Once war damage compensation was in local authority hands and the toll booths removed, work commenced on a new pier. It was opened on 19 November 1957. Designed by the council's consulting engineers, Sir William Halcrow and Partners, it was the first new pier to be built largely of reinforced concrete. Metal was hidden from view. The 1,000ft neck of the pier was carried on steel piles encased in concrete; the concrete deck was supported by steel beams, again enclosed by concrete. 'Open seating' ran along the stem toward the seaward end of the pier. The blunted arrow-shaped pier head included a three-level landing stage although, due to a calculation error, the lower level was permanently covered by the sea.[251] There was also a café, sun lounge and terraced area.

The result was a splendid pier with a traditional promenade function, but one in a modern streamlined design constructed with classic twentieth-century materials. The pier was of the past, made in the present but designed for the future.

After almost half a century, Deal Pier was in need of extensive refurbishment. The problem, of course, was the reinforced concrete. Despite its advantages in pier construction, the material is never completely happy in contact with water and salt. By 2000 it was clear that the reinforcing steel was extensively corroded and the concrete spalled (the surface eroded and breaking away). In 2004 there was major refurbishment of the pier's piles and structural supports. A limpet dam provided a dry working environment to a depth of 7m below water level. The dirty and difficult work involved removing the blistered and cracked concrete covering, grit-blasting and coating the exposed steel, and then replacing the concrete.[252] Further concrete remedial work was required in the following decade.

In 2009 the original café on the pier head was replaced with a new building, the product of a Royal In-

Deal Pier in 2002. (Fred Gray)

Views of the sea while drinking tea. The 2009 café, Deal Pier. (Copyright Niall McLaughlin Architects)

The 2009 café, Deal Pier. (Copyright Niall McLaughlin Architects)

stitute of British Architects competition won by Níall McLaughlin Architects. The award-winning design, making much use of hardwood timber, was a response to the purpose of the café – a cup of tea over the sea – the views and the 'bare bones structure' of the pier: 'the cafe's simple palate of hardwood and mass concrete both weathered well and improve with exposure. The hardwood will turn silver grey to match the concrete of the pier.'[253]

Southsea Clarence Pier

Clarence Pier, the only other replacement pier for one destroyed during the war, is the antithesis of the one

The late 1950s seaside architecture of Clarence Pier, Southsea, October 2017. (Fred Gray)

at Deal. It opened in June 1961, two decades after its predecessor was destroyed in an air raid. The extremely wide pier juts just 130ft into the Solent. Apart from being a piled structure, the designers of Clarence Pier eschewed all established pier orthodoxies. The intent and purpose was to create a big, bright and brash funfair and amusement site.

The substructure of the pier was designed by the London-based Mouchel & Partners while the superstructure was the work of two local firms of architects, A. E. Cogswell & Sons and R. Lewis Reynish. Since it opened the constant feature of the pier has been the massive steel-framed and esplanade-fronting building, with its 60ft tower, clad in blue and yellow panels. In contrast the revenue-generating side of the enterprise – the rides, arcades and food and drink outlets – is in a constant state of regeneration, reflecting new technologies, entertainments and fashions.

Modernism resurfaced

The South Bank Exhibition of the 1951 Festival of Britain championed Modernist design. Apart from commemorating the centenary of the Great Exhibition, the Festival was also intended to celebrate Britain and its people, the end of austerity, the process of reconstruction and the future. Rather than it being a beginning, some architects and designers thought the Festival a stylistic end of an era.[254] Even so, new pier architecture and interior design of the period responded to the Festival's streamlined and minimalist design ethos.

One early assertive sign of the return of Modernism to piers was at Eastbourne. There, in 1951, the old Gothic entrance kiosks were replaced with a new exhibitionist entrance building. The kidney-shaped flat roof included a broad sheltering overhang. It was topped by a curved metal frame carrying six flagpoles and a large clock. Visitors heading onto the pier passed retail units with expansive windows for looking out and in. In keeping with the Modernist aesthetics, the simple-looking new building had minimal decoration. Key elements of the Eastbourne building's design – the flat roof, the curved shape with two balancing wings for shops or a café, extensive use of glass, the streamlined and unfussy design – were taken forward by architects remodelling other piers.

Four decades later Eastbourne Pier's Modernist adventure was deemed old-fashioned. In 1991 the delightful 'Festival of Britain' architecture of the entrance was removed and replaced by a heavy Victorian pastiche of a building with nine shops.

The Royal Victoria Pier, Ventnor

The small resort of Ventnor on the Isle of Wight claimed theirs, not Deal's, was the first post-war pier, also declaring it as the 'most modern pier in Britain'.[255]

Although it had been cut in two as a defensive measure, the pier appeared to have survived the Second World War reasonably well. However, a 1948 survey condemned the structure, and the pier was largely rebuilt between 1951 and 1955. It was designed in a Modernist style by a local architect, Basil L. Phelps, and constructed by two island-based contractors. In his designs Phelps adopted a forward-looking approach, in tune with many of the stylistic ideas of the 1950s.

With two curved wings enticing visitors toward the toll booths, the new single-storey and kidney-shaped entrance building adopted and adapted the designs of the Modernist entrances to the piers at Eastbourne and Cromer. The building, 'constructed of colterro lathing rendered in coloured cement', included six shops. The total length of the new pier was 683ft. For the most part the neck of the pier was 23ft wide, although a widening at the centre was 53ft. From the shore to the pier head cast-iron piles carried welded steel beams and decking of 'greenhean' [sic], an African timber.[256] Along the pier's neck were nine 'extremely modern screen shelters'. Phelps' modern take on weather screens were constructed of wood and glass and included, at the sides, a futuristic decoration of coloured balls pierced by long metal struts.

The broader pier head, made with reinforced concrete, contained the 'entertainment arena', perhaps inspired by the designs for Weymouth's 1939 Bandstand Pier. There was 'accommodation for about 500 patrons, much of which is under cover' and 'an attractive shell bandstand'. Two flying stairways constructed of afrormosia, a timber similar to teak, led to the red-asphalted first floor 'sun deck promenade with a wonderful view of the town'. Apart from a licensed bar,

Visitors flocked to the small resort of Ventnor immediately after the war. The pier, however, remained closed, breached and was condemned in 1948. (Fred Gray collection)

A postcard sent in May 1978 shows the transformation of Ventnor's pier into an amusement pier. Structurally unsafe, the pier closed early the following decade. (Fred Gray collection)

A pier for the 1950s: a postcard of 'Ventnor from the Pier' from a photograph taken in the summer, 1960. (Copyright W. J. Nigh & Sons Limited, Shanklin I.W.)

the sun deck also contained the 'ultra modern "Calypso" coffee bar featuring outstanding decor and an entirely new coffee-making plant'.

The new pier was formally opened on 28 May 1955. It was to have a short life. Phelps' designs had not provided any space for funfair rides or an amusement arcade, by then two more certain income-generating pier attractions. The screen shelters were later removed and the open area at the entrance, and much of the neck of the pier, covered over to provide accommoda-

Wrecked again and the Ventnor Pier's Ocean Bar beyond reach of visitors. (Fred Gray)

The entrance buildings were destroyed by fire in 1985 and the pier demolished seven years later. (Fred Gray)

tion for more synthetic pier pleasures. The changes were to no avail. During the 1960s and 70s Ventnor began a spiral of decline as a seaside resort. The consequences for the pier enterprise were devastating. A structural survey of the pier in 1981 revealed that repairs and maintenance would cost £750,000. The pier closed and a fire then caused serious damage at the shore end. Various schemes to restore and reopen it – one proposal was to transform it into a health spa and another to build a cable car to link the pier with the resort's Winter Gardens – came to nothing and the pier was demolished in November 1992.[257]

Bournemouth Pier

Bournemouth Pier was excoriated by the war, with only the 1931 entrance building surviving. Over the following decades, it was reshaped again and again. Between 1946 and 53, the stripped-bare pier was restored, with the pier head totally reconstructed. Less than a decade later the pier head was again rebuilt and strengthened to carry a new theatre building with 950 seats, which opened in 1960. A year or two later a weather screen was erected along the neck of the pier between the entrance and theatre. In the following decade, surveys revealed the substructure of the pier required large-scale refurbishment. Beginning in 1979 it was rebuilt in reinforced concrete and the old entrance replaced with a far larger octagonal building.

Reconstruction work on Bournemouth Pier following the travails of the Second World War. (Marlinova Collection)

The pier as ocean liner: Bournemouth Pier Theatre, April 2010. (Author: ianpudsey. This file is licensed under the Creative Commons Attribution 3.0 Unported license)

Elisabeth Scott

Bournemouth's 1960 Pier Theatre was designed by Elisabeth Scott (1898–1972). Scott was noted for her design of the 1932 Shakespeare Memorial Theatre at Stratford-upon-Avon, the first significant public building in Britain to be designed by a female architect. Most probably Scott's theatre on the pier was also the first pier building by a woman architect. Bournemouth born, Scott returned to the resort in the late 1950s to work as a council architect. The council had made significant investment in the town's infrastructure for holidaymaking in previous decades, and the pier theatre was a further attempt to boost the resort's amenities.

Like several pier buildings elsewhere, Scott's design was reminiscent of an ocean liner. The theatre's fly tower was disguised as a ship's bridge while the sides of the building, with an undulating and protruding line cutting horizontally through striking blue ribs, suggested a vessel ploughing through waves. The roof of the building was barrel-vaulted and covered in copper. The nautical theme was continued with two 5ft tall seahorses high on the front elevation. It was as though Scott had taken the idea of the 1930s Nautical Mod-

From amusement to adventure: Bournemouth Pier, September 2015. (Author: marsupium photography. Source: Flickr. This file is licensed under the Creative Commons Attribution-Share Alike 2.0 Generic license)

erne and refashioned it for the 1960s.

In the first two decades of the twenty-first century Bournemouth Pier continued to evolve. The worn-out landing stage was replaced and made higher to combat the anticipated impact of global warming. The large late 1970s building at the pier's entrance became the Pier Amusements Family Entertainment Centre – a modern amusement arcade. Early in the new century the theatrical presentations occupying Elizabeth Scott's building struggled financially. As a result the theatre closed in 2013 and in May 2014 the building reopened as the RockReef indoor activity attraction, based on adventure sports and tagged with the slogan 'bringing the great outdoors indoors'. The transformation was a step in turning much of the pier into an adrenaline-generating activity centre; another new 2014 ride was the world's first pier-to-shore zip wire.

Despite the pier operator's focus on new ways of generating income, there were other more traditional aspects to the pier experience: deckchairs, fishing from the landing stage, and even the payment of a toll during the summer months. Apart from a huge LED sign, externally the theatre building looked much as it had

in the previous century. The seahorses continued to look down on the pier's promenaders. A year after RockReef was launched, images of Elizabeth Scott and the Pier Theatre began to be carried abroad by British citizens: architect and theatre were included in the designs for a 'creative United Kingdom' themed UK passport, introduced in December 2015.

Boscombe Pier

Just a mile and a half east of Bournemouth Pier, in the suburb of Boscombe, is the second of the resort's piers. It was the end of the 1950s before significant work took place to restore the pier from its wartime savaging and subsequent decay. Between 1958 and 1962 it was extensively remodelled, with much use made of reinforced concrete. The neck was rebuilt in the same material. A Modernist building designed by the borough architect, John Burton, was erected at the entrance. It was in reinforced concrete (of course) and was a classic of its type. A boomerang-shaped flat roof, made of a thin concrete slab, was supported by tapered pillars. The roof provided cover for the entrance, four shops, toilet blocks and, at each end, open public shel-

Boscombe Pier in June 1999. The Modernist pier was in increasing need of refurbishment and, on the pier head, the Mermaid Hall had been closed for nine years. (Fred Gray)

The closed Mermaid Hall, Boscombe Pier, 1990s. (Wayne Walters)

ters. The extensive use of blue and cream tiles complemented the natural seaside colours.

Elizabeth Scott was responsible for the low-key entertainment hall at the pier head. Although the building was shed like, it was enhanced by some of the stylistic conventions, such as the side wall ribs, she had developed for the Bournemouth Pier Theatre. Called the Mermaid Hall, the building was used for roller-skating and dancing for a few years, but was soon turned into an amusement arcade.

The old reinforced concrete pier head, which dated from the mid-1920s, was structurally increasingly unsafe. Both it and the Mermaid Hall were closed in 1990. In 2003 Bournemouth Council publicized a £9 million redevelopment scheme for the pier, which would have swept away the 1960s entrance building and the pier-head hall. Unexpectedly, in December 2004 the entrance building was architecturally listed as being of Grade II status, of 'special interest, warranting every effort to preserve' it. Some pier commentators were aghast at the listing, likening the building to 'a glorified concrete bus shelter.'[258] The listing entry states the:

… building is a design of great verve and vivacity that well demonstrates the revitalization of the British seaside resort in the 1950s … [and is] … well suited to the requirements of an architecture that combined 'sun and fun' … The sweep of the cantilevered, boomerang-shaped roof is a particularly joyous feature. It is a building that would have been despised as being exactly of its date until recently; now it is a building that can be celebrated for that very reason, and a rare example of pier architecture from these years.[259]

The neck of the remodelled and rejuvenated Boscombe Pier, May 2015. (Author: THOR. This file is licensed under the Creative Commons Attribution-Share Alike 2.0 Generic license)

The whole pier was declared unsafe at the end of October 2005. The listing led the council to alter radically the plans for the pier, and over the next two-and-a-half years the structure was extensively remodelled. The old pier head and the derelict entertainment hall were removed and replaced by a smaller pier head with an open fishing and viewing platform. The neck of the pier was re-decked and new lighting, railings and a central weather screen installed. Taken together with the restored entrance building, the result is a stream-lined promenade pier: Modernism returned!

IN THE BALANCE

The pier euphoria and success of the early post-war years proved unsustainable. The flight of holidaymakers to cheaper, warmer and more exotic foreign holiday destinations began to undermine the attractiveness of many traditional British resorts and piers. In addition, rather than taking a coach or train to the seaside, the dramatic rise in private car owner-ship – associated with rising living standards – generated a proliferation of additional ways to enjoy leisure.

The pier debate

Piers in decline became a surrogate measure of the ruination of many seaside resorts and the more general ills of society. As early as June 1963, *The Financial Times* reported it was 'hard work to keep the piers above water' and that 'many are deserted hulks, sadly rusting away in small resorts.'[260]

By the early 1970s there was an emerging if nebulous sense that seaside piers might be threatened. The writer Anthony Smith put it this way: 'The British have more of these seaward extensions, these filigrees of steel topped with planks and sentiment, than any other nation and the British will be desolated if seaside economics make them vanish from the scene.'[261]

In September 1975 *The Architects' Journal* (also known as *AJ*) devoted a themed issue to piers, linking it to European Architectural Heritage Year with its motto 'A Future for Our Past'. The journal's starting point was: 'The future of piers is uncertain. Of those remaining a few flourish, some are doomed while others have been given a temporary reprieve. Some face amputation, other more complicated operations from which they may or may not survive to enjoy a prolonged life span.'[262]

Of the piers likely to be 'disapiering', the *AJ* questioned: 'St Annes: will it survive?', 'Clevedon: will no-one come to the rescue?', 'Bangor: will the barricades ever come down?' The West Pier in Brighton, which was to close at the end of the month, faced an 'easier problem' because Brighton was such a popular place and the pier had so many opportunities to be successfully transformed. In contrast, Blackpool had 'boom piers', all three being 'outstandingly economically successful'. The pier at Shanklin appeared 'to have an assured future'. Colwyn Bay's pier was not in danger, having been fully if unsympathetically refurbished. The North Wales pier had been sold by the local council to a multi-national leisure company in 1968 and a large modern amusement arcade, in a Disney-esque style of architecture, built at the pier's entrance. In another indication of the Americanization of the British seaside, at the same time the 1930s pavilion became the Dixieland Showbar.

However, it proved extraordinarily difficult for experts – such as Michael Bradley, responsible for the *AJ*

Although much truncated, St Annes Pier survived the travails of the post-war period. June 2018. (Fred Gray)

theme piece – writing at a particular point in time, to know what lay in store for individual piers. The issue was simply that, once the early post-war boom had come to an end, seaside resorts and piers were in an endless state of flux. There were too many factors that might come into play. These ranged from the attitude, resilience and resources of owners, local authorities and pressure groups involved with specific piers through to the success (or failure) of individual resorts and far broader trends in leisure and the economy. Nothing was certain. No one knew what the future

The seemingly successful Shanklin Pier in the late 1950s. (Fred Gray collection)

Shanklin Pier was destroyed in the Great Storm of 16 October 1987 although the motley collection of entrance buildings survived. The remains were removed in 1993. By 2014 flowerbeds had replaced the kiosks. (Fred Gray)

held for individual piers, although the on-a-knife-edge suspense might last for years.

Academics might adopt opposing views. Some suggested that architecture had a role to play in countering the decline of seaside towns. The historian James Walvin argued that resorts represented 'classic examples of Victorian and Edwardian architecture and style (particularly in their theatres, piers and hotels), and it is consequently all the more important to preserve them'.[263] In contrast, the renowned historian of the seaside, John Walton, thought that the 'pier has now been left behind. Its past has vitality and social resonance: its future, sadly, may belong to the world of the museum, the preservation society and the professional purveyor of nostalgia'.[264]

Our piers were in peril, according to *The Illustrated London News* in 1981.[265] The following year *New Scientist* published an article headlined 'The end of the pier show':

One of the unique delights of the British seaside resort, and one of the high spots of Victorian civil engineering, is threatened with extinction. Our seaside piers are disappearing beneath the waves at the rate of one a year. Storms and corrosion have done the damage but negligence, complacency and fly-by-night profiteering are also to blame.[266]

The entrance to Swanage Pier in 1993. A major restoration was completed in 2019. (Fred Gray)

There was growing media recognition of the decline of the British seaside. In 1993 *The Guardian* pictured two young homeless women gazing at the ruins of Brighton's West Pier: the decay of seaside architecture in 'the last resort' was increasingly related to social changes, Britain's seaside towns were becoming 'the haunts not of the holidaymakers but of the drifter, the jobless youngster, the psychiatric patient and the lone mum'.[267] Two years later the author and journalist Simon Jenkins argued that although millions of pounds had been spent on saving piers, such as those at Bangor, Clevedon and Southend, 'most have suffered in the canon of architecture by their association with downmarket leisure, and with seaside resorts that are largely unknown territory to the denizens of Westminster and Whitehall.'[268]

As the century drew to a close the political writer and broadcaster Matthew Parris was strident and polemical in his critique, asserting that 'Britain's piers should be allowed to slip beneath the waves'. Piers were ridiculous, boring, pointless and naff structures and were 'not beautiful, novel or architecturally interesting.'[269] Parris did, though, believe that the West Pier was magnificent in its demise, 'arguably the most beautiful thing in Brighton'. Andrew Martin, writing for *The Sunday Times*, believed the future for seaside piers was amusement arcades and thrill rides, and 'it is hard to see how entertainment can be more visceral, more devoted to the quick fix, more in-your-face'.[270]

Heritage as saviour

The debate about piers and seaside towns was in the wider context of the emergence of architectural conservation and heritage movements. For example, the first meeting of the Victorian Society, with John Betjeman (1906–1984) as secretary, took place in February 1958. Betjeman, a respected and much-loved poet, writer and public figure, was deeply serious about protecting valued architecture (and townscapes) and re-

The pier at Walton-on-the-Naze survived the long post-war period, reinvented as an amusement pier. By June 2019 it had begun to reveal its age. (Fred Gray)

jecting what he saw as the selfishness, meanness and blandness of many post-war development projects.

Knighted in 1969 and Poet Laureate from 1972 until his death, Betjeman eagerly lent support to threatened seaside piers. Wonderfully quotable, he proclaimed 'the pier is Southend, Southend is the pier' and 'without the pier Clevedon would be a diamond with a flaw'. Illustrating his gift for light and accessible language, Betjeman believed more generally:

A pier is about the only place left in any town where walking is possible without having to look back all the time for oncoming vehicles. It also provides a walk on the sea without the disadvantage of being sea-sick. In fact, piers are havens of fresh air and freedom from anxiety which we can ill afford to lose.[271]

An increasing number of individuals and groups promoted piers – either individually or in general – as valued heritage that should be appreciated and protected. Passionate and vocal local campaigns to save the threatened Clevedon and Brighton West piers began in the early 1970s. Both campaigns refuted arguments for demolition and both received national media coverage.[272] In Brighton the 'We Want the West Pier' campaign was a highly organized pressure group that, toward the end of the 1970s, transformed itself into the Brighton West Pier Society (subsequently Brighton West Pier Trust), with John Betjeman and the comedian Spike Milligan as president and vice-president respectively.

In 1975, European Architectural Heritage Year, the Industrial Monuments Survey reported on Britain's surviving fifty-seven piers to the Department of the Environment, arguing that Bangor, Clevedon and Brighton West Pier, although at risk of demolition, particularly merited preservation. Two dozen other piers were also listed as worthy of preservation. Simon H. Adamson's important and innovative book *Seaside Piers*, published in association with the Victorian Society, appeared in 1977. Expert seminars about the future of piers followed; there was one in Brighton in 1978.[273]

The increasing recognition during the 1970s of seaside piers as valuable heritage assets culminated with the founding of the National Piers Society (NPS) in 1979. John Betjeman became the society's president and John R. Lloyd, the driving force behind the Brighton West Pier Trust, its secretary. The NPS developed as the key and increasingly influential body 'to promote and sustain interest in the preservation and continuing enjoyment of seaside piers.'

Government support and public funding followed in the 1980s, although it was limited to just a few proj-

Brighton West Pier was architecturally listed in October 1969 as Grade I status; the photograph shows the condition of one of the 1866 kiosks at that time. (Brighton West Pier Trust)

ects partly by the scepticism, dating back to the previous century, about the aesthetic value of piers. Then in the mid-1990s came the National Lottery Heritage Fund. What became known as the Heritage Lottery Fund (HLF) suggested the potential availability of huge levels of public funding for the restoration of piers owned by a local council or charity. The government endorsed 1996 as the 'Year of the Pier' and the NPS began its annual Pier of the Year award.

DECLINE AND DESTRUCTION

Despite sometimes almighty struggles to preserve them, piers continued to be lost throughout the rollercoaster decades.

Disappearing piers

At Cowes on the Isle of Wight the pavilion on the never very successful Victoria Pier was removed in 1951 and the pier dismantled a decade later. The resort of New Brighton at the mouth of the River Mersey ex-

perienced traumatic decline from the mid-1960s. The last ferry across the Mersey ran in 1971. The pleasure pier closed in 1972, was listed as architecturally important in 1975 and was demolished three years later.

The once splendidly successful Morecambe was plunged into a maelstrom of decline.[274] Visitor spending, at constant values, fell catastrophically from £46.6 million in 1973 – a year when the resort was already in decline – to £6.5 million in 1990. The resort and its piers could not survive. The landward half of the town's West End Pier was wrecked in a November 1977 storm and the remainder demolished the following year. The resort's Central Pier survived for longer despite decay, closure and fires. However, the pavilion was destroyed in a conflagration in March 1991 and the remains of the pier removed a year later.

The pier at Rhyl, on the north Wales coast, was closed for safety reasons in 1966 and dismantled in March 1973. Redcar Pier was also closed as unsafe, on this occasion in 1980, and demolition followed in 1981. On the Isle of Wight, apart from the demise of Ventnor's pier, the pier at the nearby resort of Shanklin

Fleetwood Pier in 2000, at the dawn of the new millennium. In less than a decade it had disappeared. (Fred Gray)

was wrecked in the Great Storm of 16 October 1987 and demolished in 1993. Southampton Royal Pier closed at the end of 1979. Derelict and decaying, it survived for almost two decades. Then, in 1997, the pavilion and bandstand were destroyed by fire and much of the pier neck left a twisted ruin following another fire five years later. The haunting derelict remnants of the pier remained into the present century although away from the body of the pier, the Art Deco gatehouse survived and was used as a restaurant.

At Fleetwood the pier that had provided the full stop to the golden age of pier building experienced a familiar pattern of hoped-for renewal interrupted by continuing decline and closure; the pier closed for the third time since the war in 2006, was then gutted by fire, and the remains demolished in 2008, two years short of the centenary of its opening.

Apart from the memories of people who walked over the decks of these vanished piers there are also often surviving archaeological remains: perhaps a broken pile revealed at low tide, a section of pier railing

or seat in a public garden, or a fragment of ornamental cast iron or weathered timber displayed in a pier lover's home.

Tempest

The threat from stormy weather and seas to seaside piers, increasingly precarious and fragile, intensified throughout the rollercoaster years. As the economic

Lowestoft's Claremont Pier battered by a storm in October 1996. (Fred Gray)

maelstrom facing piers deepened, so the challenge of reconstruction after major storm damage became greater.

The 'Great East Coast Floods' of 31 January 1953 killed 307 people, with 30,000 others evacuated from low-lying land. At Hunstanton sixty-six people died, many of them American service families living in bungalows on the beach. Despite the human disaster, east coast piers came through the tempest surprisingly unscathed. Those at Skegness, Hunstanton and Southwold all suffered damage with, at Southwold, the seas sweeping slot machines from the pier's amusement arcade. The destruction wreaked on Cromer Pier and Margate Jetty was greater. At Cromer, the pavilion theatre, lifeboat station and parts of the deck were devastated; government compensation enabled the rebuilding of the pavilion and the theatre reopened for the 1955 summer season. Much of the decking on Margate Jetty was punched upwards, shattered and stripped from the pier by savage waves. Despite the significant damage the Jetty decking was renewed and some of the piles damaged in the storm flood repaired by filling them with concrete.[275]

Almost exactly twenty-five years later another east coast tempest of similar magnitude, the storm surge of 11 January 1978, had far more significant consequences for piers.[276] Those at Hunstanton, Herne Bay and Margate were wrecked and others, including the structures at Clacton and Skegness, suffered major damage.

The storm-surge ravaging of the pier at Hunstanton was so extreme that some of the iron piles ripped from the seabed were found more than five miles away. The local council subsequently dismantled what remained of the structure out to sea. The two-storey Pier Entertainment Centre dating from 1964 and on the site of the earlier entrance buildings survived, no doubt because of its location on the landward end of the beach. Just two iron piles and a short length of surviving wooden decking rather tremulously bridged the low seawall to peak meekly at the sea.

Margate Jetty had become so decrepit and unsafe that it was closed to the public in 1974. The storm four years later provided the *coup de grâce,* with only the

The Pier Amusement Centre without its pier. Although the building was destroyed by fire in 2002, another Hunstanton Pier family entertainment centre occupies the site. (Fred Gray)

lifeboat house and Jetty extension surviving. Despite the destruction, the remains proved determinedly resistant to removal – even by explosives – and the Jetty extension became a stranded offshore island for another two decades before it finally disappeared in 1998.

The £100,000 storm damage to Clacton Pier included the demise of the 1928 Ocean Theatre with its proud history of variety shows. At Cleethorpes, 150 disabled and elderly people enjoying the pantomime in the pier's pavilion were temporarily stranded. The 1978 storm also led to fundamental changes to the pier at Skegness. Much of the long neck of the pier was washed away and the pier head with its theatre (the original 1881 saloon, although much modernized and altered) left isolated. Ambitious plans to reconnect the two parts of the pier with a monorail and construct a large new pier-head theatre came to nothing, and a

The shortest pier? The remains of the pier survived on Hunstanton seafront long after the storm surge of 1978. (Fred Gray)

Margate Jetty looking solid and secure; it was destroyed in 1978. (Fred Gray collection)

The entrance to Skegness Pier's huge family entertainment centre, summer 2000. (Fred Gray)

The surviving promenade over the beach, Skegness Pier, summer 2000. (Fred Gray)

combination of demolition and fire resulted in the removal of the offshore remains by early 1986. Subsequently, Skegness Pier continued its development as a large land and beach-bound amusement and funfair enterprise removed from the perils of the sea, the remains of the Victorian pier neck providing a short promenade over the beach.

Compared with what happened in 1953, the 1978 tempest was associated with far greater pier loss and devastation. The storm, as a catastrophic event, was the immediate cause, the catalyst of destruction. However, the underlying factors undoubtedly related to the failure of pier enterprises during the post-war period and many years of underinvestment in maintenance and renewal. Even without the storm, piers in what had become lost resorts were in terminal decline. The storm was the means to the end. In places where reconstruction might have been possible – for example, at Skegness – there was simply no appetite for it.

Piers in limbo

Although it is bound up with increased risk – of arson, for example – and with greater uncertainty and trepidation about the future, there is no inevitability to what follows the closure of a pier. Sometimes closure

is the spur needed for restoration and recovery. Occasionally, despite, or rather because of, the best endeavours of the supporters and advocates, a pier falls into limbo, a state of seemingly interminable closure. Neither the demolitionists nor restorers have sufficient leverage to determine events. Each pier in limbo has its own unique history, of battles for survival, preservation and renewal.

Over often long periods of time, with minimal intervention to stabilize or repair the structure, a natural process of decay occurs. The process generates a powerful and often contradictory mixture of emotions and perspectives. For some people, a ruined pier is an eyesore that should be swept away. A ruin may be perplexing: why did it happen and who allowed it to happen? For other viewers, a ruin may be an intriguing, mysterious, appealing or romantic spectacle.

Weston-super-Mare's Birnbeck Pier was closed as unsafe in 1994. A year later the *Sunday Times* described how it 'stands closed and semi-derelict since the Welsh steamers departed'.[277] Over the subsequent quarter of a century, the pier has been reclaimed and ruined by nature, 'a beautiful, if heartbreaking, sight'.[278] Brighton's West Pier experienced a similar process of

The ruined Birnbeck Pier, October 2011. (Photograph by Mike Peel. This file is licensed under the Creative Commons Attribution-Share Alike 4.0 International license)

natural repossession while its fate was being determined in the period between its 1975 closure and 2003. There has been more intervention to stabilize the Queen's Pier at Ramsey, on the Isle of Man, since its 1991 closure. Nonetheless, the consequences of decay and corrosion are obvious, making the pier 'a magnificent, if sorry, sight'.[279]

SURVIVAL AND REVIVAL

The underlying issue during the rollercoaster years was exactly the same as it had been in previous eras and is today. How did the economics of a pier as an enterprise – whether in the private, public or not-for-profit sector – stack up? Was the revenue generated from pier users adequate given the varied funding demands? And if it wasn't, what other sources of funding were available? Apart from everyday running costs such as wages, maintenance demands were continual and at times combined with bills associated with repairs for specific damage. Such costs were higher for historic ageing structures, especially where a pier was architecturally listed. And then there was the issue of investment in new attractions or buildings to ensure a pier enterprise remained competitive. The target of an annual profit or surplus might easily be missed.

Even when piers stayed afloat, during the long post-war period there was an accumulation of changes to the traditional pleasure pier business. Although the speed of change varied from resort to resort and pier to pier, by the mid-1970s most of the pavilions, concert halls, theatres and ballrooms that adorned piers had lost their original purpose. Similarly, where they survived, the pleasure-steamer landing stages (except as fishing platforms), bathing stations for public fun in the sea and diving boards previously used by aquatic entertainers were for the most part redundant and increasingly decrepit.

A musical intermission

For a relatively brief interlude in some seaside towns the pier ballrooms and theatres, as the largest venues available, were put to new uses, hosting the explosion of pop and rock music groups and individual artists playing live during the 1960s and 70s. The roll call of bands performing in the Hastings Pier ballroom during the two decades would have filled a rock and pop hall of fame. In 1964 and 65, The Rolling Stones, The Who, The Kinks and The Honeycombs were amongst the array of artists who played in what was described as 'an aircraft hanger at the end of a sixpenny bus ride from the promenade'.[280] Hastings Pier missed out on The Beatles, however, with a changed schedule and their increasing fame putting paid to an appearance planned for 1962.

Along the coast at Worthing patrons using the pier pavilion in the 1960s could appreciate performances by the resort's municipal orchestra (it survived until 1978) and, if they had eclectic musical tastes, also enjoy a rock group; for example, Jimi Hendrix played there on 23 February 1967.

A decade earlier the jukebox was a temporary salvation for the much smaller Clevedon Pier. At the behest of the piermaster one was installed in the pier's tiny pavilion. For about a decade the jukebox became the centre of a new way of life, focussed on dancing on the pier, for the town's teenagers – a newly emerged social grouping and cultural force.[281] Visitor numbers to the pier increased from 45,000 in 1956 to 83,000 in 1959.[282]

These musical and dancing episodes were enjoyed in large part by local young people. Their experiences help explain 'the significance of the pier as a leisure space to various local groups across the decades', and the continuing attachment and commitment to a local pier as a community asset.[283] (In 2019 there were nightclubs on the piers at Aberystwyth and Bognor Regis and on Claremont Pier, Lowestoft.)

The tiny pavilion on the pier head, Clevedon Pier.
(Wayne Walters)

Hastings on the slide

There were other possibilities for owners of multi-purpose piers to explore. Back in Hastings, for example, the rock band Pink Floyd appeared in the pier's ballroom on 20 January 1968. At the time the pier was 'open for your pleasure all the year', with other attractions including a bingo club and prize bingo, angling, amusement arcades, a shooting range, tenpin bowling and licensed bars. There was even a pier school of dancing, held on Monday and Friday evenings in the restaurant.

By then the entrance to the pier was home to the Triodome, a huge circular domed hall made of aluminium alloy. The building's original purpose was to house two attractions celebrating the Battle of Hastings millennium: a new 'Hastings Embroidery' and a diorama of the 1066 battlefield. The structure's subsequent history was chequered. It became a 'Zooquaruim', was then rebranded as the 'Safari-Dome Zoo' but by 1974 had become an amusement arcade. It was removed from the pier in 1986. Later in the same decade, the

Hastings Pier in 1966, with the Triodome housing the 'Hastings Embroidery'. (Fred Gray collection)

The pretence of a successful pier. Storm clouds gathering over Hastings Pier, July 1998. (Fred Gray)

Hastings Pier, September 2002. (Fred Gray)

best the ballroom could offer were 1960s nostalgia nights.

From then and into the new century, on the surface the pier remained largely unchanged as an architectural spectacle. However, new coats of white paint covered an increasingly frail business and perilous structure. The pier experienced changing ownership, increasing decay and fears about safety, hopes for renewal generated and then dashed, and the growing apprehension of local people for the future of their (privately owned) pier.

Blackpool's three piers

It was at Blackpool where, post war, the traditional pleasure pier business of variety shows, music and dancing was sustained for longest. Many of the artistes working on the resort's piers later became household names in the television age. However, as the pier business developed in new ways, all three piers continued to evolve architecturally.

As early as 1949 on the Central Pier, the large dancing arena was transformed into an open-air theatre. The 1903 White Pavilion at the entrance to the pier was demolished in 1966 and, two years later, the Dixieland Showbar and Golden Goose amusement arcade opened. The curious low-level jetty extension designed for steamer access at low tide had long been redundant; damaged in storms, it was demolished in

The remains of the Blackpool Central Pier 1868 low-level jetty revealed at low tide, late June 2009. (Fred Gray)

stages in 1968 and 1975. The South Pier, too, continued as a performance pier after the war. Then, in 1963, the theatre at the entrance to the pier was converted into an amusement arcade. The imposing 1896 Grand Pavilion was destroyed in a conflagration in 1964 although a replacement building, a purpose-designed theatre, was quickly constructed. Away from the entrance building, architecturally the North Pier changed least over the long post-war period, the 1930s theatre and sun lounge on the pier head surviving to the present day.

In 1967 all three piers were acquired by a rapidly expanding hotel and catering company that, in 1970, became known as Trust Houses Forte (THF). Steadily developing as a transnational corporation, the company's piers portfolio was a tiny part of THF's business. Still, the company was confident enough about the commercial prospects to buy piers elsewhere including Colwyn Bay, Llandudno, Southsea (South Parade Pier) and Eastbourne.

The managing director of the THF leisure division believed, in 1975, that the success of a pier was assured, 'when you have a good resort like Blackpool and you provide what people want.'[284] THF continued to differ-

entiate what each Blackpool pier offered to holidaymakers. The North Pier 'is treated respectfully with 3,000 deck chairs rhythmically disposed for sun-worshippers' and retained the theatre, café, and sun lounge at the seaward end. The other two piers were more intensively built up to 'cater for a younger clientele. On South Pier, children's trampolines and games stretch out from the bulges and along the cluttered deck.'

A few years later, in 1981, the writer and broadcaster Ray Gosling thought all three piers 'are all strong as rock'. The South Pier focussed on children's entertainments, the Central was 'very razzmatazz' with amusements, while 'the North still looks good and much as it was, a spectacle in itself as a pier should be – a combination to delight the eye of motion and stillness.'[285]

THF's interest in piers was not sustained for long. Its pier portfolio was sold to the First Leisure Corporation, a diverse company, in 1983 and the new owners set about transforming all three piers. Las Vegas-style changes to the Central Pier included a new entertainment centre, originally called Maggie May's Showbar and, in 1990, the installation of a giant Dutch-built Ferris wheel on a much-strengthened substructure. On the South Pier, the 1970s theatre was swept away in 1998 and the pier head turned into the 'adrenaline zone of white-knuckle rides'. During the 1980s the entrance to the North Pier was transformed with an architecture of Victorian nostalgia, with the new building providing the home for a cabaret bar (rather confusingly called Merrie England), amusement arcade and shops.

Although the North Pier retained key aspects of its earlier architecture, all three Blackpool piers reached the turn of the century transformed as visual spectacles and business enterprises. By then the ownership of the piers had changed yet again, coming under the control – together with Blackpool's Tower and Winter Garden complex – of an Isle of Man business tycoon.

Brighton's Palace Pier

The Palace Pier's early post-war rejuvenation was no guarantee of continuing success. By the early 1970s, the pier was tired and rundown. A music hall variety show had run during the 1973 summer season. The derelict and unused landing stage was being dismantled that autumn when a barge used in the work broke

free during a sudden and fierce storm on 19 October, battering a corner of the pier head, smashing twenty-five piles, toppling the helter-skelter into the sea and causing a corner of the magnificent 1901 theatre building to lurch seaward and drop 2ft. Repairs were carried out but the theatre stayed dark.

In February 1984 the pier was purchased by the Noble Organisation, a company with diverse leisure, gaming and amusement interests. New policies were introduced including free admission and use of deckchairs and a ban on angling. A year later a £7.5 million refurbishment and development programme was announced. The plan was to turn 'a wonderfully dilapidated, terminally rusty, semi-surreal strip of aged amusement arcades into a 1980s leisure and entertainment venture.'[286]

As part of the programme of work the theatre was to be dismantled and put into storage while the substructure was being renewed. Once returned, the building was to be jacked up and an extra floor inserted for fairground rides including a ghost train and dodgems. The theatre was removed in 1986. The structure then mysteriously disappeared from public view

The autumn 1973 damage to the Palace Pier, Brighton. (Fred Gray collection)

and scrutiny although fragments, including some Oriental domes from the roof, turned up in local recycling yards. The plain oval Triodome from Hastings Pier then magically reappeared on the site where the theatre had stood and began to perform as a large amusement arcade.

The pier's new owners pressed ahead with other aspects of their development plan. A new and much larger entrance was built with a crescent of fast-food outlets. Existing pier buildings including the Palace of Fun were refurbished and the old timber cladding replaced with synthetic materials. In 1995 the pier head was massively enlarged, to cover the footprint of the old landing stage, and used as the site for a large funfair. In little more than a decade the 'semi-surreal' pier had, indeed, been transformed into a bright new amusement and funfair centre above the waves.

The municipal pier

When owned by a local council a pier can be a long time in politics, endlessly tossed about by electoral, political and financial considerations. As the piers at Herne Bay, Southend, Cromer, Bangor and Clevedon illustrate, depending on local circumstances municipal support might waver or be withdrawn but on other occasions be resilient and constant. Whatever the situation, the implications were significant for the future of a pier and its architecture.

Herne Bay

The pier at Herne Bay had been in local authority ownership since 1909. Never satisfactorily restored after the Second World War, in September 1968 the long stem of the pier was designated as unsafe and closed to the public. The council had no appetite to spend the money necessary to rebuild it. Then, in 1970, the landward-end Grand Pavilion was destroyed by a fire. The political support for a replacement building was on more solid ground. However, the designs for a large

Herne Bay Pier c.1950s The Grand Pier Pavilion was destroyed by fire in 1970. (Fred Gray collection)

replacement pavilion, including an aquarium, sports room, skating rink and a 100ft-high tower, were deemed too expensive. Instead a cheaper, but nonetheless startlingly modern sports building, designed by John C. Clague, was erected for the local authority. The new building, formally named the Pier Pavilion Leisure Centre although subsequently nicknamed the Cowshed by local people, included a multi-purpose sports hall, squash courts and sauna. It was opened by former Prime Minister Edward Heath in 1976.

As for the remainder of the pier, two sections were washed away in the 1978 storm surge and further parts of the neck removed by storms the following winter. In 1980 the remains of the neck were demolished. Too difficult to remove, the slowly disintegrating pier head,

Herne Bay Pier with its retail village of beach huts, July 2018. (Author: @UnfoundMatt. This file is licensed under the Creative Commons Attribution-Share Alike 4.0 International license)

with its 1899 refreshment room topped by a Moorish dome, remained out to sea. As a ruin it survives today, marked by a solar-powered navigation light.

Declared unsafe and condemned, the 1976 sports pavilion on the surviving stub of the pier was demolished in 2012. The following year the vacated pier remnant was transformed into a unique 'beach hut village', occupied by thirty-two seaside businesses. By then the increasingly vocal and active Herne Bay Pier Trust, with the objective of the preservation, renovation, reconstruction and enhancement of the pier, proposed alternative visions for the pier's future.

Southend Pier

At Southend the number of people visiting the pier rose from 4.5 million in 1946 to a heady 5.75 million in 1949. Exactly two decades later the figure had fallen to 1.25 million. There followed a period of tremulous political decision-making. In 1974 the spiral of decline led the town's borough treasurer to recommend the pier be taken apart and sold for scrap, so removing any temptation the council might have to spend money on

it.[287] Fire followed fire and it was touch and go whether the council would maintain its commitment to the pier. In 1980 it was announced that the pier would be closed with demolition considered unless the pier could be leased to an external organization.[288]

The pier survived into the new century however, with the council commitment increasingly steadfast. In 2017, 350,000 visitors paid to enjoy the pier.[289] By then the architecture of the pier had been revitalized. The most significant new building, the result of an architectural competition, was the 2012 'Royal Pavilion', a cultural and visitor centre with a multi-purpose main hall, café and exterior terrace. Constructed off site, the building was barged along the Thames the twenty miles from Tilbury and then craned on to the pier head.[290] The designers, White Arkitekter, argued the pavilion was a 'radical deviation from the traditional architecture of Southend. Harmonizing with the windswept site, the Royal Pavilion is, once again, a focal point for cultural life in the town.'[291] Winning a Royal Institute of British Architects (RIBA) award in 2013, the judges commented:

The world's longest pleasure pier, photographed late April 2010, reaches out from Southend across the sand and mud – here covered by water – of the Thames estuary. (Fred Gray)

Southend Pier Cultural Centre, August 2012. The building is now called the Royal Pavilion. (By Luke Hayes/Sprunt Architects – Luke Hayes. This file is licensed under the Creative Commons Attribution-Share Alike 3.0 Unported license)

While strikingly modern, the new building is essentially a pavilion in the tradition of Victorian pier architecture. Its folded, faceted form is determined partly by the steel structure required to spread the building's load evenly over the pier's 100-year old cast iron piles. The building is clad in materials chosen to withstand the hostile marine environment.[292]

Cromer Pier

Cromer Pier provides a remarkable illustration of an enduring struggle to survive and prosper, despite adversity and battering. In 1975, the consultant engineer for the pier commented bleakly that 'I think it's OK now. But with the best will in the world I doubt if it will still be here in 30 years' time.'[293] Over the long

post-war period major storm damage occurred in 1949, 1953, 1976, 1978, 1990, 1993, 2005 and 2013. During the 1993 storm the pier was sectioned again, this time accidentally, when a 100-ton rig-barge destroyed part of the neck of the pier, isolating the pier head.[294] On each occasion the pier has suffered storm damage, the local authority owners, aware of the pier's importance to the town's tourist economy and its iconic status and symbolic role, have repaired and renewed the structure.

2019 marked the fortieth anniversary of the 'Seaside Special' variety show in the pier's Pavilion Theatre: 'the last full-season "end-of-the-pier" variety show left in the world'.[295]

The failure of previous protective measures, Cromer Pier 1993. (Wayne Walters)

Major damage to Cromer Pier, 1993. (Wayne Walters)

Compact, graceful and well maintained, Cromer Pier in June 2000. (Fred Gray)

Cromer Pier's Pavilion Theatre in June 2000, home to the long-running 'Seaside Special' summer variety show and, at the pier head, the 1998 lifeboat house. (Fred Gray)

Bangor Garth Pier

Immediately after the Second World War, Bangor City Council was ambivalent about the future of the decayed Bangor Garth Pier. However, the council did not have the powers required to demolish the pier and the structure remained in its care. In the late 1960s the council attempted to sell the pier to the private sector, but these plans were thwarted because of the pier's low potential for income generation. Safety concerns led to its closure in April 1971. Then came local government reorganization and a new public owner of the pier, Grade II* listing in 1984 and the transfer of the pier, for a nominal fee of one penny to Bangor City Council. Following a vigorous if arduous fundraising campaign restoration work at last began in October 1982; it was to last until 1988 and cost £3.5 million.

On the pier's centenary, in 1996, the community council confirmed that following the 1982 restoration, the promise to the people of Bangor was that 'the cost of maintenance will be met by the pier itself … [which] … will stand on its own strong, elegant legs, hopefully making a profit'.[296] The pier's limited income generation potential meant the promise could not be fulfilled. Instead, the council continued its stewardship of the pier. A four-year restoration plan began in August 2017, although again with uncertainties about the extent of the work required and its cost. By April 2019 £1.3 million from the city council's reserves had been spent on the refurbishment of the pier.

A classic promenade pier, Bangor Garth from across the Menai Straights. (Geoffrey Mead)

Bangor Garth Pier, September 2014. (Wayne Walters)

Clevedon – a pier in trust

An alternative to private and municipal ownership models is for a pier to be owned by a charitable trust, on behalf of the local community. The most sustained and successful example of a pier held in trust is Clevedon.

In October 1970 two complete spans – a total of 200ft – of Clevedon's elegant wrought iron pier, then owned by the council, collapsed into the sea. The seemingly disastrous episode occurred during poorly carried out weight testing of the structure required to obtain insurance cover. The immediate consequence was the closure of the pier. But the event also revealed a groundswell of support for the pier and its repair; within two years a trust to preserve the pier had been established. In 1979 the local authority owners, Woodspring District Council, a body that ironically had the statutory duty to enforce the maintenance of listed buildings, voted to demolish the pier.

A public inquiry to decide on the pier's fate took place in March 1980. The Poet Laureate, Sir John Betjeman, riding to the defence, described Clevedon as 'being the most beautiful pier in England'.[297] The inquiry's inspector judged that the pier should be saved, finding that it was an 'exceptionally important build-

ing' with a 'unique' and 'delicate design'.[298] The district council then absolved itself from direct responsibility for the pier, granting what was to become the Clevedon Pier and Heritage Trust a ninety-nine-year full repairing lease on the structure. Its aesthetic value demonstrated, major funding for restoration was secured from English Heritage and the National Heritage Memorial Fund.

Extraordinarily, in 1985 the pier then disappeared from Clevedon. It was dismantled and removed by barge for refurbishment in a disused dock six miles away. Re-erected on new foundations in 1988 and re-decked the following year, it wasn't until the late 1990s that sufficient public funding was obtained to restore and return the pavilion and shelters to the pier head. The reconstructed pier, remade at a cost exceeding £4 million, was formally reopened on 25 May 1998. In 2001 the pier was architecturally listed as being of Grade I 'exceptional interest' status. An innovative new visitor centre opened in 2016. Seeking to avoid the repair bills of the past, the pier trust also planned a twenty-year maintenance programme, dependent on the ambitious target of generating an annual £100,000 surplus.

Clevedon Pier undergoing restoration, early 1990s. (Fred Gray)

Clevedon Pier, September 2008. (Author: mattbuck. This file is licensed under the Creative Commons Attribution-Share Alike 2.0 Generic license.)

Blackpool North Pier, June 2018. (Fred Gray)

Blackpool South Pier, June 2018. (Fred Gray)

Blackpool Central Pier, June 2018. (Fred Gray)

Blackpool Central Pier, June 2018. (Fred Gray)

Chapter Eight

PROSPECT

What of the not-too-distant future for seaside piers? Some of the significant individual pier developments during the first two decades of the twenty-first century – including those explored in the previous chapter – allow us to tease out some pointers to what may happen next. Piers have been lost, but other ruined piers have been restored. Remarkably, new piers have also been built. There are indications of the development of a twenty-first century architecture for pleasure buildings over the sea.

FOUND AND LOST

Southwold Pier

A new century dawned and, extraordinarily, a new pier for the most family-centred of resorts, Southwold. By the 1980s Southwold Pier, having been whittled away by the action of storms, was a shadow of the original. New private-sector owners took over in 1987 and restored the 1936 entrance building the following year. In 1999 work started on a new 620ft pier designed by locally based architect Brian Haward.

The new pier, completed in 2001, included a T-shaped pier head and, on the neck, four low-key buildings – stylistically very at home in the small resort famous for its beach huts.[299] *The Times* believed Southwold showed piers had renewed meaning for the seaside, proclaiming it was evidence that 'a seaside icon is on the way back'.[300] As a new pier it had none of the costs and disadvantages of maintaining an ageing, historic structure. Despite its understated character, there was a keen appreciation of how best to generate income. Attractions included a 'family entertainment centre' (FEC) and other arcades – including one featuring automata, 'one of the most unique and eccentric collections of interactive machines in the world' – and various food and drink and retail outlets.[301]

Felixstowe Pier

Although Felixstowe Pier was branded in 2019 as 'Great Britain's newest pier', the structure was a combination of a completely new root-end pier and the relics of the decayed (and too expensive to remove) long pier neck.[302] The old substructure of ageing reinforced concrete piles was replaced with a new one of driven steel piles and precast concrete beams and slabs. The new substructure carried a large eye-catching and

Left: The extraordinary open expanse at the end of the renewed Hastings Pier, September 2017. (Fred Gray)

A new pier for the new millennium: Southwold Pier

The old pier in truncated form, October 1996. (Fred Gray)

The pier grows longer, summer 2001. (Fred Gray)

Summer 2000: the new pier progresses. (Fred Gray)

Almost finished, summer 2001. (Fred Gray)

A grandstand position, summer 2000. (Fred Gray)

Summer 2001. (Fred Gray)

Waiting for the water clock to perform, summer 2001. (Fred Gray)

The entrance to Felixstowe Pier, June 2013. (Wayne Walters)

The new Felixstowe Pier, June 2019. (Fred Gray)

Felixstowe Pier, the new shore-end building and the surviving older pier stretching into the sea, June 2019. (Fred Gray)

income-generating entertainment pavilion surrounded by a boardwalk.[303] The building, constructed using modern materials, housed an FEC described as 'an authentic British seaside gaming experience with twinkling arcades and mini retro-style tenpin bowling' and a café-bar with views of sea and coast.[304]

The new pier officially opened in October 2017 as part of a wider remaking of the seafront plaza.[305] In design terms the pavilion referenced the innovative 1903 Art Nouveau pavilion on Great Yarmouth's Wellington Pier (a building that had also been reconstructed a few years earlier). The twin towers at the entrance to the building framed a large nostalgically themed seascape mural made of vinyl rather than glass.

Grand Pier, Weston-super-Mare

The large warehouse-like Modernist pavilion on the Grand Pier was destroyed in a fire on 28 July 2008, the conflagration also causing significant damage to the remainder of the pier. The replacement pavilion, designed by Bristol-based Angus Meek Architects, opened on 23 October 2010. Echoing some design elements from the destroyed building, such as four corner towers, the futuristic replacement had twice the floor space and accommodated both modern thrill rides such as 'Robocoaster' and 'Sidewinder', traditional fairground attractions including both a ghost train and helter-skelter, and places to eat and drink.[306] A covered walkway along the stem of the pier provided weatherproof access to the pier-head pavilion.

Hastings Pier

In 2008 Hastings Pier was closed – once again – as unsafe and then destroyed by fire on 5 October 2010. An intense and popular local campaign led to the council compulsorily purchasing the pier from the absentee private owners, and then transferring it on to the Hastings Pier Charity, an innovative form of community ownership argued to be 'a best-practice model of community-led regeneration for seaside piers.'[307] This involved 'a dedicated, transparent charitable ownership, coupled with local, co-operative-style membership and a strongly commercial and entrepreneurial management approach. The energy, passion and ambition has come from local people.'[308]

The pier reopened on 27 April 2016 following the expenditure of £14.2 million, including £13 million from the Heritage Lottery Fund (HLF) and £590,000 from shares bought by individuals supporting the pier. Much of the funding was used to restore the substructure. In a most modern interpretation of a promenade pier, a wide and open deck covered much of the footprint of the old pier. The single new building, clad in timber salvaged from the destroyed pier, was a visitor

The morning after: the still smouldering ruins of Hastings Pier. (Fred Gray collection)

and education centre with a rooftop viewing platform. The restored curved band enclosure shelter from 1911 (the only part of the superstructure to survive the fire) was remodelled into a café-bar. It was projected that the pier would attract 325,000 visitors a year with the major income source from events such as open-air concerts and festivals on the pier's vast deck; in the opening fortnight an estimated 75,000 people visited the pier.

In 2017 the RIBA awarded the annual Stirling prize for the best new building in the UK to Hastings Pier by dRMM Architects. Dubbed 'the people's pier' by the

The renewed Hastings Pier rested on the substructure of the old, September 2017. (Fred Gray)

The visitor and education centre, September 2017.
(Fred Gray)

chair of the prize committee, the RIBA described the pier as a 'phoenix risen from the ashes', with the architects having 'carefully restored and creatively reimagined the Victorian pier as a contemporary multipurpose space'.[309]

There was then an unexpected twist in the rebirth of Hastings Pier. In November 2017, days following the award of the architecture prize, the charity running the pier was bankrupt and in administration. Despite the considerable community support for the pier and the large amount of public funding spent on remaking and reshaping the structure, in June 2018 the pier was perversely sold for £60,000 to a private company controlled by the same individual who owned the nearby Eastbourne Pier.[310] In less than a decade the pier was owned, in sequence, privately, by the local authority, by a community organization and then privately again. In June 2019 the new building designed as a visitor and education centre became an amusement arcade: it seemed that the pier was unable to shake off the spectre of its former self.

Southsea South Parade and Penarth Piers

With a common stylistic heritage, Penarth Pier and Southsea South Parade Pier were both refurbished. However, different ownership models led to fundamentally different pier uses.

Hastings Pier in September 2017 with rain on the horizon. Within two months the pier was recognized as the best new building in the UK and the charity running the pier was bankrupt. (Fred Gray)

Southsea South Parade Pier in October 2017, shortly after reopening following its 2012 closure. (Fred Gray)

At Southsea the pier was closed as unsafe in 2012. Although a community organization attempted to buy the pier, it was sold to new private owners. The refurbished pier reopened in 2017 as a multi-purpose amusement attraction with arcades and a bar with a programme of live entertainment; a funfair was added in 2019. In contrast, at Penarth the council owned the pier with restoration work being publicly rather than privately funded. Major repairs to the substructure occurred in the late 1990s and early in the new century the pavilion also required extensive refurbishment. Run by a not-for-profit organization, the pavilion was redeveloped as a multi-functional space for exhibitions, live music and theatre, and cinema screenings. Externally, new ornamental zinc tiles replaced the faded green paint on the pavilion's roof and domes, and dramatically changed how the building looked.[311] In August 2014 Penarth Pier was voted the 'most special place in Wales'.

Penarth Pier in May 1998. The restored pier reopened a few days later. It was more than a decade before the pavilion was refurbished. (Fred Gray)

The restored pavilion, Penarth Pier, October 2013. (Author: Ben Salter. Source: Flickr. This file is licensed under the Creative Commons Attribution 2.0 Generic license)

Victoria Pier, Colwyn Bay

A long period of decline was associated with frequent changes in the private ownership of the pier. It was closed as unsafe in 2008 and sections collapsed during subsequent storms. In 2012 the pier came into municipal ownership and unsuccessful proposals were made to restore the structure with HLF funding. Meanwhile, with the exception of nine piles at the root end of the structure, by May 2018 the desolate remains had been removed. Attempting to clutch on to some essence of the old pier, elements of the fabric including decorative cast iron were salvaged. The remnants of the 1934 pavilion murals by Ravilious and Adshead were also saved in the hope that they might be conserved.[312]

In March 2019 the local authority and Colwyn Victoria Pier Trust were working together on plans for a truncated pier. To be built on the surviving landward-end piles and incorporating retained components from the old pier, the new structure was to act as an interpretation platform for its history.[313] It was to be the first step in ambitions to build a new larger pier with a pavilion.

Brighton West Pier

In 1998 the HLF agreed to provide 'in principle' a grant of £14.5 million for the restoration of the pier by the West Pier Trust. Despite the promise of a renewed pier a quarter of a century after its closure, the restoration scheme was dragged into a quagmire of bureaucratic dithering, opposition from the owners of the neighbouring Palace Pier, political lobbying, planning inquiries and public protest.[314] Then, in an eighteen-month period ending in June 2004, the pier's theatre and concert hall were destroyed in two violent storms and two arson attacks. The visually dramatic images received international media coverage, while locally each event drew hundreds of spectators to gaze, record and scavenge for remnants of the structure.

Following the devastation, the two most significant national bodies for the historic environment locked horns to contest the future of the pier. Despite the damage, English Heritage, responsible for protecting the historic environment, initially remained supportive, arguing 'The West Pier was the most important pleasure pier ever built in terms of its climactic and

The remains of the Victoria Pier, Colwyn Bay, August 2017. (Copyright holder: Reading Tom. Source: Flickr. This file is licensed under the Creative Commons Attribution 2.0 Generic license)

The arson attack on the West Pier, March 2003. (Fred Gray)

The dramatic removal of the detritus of the West Pier Concert Hall, February 2010. (Fred Gray)

seminal engineering design, its architectural ambition and as an enduring social symbol of Brighton as the acme of seaside resorts.'[315]

The HLF, though, took the alternative view and withdrew its financial support, arguing the project was by then too risky and uncertain. A scathing *Daily Telegraph* editorial in July 2004 saw the West Pier 'tragedy' as 'a parable for everything that is wrong with Britain'.[316]

The West Pier and the restoration project were both lost. And yet by 2019 the site had been reborn as a place for spectacular seaside architecture. The root end of the pier became the location of the 2016 British Airways i360, an innovative and slender 162m-high moving ob-

servation tower.[317] Described by the designer, David Marks of Marks Barfield Architects, as a vertical pier, the vision 'was to follow in the spirit of the original pier, inviting visitors to walk on air and gain a new perspective of the city, just as in the past they walked on water.'[318] The i360 was an ideal platform from which to view, just off shore and in a state of active collapse, the skeleton of the West Pier theatre and pier head. Close by, the promenade was enlivened by a 'golden spiral' sculpture made of salvaged pier columns. The West Pier Trust was also actively seeking to restore and re-erect a surviving 1866 kiosk from the pier – the world's oldest extant pleasure pier building.[319]

View of the ascending pod and the slender tower, British Airways i360, Brighton, August 2018. (Fred Gray)

A bird's-eye view from the i360 pod of the transitional zone between land and sea and the 'golden spiral' made from the West Pier's cast-iron columns. Brighton, July 2018. (Fred Gray)

AND THEN?

The evidence of the first two decades of the twenty-first century strongly suggests that, contrary to the views of commentators from the 1970s onwards, it will not be the end of the pier. Piers will continue to provide a defining characteristic and architectural feature of many British seaside resorts. They will continue to be a focus of cultural and economic life and a source of local identity. There will be new piers, restored piers and, as in the case of the Brighton seafront observation tower, reinterpretations of the essence of the pier. Piers may also be lost, although as the examples from Colwyn Bay and Brighton demonstrate, vanquished piers may live on in spirit and at times even be resurrected in a new form. However, as the life stories of piers recounted in this book demonstrate, it would be foolhardy to predict a specific future for any individual pier: what happens is conditional on so much else that nothing is certain.

Gathering together strands of evidence from the last quarter of a century indicates two extreme types of contemporary pier enterprise: amusement piers and civic piers will help guide and determine future pier prospects. At either end of a continuum – and there are blends of the two in between – amusement and civic piers have fundamentally different ownership and financial underpinnings, contrasting functions and purpose and, frequently, different architectural manifestations.

Amusement piers

Amusement piers are privately owned and, necessarily, commercially orientated. The root to financial success of amusement piers is through major investment in year-round, all-weather artificial attractions. The single most important feature of amusement piers is the ubiquitous 'family entertainment centre'. Both 'family entertainment' and 'seaside entertainment' become shorthand surrogate (and for some, misused) terms for an amalgam of activities focussing on amusement and gaming machines and arcade games, attractions such as tenpin bowling and adventure golf and, housed indoors or in the open air, funfair and thrill rides – often the more extreme the better – and adventure playgrounds. All these entertainments are also usually associated with diverse family-orientated food and drink outlets.

To succeed FECs need to attract and retain visitors from a local and regional market. Apart from the entertainments on offer they depend on outstandingly visible and attractive locations. A pier, with an extreme setting and spectacular architecture, is a magnetic attraction in its own terms. The requirement to provide year-round, all-weather entertainments necessitates large indoor spaces: pier entertainment buildings are ideal. At best, a pier and an FEC become highly accommodating bed fellows. And the glue in the relationship between pier and FEC is the amusement machine. In 2017 the amusement and gaming machine trade body, BACTA, believed: 'The biggest revenue stream for Britain's piers – and the only one that can be relied upon all year round – is coin operated amusements.'[320]

In 2019 the most successful contemporary amusement pier was Brighton Palace Pier (the name changed in 2016). With an estimated 4,684,000 visitors in 2017 the pier was the most popular free attraction outside London, ranking fourth after the British Museum, Tate Modern and National Gallery. In 2016 it accommodated 350 arcade machines and eighteen funfair rides.[321] In 2019 the pier proclaimed that 'above the deck the latest video games, thrill rides and retail shops ensure that our customers experience the best of seaside entertainment.'[322] With the Palm Court fish and chip restaurant, Victoria's Bar and Horatio's Bar, and numerous smaller food kiosks, enticing visitors to eat and drink was an important means of extending the

Brighton's Palace Pier, June 2019. (Fred Gray)

The Brighton Palace Pier 'Palace of Fun' in June 2019. The much changed 1920s building began life as the Winter Gardens. (Fred Gray)

The view back to Brighton, Palace Pier, June 2019. (Fred Gray)

In July 2014 Sandown Pier was advertised with the strapline 'a whole day's fun in one'. (Fred Gray)

Clacton Pier in June 2019. (Fred Gray)

Apart from a large and revitalized family entertainment centre with attractions including adventure golf and bowling, Clacton Pier retained a traditional funfair, June 2019. (Fred Gray)

length of a visit and generating income. The pier wasn't simply a regional FEC; much of the success was rooted in Brighton's standing as a seaside resort with a large number of young international visitors.

The commercial amusement pier model could adopt different guises. Southsea's Clarence Pier, opening in 1961, was the prototype purpose-designed amusement pier, a harbinger of things to come. For the Grand Pier at Weston-super-Mare and Felixstowe Pier, the amusement pier strategy promised sufficient revenue to allow investment in large modern pier entertainment buildings. Although new amusement pier buildings utilize modern building and design ideas, techniques and materials, stylistically the architectural references have been to pier pleasure buildings of the past. The use of imposing frontages, prominent towers and bright, white materials all act to emphasize the striking and attractive nature of a building. Add the location, by or over the sea, and the experience is removed from the everyday world.

As at Brighton and Southsea, much the same effect was achieved by refurbishing existing pleasure pier buildings. By 2019, the owners of Clacton Pier had revitalized the large old 1930s entertainment buildings,

reinventing them as fit for a successful modern amusement pier. At another extreme, Southwold Pier used the same ingredients to produce an altogether lower-key amusement pier. The financial viability of even the tiny pier-like structure at Burnham-on-Sea depended on its FEC.

Civic piers

Municipally- or community-owned civic piers, in contrast to amusement piers, are based on an alternative premise. Whether owned by a local authority or a not-for-profit pier trust, as iconic structures civic piers may be valued as irreplaceable physical heritage, for their symbolic status or as crucial community assets. Civic piers may also have a significant role in ensuring the success of the tourist economy, the cultural life of a seaside town, or the physical regeneration of a seafront.

Piers in local authority ownership – examples range from Deal, Worthing, Bangor and Southport to Cromer, Southend, Bournemouth and Boscombe – depend on continuing public funding that is often hidden from view. Pier entertainment buildings might be contracted out or leased to specialist commercial companies: the entertainments provided on Bournemouth Pier edge along the continuum toward the amusement

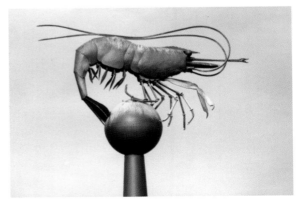

Public art marking the entrance to Southport Pier, 1994. (Fred Gray)

pier model. In contrast the pavilion on Penarth Pier, run by a not-for-profit company, has a strong focus on community use.

Piers in civic ownership, including those at Deal, Southend and Southport – and at least at the moment of its rebirth, Hastings – also demonstrate the emergence of an original twenty-first century architecture of pier buildings. These new pavilions over the waves, often the result of architectural competitions, serve various purposes – as cafés, visitor centres, education venues and civic spaces – but are characterized by their streamlined aesthetic respecting both the tradition and nature of piers. Such buildings, while very different from the new amusement pier pavilions, are equally appropriate embellishments to contemporary piers.

Lottery funding has helped revolutionize the funding possibilities for civic piers. At Southport, the HLF was a major contributor to the wholesale reconstruction of the pier – which was dismantled and then remade – between 2000 and 2003.[323] The pier at Saltburn was similarly remade with funding from the lottery and European Union. In 2019 it was estimated that since its inception the HLF has awarded almost £24 million – surely an underestimate – to pier-related projects.[324] However, the process of accessing funding was arduous and often, as in the case of the Victoria Pier, Colwyn Bay, unsuccessful.

By 2019 just two piers had been successfully restored through community ownership. Clevedon, dis-

cussed in the previous chapter, was established as an exceptional success, although it still faced the formidable challenge of funding continuing maintenance. At Swanage, following an eighteen-month regeneration project, the simple small, wooden pier reopened on 3 April 2019. Owned and run by Swanage Pier Trust, the

The demolition of the old pier head, Southport, late 1990s. (Wayne Walters)

The 2002 new pier pavilion at Southport by shedkm architects. (Courtesy Chris Brink & shedkm)

The remarkable start of the remaking of Southport Pier, late 1990s. (Wayne Walters)

The startling modern pavilion at Southport is built on a new extension to the pier. (Courtesy Chris Brink & shedkm)

restoration, in large part funded by the HLF, included replacing many of the wooden piles and the construction of a new visitor centre.[325]

Portent

As the examples of Brighton's West Pier and Hastings Pier illustrate, the relationships between private, public and not-for-profit organizations with pier interests may chafe against each other, sometimes in sore, unproductive and ultimately destructive ways. Even if privately owned, local people often believe that a pier belongs to them and is a community asset to be enjoyed and safeguarded for future generations. Such passionate local support and community interest is an often unappreciated asset but one that, while seemingly holding promise for the future, is difficult to translate into successful and enduring community ownership.[326]

Whether amusement piers or civic piers, cherishing, maintaining and renewing old, fragile and at-risk structures will continue to be expensive and technically demanding.[327] In the case of Cromer Pier, in 2019 it was reported that the relatively small local authority owner and custodian continued to invest approximately £500,000 per annum to preserve and maintain its listed structure.[328] In the same year the three Blackpool piers, privately owned by a family business, were 'under threat, as their attractions generate insufficient revenue' to fund the required maintenance.[329] The issue at Blackpool was a combination of the specifics of restoring and maintaining three large nineteenth-century piers, the difficulty of appealing to sufficient visitors given the resort's rival attractions and long-term changes to the town's visitor base.

The perpetual battle for a pier's survival will be made more formidable by climate change. Although the speed and extent of change is uncertain, sea level rises will both continue and accelerate, and 'storminess' – the frequency and intensity of storms, storm surges and the height of extreme waves – will increase.[330] Average temperatures

Saltburn Pier, late February 2019. The pier reopened in July 2001 after being dismantled, restored and re-erected. The cliff lift provides a gentle means of access to and from the pier. (Fred Gray)

will rise and there will be more periods of intense heat and sun. Pier architecture and engineering will necessarily evolve and adapt to meet challenging environmental circumstances. Piers may become places to storm watch or escape from intense onshore heat. New ideas and new materials may produce innovative twenty-first century versions of Victorian pier weather screens or inter-war sun decks. New challenges may become opportunities for a new architecture of British seaside piers.

The foundations of pleasure, Brighton Palace Pier, June 2019. (Fred Gray)

ENVOI

For two centuries the British seaside pier has survived and enjoyed a tumultuous history. In varied forms and guises around the coast of Britain, it has provided, at times, an astonishing architectural feast and engineering spectacle. On other occasions, and despite the edge-of-the-land coastal setting, the pier has been a rather mundane sight. Designed to subdue and consume nature, the pier has also been left hapless, distraught and ruined by the elements. It is an environment-bridging, shapeshifting, perilous and impermanent structure.

The pier is a stage, a transit point, between land and sea and is a stage for performance, display and spectating. It has been a place of staid promenade and genteel society, the most natural and most synthetic of pleasures, and rambunctious amusement. It has seen the sight and been a site of sometimes extraordinary, sometimes breathtaking and sometimes ridiculous entertainment.

The pier may be a place of recreation and leisure, enjoyment and excitement, romantic and sexual encounter, boredom and loneliness, danger and fear, of no return, of coming home, of new possibilities. As a place of horizons and perspectives, where the relationship between society and nature is exposed and extreme, the pier allows the natural world to be contemplated and questioned. The abiding pier pleasures, first learnt in the nineteenth century and equally accessible to the contemporary seaside visitor, include the excitement of walking on water and peering below at the surging and mysterious sea. The pier encourages us to speculate about ourselves and about others, on other places, real and imaginary, and about other times, past and future.

REFERENCES

1. Walking on Water: Introducing British Seaside Piers

1 Simon H. Adamson, *Seaside Piers* (London, 1977), p. 110.
2 Anthony Wills and Tim Phillips, *British Seaside Piers* (Swindon, 2014), p. 28.
3 Alain Corbin, *The Lure of the Sea: The Discovery of the Seaside in the Western World 1750–1840* (Cambridge, 1994).
4 Ibid., p. 62.
5 Ibid., p. 263.
6 Kate Flint, *The Victorians and the Visual Imagination* (Cambridge, 2000), pp. 285–6.
7 John Hassan, *The Seaside, Health and the Environment in England and Wales since 1800* (Aldershot, 2003), pp. 76–8.
8 J. Whyman, 'Water communications to Margate and Gravesend as coastal resorts before 1840', *Southern History*, iii (1981), pp. 111–38.
9 John K. Walton, *The English Seaside Resort: A Social History 1750–1914* (Leicester, 1983).
10 John H. Clapham, *An Economic History of Modern Britain: Free Trade and Steel 1850–1886* (Cambridge, 1952), p. 518.
11 Walton, *English Seaside Resort*, p. 173.
12 Ibid.; John K. Walton, *The British Seaside: Holidays and Resorts in the Twentieth Century* (Manchester, 2000).
13 John Benson, *The Rise of Consumer Society in Britain, 1880–1980* (London, 1994).
14 Walton, *English Seaside Resort*, pp. 164–6.
15 *Preston Chronicle*, 23 May 1863.
16 Felicity Stafford and Nigel Yates, *The Later Kentish Seaside* (Gloucester, 1985), p. 24.
17 Clapham, *Free Trade and Steel*, p. 518.
18 *The Standard*, 11 November 1864.
19 John Field, 'The Battle of Southsea', *The Portsmouth Papers*, 34 (1981).
20 John F. Travis, *The Rise of the Devon Seaside Resorts 1750–1900* (Exeter, 1993), p. 184.
21 David Cannadine, *Lords and Landlords: The Aristocracy and the Towns 1774–1967* (Leicester, 1980), p. 355.
22 John K. Walton, 'British Tourism Between Industrialization and Globalization', in *The Making of Modern Tourism: The Cultural History of the British Experience, 1600–2000*, ed. Hartmut Berghoff, Barbara Korte, Ralf Schneider and Christopher Harvie (Basingstoke, 2002), pp. 109–31.
23 Marie-Christine Grasse, *Coups de Soleil & Bikinis* (Milan, 1997), p. 43.
24 Ibid., p. 63.
25 Ken Worpole, *Here Comes the Sun. Architecture and Public Space in Twentieth-Century European Culture* (London, 2000), p. 14.
26 Bernard Toulier, Corinne Belier and Franck Delorme, *Tous à la Plage!: Villes Balnéaires du XVIIIe Siècle à nos Jours* (Paris, 2016), pp. 54–5.
27 Guy Junien Moreau, *Le Casino de la Jetée-Promenade* (Nice, 1993).
28 Frederick Treves, *The Riviera of the Corniche Road* (London, 1921), pp. 15–16.
29 Wilhelm Huls and Ulf Böttcher, *Bäderarchitektur* (Rostock, 1998).

2. Making Piers: People, Materials and Techniques

30 'Marine Terrace', www.picturemargate.org.uk, accessed 1 May 2019.
31 Paul Dobraszczyk, *Iron, Ornament and Architecture in Victorian Britain: Myth and Modernity, Excess and Enchantment* (London, 2014).
32 Paul Dobraszczyk, 'Historicizing Iron: Charles Driver and the Abbey Mills Pumping Station (1865–68)', *Architectural History*, 49 (2006), pp. 223–256, p. 226.
33 E. Graeme Robertson and Joan Robertson, *Cast Iron Decoration: A World Survey* (London, 1977), p. 18.
34 *The Engineer*, 16 January 1880.
35 Personal communication from Martin Easdown, 29 July 2019.
36 Martin Easdown, *Lancashire's Seaside Piers* (Barnsley, 2009).
37 Martin Easdown and Darlah Thomas, *Piers of Wales* (Stroud, 2010), p. 155.
38 Dobraszczyk, *Iron, Ornament and Architecture*, p. 149.
39 'Arnold England', www.manchestervictorianarchitects.org.uk, accessed 1 February 2019.
40 www.manchestervictorianarchitects.org.uk, accessed 9 January 2019.
41 'John Dent Harker', www.manchestervictorianarchitects.org.uk, accessed 1 February 2019.
42 *The Engineer*, 12 March 1875.
43 Robertson and Robertson, *Cast Iron Decoration*.
44 Simon H. Adamson, *Seaside Piers* (London, 1977); Cyril Bainbridge, *Pavilions on the Sea: A History of the Seaside Pleasure Pier* (London, 1986).
45 Faye Watson Davies, 'Does the Name Eugenius Birch Mean Anything to You? The Life and Selected Works of Eugenius Birch 1818–1884', Postgraduate Diploma, Conservation of Historic Buildings, Architectural Association (2015), p. 62.
46 M. Noel Ridley, 'Promenade Piers', *The Structural Engineer*, XII, 2 (1934), pp. 106–10.
47 Personal communication from Nigel Hosker, HOP Consulting Ltd, 28 June 2019.
48 *The Architect and Building News*, 23 September 1927.
49 *The Engineer*, 12 March 1875.
50 R. A. Otter, ed., *Civil Engineering Heritage: Southern England* (London, 1994), p. 165.
51 Peter Cross-Rudkin et al., eds., *A Biographical Dictionary of Civil Engineers in Great Britain and Ireland: Volume 2: 1830–1890* (London, 2008), pp. 544–5.
52 Alan J. Lutenegger, 'Historical Development of Iron Screw-Pile Foundations: 1836–1900', T*he International Journal for the History of Engineering and Technology*, 81:1 (2011), pp. 108–128.
53 *The Engineer*, 12 March 1875.
54 Martin Easdown, *Yorkshire's Seaside Piers* (Barnsley, 2008), p. 15.
55 Martin Easdown, *Piers of Sussex* (Stroud, 2009), p. 37.
56 *The Morning Post*, 6 August 1872.
57 Nigel Winterbottom, 'Brighton Pier, UK – innovation in renovation',

Proceedings of the Institution of Civil Engineers – Engineering History and Heritage, 167, 2 (2014), pp. 100–10.
58 *The Engineer*, 12 March 1875.
59 *The Illustrated London News*, 18 August 1860.
60 Adamson, *Seaside Piers*, p. 68.
61 Easdown, *Lancashire's Seaside Piers*, p. 124.
62 Personal communication from Nigel Hosker, HOP Consulting Ltd, 28 June 2019.
63 *Preston Chronicle*, 23 May 1863.
64 Easdown, *Yorkshire's Seaside Piers*.
65 *The Times*, 4 August 1868.
66 Fred Gray, *Walking on Water: The West Pier Story* (Brighton, 1997), p. 29.
67 J. E. Breakell et al., *Management of accelerated low water corrosion in steel maritime structures* (London, 2005); R. E. Melchers and R. J. Jeffrey, 'Accelerated low water corrosion of steel piling in harbours', *Corrosion Engineering, Science and Technology*, 48, 7 (2013), pp. 496–505.

3. Agreeable Promenades and Pioneer Piers
68 Jane Austen, *Persuasion* (London, 1932), p. 81.
69 Richard Bull, *Lyme's Battle with the Sea: Part 1: The Cobb Breakwater* (Lyme Regis, 2015) p. 2.
70 Austen, *Persuasion*, p. 94.
71 George Roberts, *The History of Lyme-Regis, Dorset, from the Earliest Periods to the Present Day* (Lyme Regis, 1823), p. 173.
72 Emma Boast, 'Margate Pier – The Pier Structure', www.thanetarch.co.uk, accessed 8 March 2019.
73 Anonymous, *The Visitor's Guide to the Watering Places* (London, 1841), p. 159.
74 Richard Fischer and John Walton, *British Piers* (London, 1987), p. 12.
75 Anonymous, *An Historical Guide to Great Yarmouth in Norfolk* (Yarmouth, 1806), p. 22.
76 Anonymous, *An Historical Guide to Great Yarmouth in Norfolk* (Yarmouth, 1817), p. 22.
77 John Preston, *The Picture of Yarmouth* (Yarmouth, 1819), p. 13.
78 Kathryn Ferry, '"The Maker of Modern Yarmouth": J. W. Cockrill', in *Powerhouses of Provincial Architecture 1837–1914*, ed. Kathryn Ferry (London, 2009), pp. 45–58.

79 Ward and Lock, *Great Yarmouth, 1911–12* (London, 1911), p. 16.
80 Anonymous, *The Visitor's Guide to the Watering Places*, p. 161.
81 Ibid.
82 Allan Brodie, 'The Brown family adventure – seaside holidays in Kent in the mid-nineteenth century', *Journal of Tourism History*, 5, 1 (2013), pp. 1–24.
83 Marian Lane, *Piers of the Isle of Wight: A Nostalgic View* (Isle of Wight, 1996).
84 Simon H. Adamson, *Seaside Piers* (London, 1977), p. 110.
85 Quoted in Martin Easdown and Linda Sage, *Piers of Hampshire and the Isle of Wight* (Stroud, 2011), pp. 105–6.
86 A. W. Skempton, ed., *Biographical Dictionary of Civil Engineers in Great Britain and Ireland. Volume 1: 1500–1830* (London, 2002), pp. 85–7.
87 John George Bishop, *The Brighton Chain Pier: In Memoriam* (Brighton, 1897), p. xviii.
88 Stella Beddoe, '"Hung Like a Fairy Fabric O'er the Sea …" The Brighton Chain Suspension Pier' in *Brighton Revealed Through Artists' Eyes c.1760–c.1960* ed. David Beevers (Brighton, 1995), pp. 40–3, p. 40.
89 *The Times*, 2 December 1823.
90 Alain Corbin, *The Lure of the Sea: The Discovery of the Seaside in the Western World 1750–1840* (Cambridge, 1994), p. 265.
91 *New Monthly Magazine*, LXI (1841), p. 168, quoted in Edmund M. Gilbert, *Brighton: Old Ocean's Bauble* (London, 1954), p. 129.
92 William Makepeace Thackeray, *The Newcomes* (London, 1893), pp. 102–3.
93 John H. Clapham, *An Economic History of Modern Britain: The Early Railway Age 1820–1850* (Cambridge, 1959), p. 8.
94 Beddoe, 'The Brighton Chain Suspension Pier', p. 41.
95 Bishop, *The Brighton Chain Pier*, p. 23.
96 Beddoe, 'The Brighton Chain Suspension Pier'.
97 Easdown and Sage, *Piers of Hampshire and the Isle of Wight*, p. 120.
98 *The Times*, 7 December 1896.
99 Easdown and Sage, *Piers of Hampshire and the Isle of Wight*, pp. 125–6.
100 John William Burrows, *Southend Pier and Its Story: 1829–1835–1935* (Southend-on-Sea, 1936), p. 2.

101 Ibid., p. 15 and p. 30.
102 Martin Easdown, *Piers of Kent* (Stroud, 2007), p. 45.

4. Revolution: Iron Takes Over
103 Anonymous, *The Visitor's Guide to the Watering Places* (London, 1841), p. 1.
104 Robert Peirce Cruden, *The History of the Town of Gravesend in the County of Kent and of the Port of London* (London, 1848), p. 501.
105 Ibid., p. 505.
106 Anonymous, *The Visitor's Guide to the Watering Places*, p. 11.
107 Ibid., p. 531.
108 John Baldry Redman, 'The Terrace Pier, Gravesend', *Minutes of Proceedings of the Institution of Civil Engineers* (1845), pp. 222–50, p. 229.
109 Kathryn Ferry, 'Palaces on the Sea', *Country Life*, 11 July 2018, pp. 90–94.
110 Martin Easdown and Linda Sage, *Piers of Hampshire and the Isle of Wight* (Stroud, 2011), pp. 65–8.
111 *The Builder*, 22 September 1855.
112 *Preston Chronicle*, 23 May 1863.
113 'The opening of Southport Pier', *The Illustrated London News*, 18 August 1860.
114 Anonymous, 'On the south coast', *Fun*, 11 June 1864.
115 *Preston Chronicle*, 23 May 1863.
116 'The opening of Blackpool Pier', *The Illustrated London News*, 30 May 1863.
117 'New promenade pier at New Brighton', *Liverpool Mercury*, 11 June 1867.
118 'The opening of Blackpool Pier', *The Illustrated London News*.
119 Martin Easdown and Darlah Thomas, *Piers of Wales* (Stroud, 2010), p. 51.
120 'On the Welsh coast', *The Sphinx*, 2 September 1871.
121 Fred Gray, *Walking on Water: The West Pier Story* (Brighton, 1997); Fred Gray, *Designing the Seaside: Architecture, Society and Nature* (London, 2006).
122 *The Brighton Herald*, 4 July 1863.
123 Gray, *Walking on Water*, p. 16.
124 Ibid.
125 *The Brighton Examiner*, 9 October 1866.
126 *The Builder*, 13 October 1866.
127 *The Brighton Herald*, 8 April 1865.
128 *The Brighton Herald*, 1 April 1865.

129 *The Builder*, 13 October 1866.
130 *The Brighton Examiner*, 9 October 1866.
131 'Opening of the West Pier at Brighton', *Morning Post*, 8 October 1866.
132 Ibid.
133 Helen Hughes, 'Brighton West Pier Kiosk: Architectural Paint Investigation', Report for Brighton West Pier Trust, January 2018.
134 Jessica Rutherford, *A Prince's Passion: The Life of the Royal Pavilion* (Brighton, 2003), pp. 156–67.
135 *Penny Illustrated Paper*, 8 June 1867.
136 *Monmouthshire Merlin*, 8 June 1867.
137 Quoted in Martin Easdown, *Lancashire's Seaside Piers* (Barnsley, 2009), pp. 20–21.
138 *Liverpool Mercury*, 11 June 1867.
139 *The Engineer*, 23 April 1869.
140 Paul Wells and Sylvia Endacott, *Glimpses of Bognor Regis Pier* (Bognor Regis, 1998), p. 3.
141 John William Grover, 'Description of a Wrought-Iron Pier at Clevedon', *Minutes of Proceedings of the Institution of Civil Engineers*, 32 (1871) pp. 130–6, p. 130.
142 Roger Cragg, ed., *Civil Engineering Heritage: Wales and West Central England* (London, 1997), pp. 116–17.

5. The Golden Age of Seaside Piers

143 Martin Easdown, *Yorkshire's Seaside Piers* (Barnsley, 2008), p. 68.
144 Steve Peak, *A Pier Without Peer: The History of Hastings Pier* (Hastings, 2016), p. 59.
145 *The London Journal*, 21 September 1872.
146 *The Morning Post*, 6 August 1872.
147 Peak, *A Pier Without Peer*, p. 65.
148 'Obituary. Eugenius Birch', *Minutes of the Proceedings of the Institution of Civil Engineers*, 78 (1884), pp. 414–16.
149 Martin Easdown, *Lancashire's Seaside Piers* (Barnsley, 2009), p. 108.
150 Lynn F. Pearson, *The People's Palaces: Britain's Seaside Pleasure Buildings* (Buckingham, 1991); Easdown, *Lancashire's Seaside Piers*, pp. 101–4.
151 Quoted in Simon H. Adamson, *Seaside Piers* (London, 1977), p. 40.
152 Easdown, *Yorkshire's Seaside Piers*.
153 Martin Easdown and Linda Sage, *Piers of Hampshire and the Isle of Wight* (Stroud, 2011), pp. 210–11.
154 *The Times*, 9 August 1880.
155 Anthony Wills and Tim Phillips, *British Seaside Piers* (Swindon, 2014), pp. 192–3.
156 Easdown, *Lancashire's Seaside Piers*, p. 141.
157 John MacKenzie, *Orientalism: History, Theory and the Arts* (Manchester, 1995), p. 71.
158 Edward W. Said, *Orientalism* (London, 1978), p. 3.
159 David Cannadine, *Ornamentalism. How the British Saw Their Empire* (London, 2001).
160 MacKenzie, *Orientalism*, p. 94. See, also, Patrick Conner, *Oriental Architecture in the West* (London, 1979) and Raymond Head, *The Indian Style* (Chicago, 1986).
161 Paul Dobraszczyk, *Iron, Ornament and Architecture in Victorian Britain: Myth and Modernity, Excess and Enchantment* (Farnham, 2014), p. 150.
162 Kenneth Lindley, *Seaside Architecture* (London, 1973), p. 42.
163 Michael Paris, *Warrior Nation. Images of War in British Popular Culture, 1850–2000* (London, 2000).
164 Christiana Payne, 'Seaside Visitors: Idlers, Thinkers and Patriots in Mid-Nineteenth-Century Britain', in *Water, Leisure and Culture. European Historical Perspectives*, ed. Susan C. Anderson and Bruce H. Tabb (Oxford, 2002), pp. 87–104, p. 92.
165 Stephen V. Ward, *Selling Places: The Marketing and Promotion of Towns and Cities 1850–2000* (London, 1998), p. 60.
166 *The Monthly Magazine*, 30 July 1812.
167 *The Illustrated London News*, 30 October 1858.
168 Peak, *A Pier Without Peer*, p. 59.
169 *The Builder,* October 1885.
170 *The Daily Telegraph*, 20 October 1893.
171 Easdown, *Piers of Kent*, pp. 76–7.
172 Chris Mawson and Richard Riding, *British Seaside Piers* (Hersham, 2008), p. 111.
173 Peak, *A Pier Without Peer*, pp. 118–19.
174 Lindley, *Seaside Architecture*; Lynn F. Pearson, *Amusement Machines*
(Princes Risborough, 1992).
175 Albert Bullock and Peter Medcalf, *Britain in Old Photographs: Palace Pier, Brighton* (Stroud, 1999).
176 Fred Gray, *Walking on Water: The West Pier Story* (Brighton, 1997), p. 61.
177 Paul Wells and Sylvia Endacott, *Glimpses of Bognor Regis Pier* (Bognor Regis, 1998), p. 3.
178 Easdown, *Lancashire's Seaside Piers* p. 117.
179 *The Engineer*, 27 May 1887.
180 *The Building News*, 19 July 1901.
181 *The Stage*, 11 July 1901.
182 M. Noel Ridley, 'Dovetail Corrugated Sheeting', *The Concrete Institute, Transactions and Notes*, X (1923), pp. 1–27.
183 M. Noel Ridley, 'Promenade Piers', *The Structural Engineer*, XII, 2 (1934), pp. 106–10.
184 Mawson and Riding, *British Seaside Piers*, p. 128.
185 Pearson, *The People's Palaces*, p. 27.
186 Ibid.
187 *The Stage*, 18 July 1901.
188 Easdown, *Lancashire's Seaside Piers*, p. 94.
189 Pearson, *The People's Palaces*, p. 28.
190 Wills and Phillips, *British Seaside Piers*, p. 93.
191 Martin Easdown, *Piers of Sussex* (Stroud, 2009), p. 145.
192 Mawson and Riding, *British Seaside Piers*, pp. 48–51; Wills and Phillips, *British Seaside Piers*, pp. 113–19.
193 Pearson, *The People's Palaces,* p. 27; Mawson and Riding, *British Seaside Piers*, p. 48.
194 Boulton & Paul, Manufacturers, *Rose Lane Works, Norwich: Catalogue 43* (Norwich, 1888).
195 Pearson, *The People's Palaces*.
196 Kathryn Ferry, '"The Maker of Modern Yarmouth": J. W. Cockrill', in *Powerhouses of Provincial Architecture 1837–1914*, ed. Kathryn Ferry (London, 2009), pp. 45–58, p. 49.
197 'British Uralite Company', www.graces guide.co.uk, accessed 31 August 2018.
198 Kathryn Ferry, 'The Maker of Modern Yarmouth'.
199 Judith Martin, 'Cockrill-Doulton Patent Tiles', www.buildingconservation.com, accessed 31 August 2018.

200 Pearson, *The People's Palaces*, p. 57.
201 Ibid., p. 28.
202 Ibid., p. 97.
203 Ibid., p. 95.
204 Nikolaus Pevsner and Bill Wilson, *The Buildings of England: Norfolk 1: Norwich and North-East* (Yale, 1997), p. 527.
205 Easdown, *Yorkshire's Seaside Piers*, p. 84.
206 Easdown, *Piers of Sussex*, pp. 149–52.

6. Piers and the Sunny Seaside
207 Fred Gray, '1930s Architecture and the Cult of the Sun' in *Modernism on Sea: Art and Culture at the British Seaside*, ed. Lara Feigel and Alexandra Harris (Oxford, 2009), pp. 159–76, p. 165.
208 Fred Gray, *Designing the Seaside: Architecture, Society and Nature* (London, 2006), pp. 76–72.
209 Ibid.
210 Wesley Dougill, 'The British Coast and Its Holiday Resorts', *The Town Planning Review*, 16 (1935).
211 Malcolm Muggeridge, 'Bournemouth', in *Beside in Seaside*, ed. Yvonne Cloud (London, 1934), pp. 108–44, p. 134.
212 Ivor Brown, *The Heart of England* (London, 1935), pp. 15–16.
213 Dougill, 'The British Coast', p. 278.
214 'Leisure at the Seaside', *The Architectural Review*, 80 (1936).
215 *Sunny Southport Official Guide 1938–39* (Southport, 1938), p. 15.
216 *The Municipal Review*, September (1936).
217 *The Daily Telegraph*, 2 August 1934.
218 *The Daily Mail*, 31 July 1937. See also Chris Mawson and Richard Riding, *British Seaside Piers* (Hersham, 2008), p. 27.
219 *The Daily Mail*, 19 August 1939.
220 'The Worthing Pier Pavilion', *The Architect and Building News*, 12 November 1926.
221 Ibid.
222 Ward Lock, *Worthing and District* (London, c.1927), p. 20.
223 Sally White, *Worthing Pier: A History* (Worthing, 1996), p. 8.
224 'Worthing Amenities. Opening of the New Pier Pavilion of Novel Design', *The Municipal Review*, October (1935).

225 Ward Lock, *Worthing and District*, p. 23.
226 Martin Easdown and Darlah Thomas, *Piers of Wales* (Stroud, 2010), pp. 137–53.
227 'The New Pier Pavilion, Colwyn Bay', *The Architect and Building News*, 1 June 1934, www.victoriapier.co.uk, accessed 1 June 2019.
228 Ibid.
229 Helen Binyon, *Eric Ravilious: Memoir of an Artist* (Guildford, 1983), p. 70.
230 'The New Pier Pavilion, Colwyn Bay', *The Architect and Building News*.
231 Alastair Fairley, *De La Warr Pavilion: The Modernist Masterpiece* (London, 2006), p. 45.
232 Ibid., pp. 78–82.
233 Steve Peak, *Hastings Pier: A Pier Without Peer* (Hastings, 2016), pp. 164–5.
234 Easdown and Thomas, *Piers of Wales*, pp. 11–24.
235 Ray Gosling, 'Our piers in peril', *The Illustrated London News*, December, 1981.
236 Mawson and Riding, *British Seaside Piers*, p. 112; Wills and Phillips, *British Seaside Piers*, p. 255–6.
237 Martin Easdown, *Lancashire's Seaside Piers* (Barnsley, 2009), pp. 144–5.
238 Bruce Peter, *Form Follows Fun: Modernism and Modernity in British Pleasure Architecture, 1925–1940* (Abingdon, 2007).
239 Mawson and Riding, *British Seaside Piers*, p. 114; Wills and Phillips, *British Seaside Piers*, pp. 259–61.
240 Richard Fischer and John Walton, *British Piers* (London, 1987), p. 28.
241 A. P. Herbert, *The War Story of Southend Pier: The Battle of the Thames* (Southend-on-Sea, 1945), p. 7.
242 Peak, *Hastings Pier*, p. 179.
243 C. H. Bishop, *Folkestone: The Story of a Town* (Folkestone, 1973), pp. 138–9.
244 Mawson and Riding, *British Seaside Piers*, p. 61; Easdown and Thomas, *Piers of Wales*, p. 86.
245 Martin Easdown and Linda Sage, *Piers of Hampshire and the Isle of Wight* (Stroud, 2011), p. 61.
246 Ibid.

7. The Rollercoaster Years
247 Martin Farr, 'Decline beside the seaside: British seaside resorts and de-

clinism', in *Mass Tourism in a Small World*, ed. David Harrison and Richard Sharpley (Wallingford, 2017), pp. 105–17.
248 Clacton Urban District Council, *Holiday Time at Clacton-on-Sea* (Clacton, 1947), pp. 16–17.
249 Steve Peak, *A Pier Without Peer: The History of Hastings Pier* (Hastings, 2016), pp. 189–90.
250 Martin Easdown, *Yorkshire's Seaside Piers* (Barnsley, 2008), p. 55.
251 Martin Easdown, *Piers of Kent* (Stroud, 2007), p. 99.
252 Ibid.
253 'Deal Pier, Kent', www.niallmclaughlin.com, accessed 2 April 2019.
254 Mary Banham and Bevis Hillier, *A Tonic to the Nation: The Festival of Britain 1951* (London, 1976), p. 11.
255 'Ventnor's claim to first post-war pier', *The Surveyor*, 31 May 1958.
256 Ibid.
257 Ventnor and District Local History Society, *The Harbour and Piers of Ventnor 1843–1988* (Ventnor, 1989), and Martin Easdown and Linda Sage, *Piers of Hampshire and the Isle of Wight* (Stroud, 2011), p. 151.
258 Chris Mawson and Richard Riding, *British Seaside Piers* (Hersham, 2008), p. 19.
259 'Neck or Entrance Building at Boscombe Pier', www.historicengland.org.uk, accessed 1 March 2019.
260 *The Financial Times*, 14 June 1963.
261 Anthony Smith, *Beside the Seaside* (London, 1972), pp. 249–50.
262 'The pleasure of piers', *The Architects' Journal*, 24 September 1975.
263 James Walvin, *Beside the Seaside* (London, 1978) pp. 152–3.
264 Richard Fisher and John Walton, *British Piers* (London, 1987), p. 30.
265 Ray Gosling, 'Our piers in peril', *The Illustrated London News*, December 1981.
266 Fred Pearce, 'The end of the pier show', *New Scientist*, 4 February 1982.
267 *The Guardian*, 26 July 1993.
268 *The Times*, 10 June 1995.
269 Matthew Parris, 'Why Britain's piers should be allowed to slip beneath the waves', *The Spectator*, 29 November 1997.
270 *The Sunday Times*, 25 August 1996.

271 Cyril Bainbridge, *Pavilions on the Sea: A History of the Seaside Pleasure Pier* (London, 1986), p. 17.

272 Eric Underwood, *Brighton* (London, 1978), pp. 156–8; Fred Gray, *Walking on Water: The West Pier Story* (Brighton, 1997), pp. 75–6.

273 Basil J. Rushton, 'Piers – a future in the past', *Portico*, Winter (1978).

274 Roger Bingham, The Lost Resort?: *The Flow and Ebb of Morecambe* (Cartmel, 1990).

275 Easdown, *Piers of Kent*, p. 73.

276 J. A. Steers et al., 'The Storm Surge of 11 January 1978 on the East Coast of England', *The Geographical Journal*, 145, 2 (1979).

277 *The Sunday Times*, 23 July 1995.

278 Anthony Wills and Tim Phillips, *British Seaside Piers* (Swindon, 2014), p. 252.

279 Ibid., p. 170.

280 Andre Palfrey-Martin, 'Memories of a music maker', in Peak, *Hastings Pier*, pp. 203–224, p. 206.

281 Lavinia Brydon, Olu Jenzen and Nicholas Nourse, '"Our Pier": leisure activities and local communities at the British seaside', *Leisure/Loisir*, 43, 2 (2019).

282 'The History of Clevedon Pier', www.clevedonpier.co.uk, accessed 1 June 2019.

283 Brydon et al., 'Our Pier', p. 207.

284 'The pleasure of piers', *The Architects' Journal*.

285 Gosling, 'Our piers in peril', p. 59.

286 Lewis Blackwell, 'Transforming a penny arcade', *Building Design*, 8 February 1985.

287 Gosling, 'Our piers in peril'.

288 Martin Easdown, *Southend Pier* (Stroud, 2007).

289 'Most visited paid attractions – East 2017', www.visitbritain.org, accessed 1 May 2019.

290 Thomas Lane, 'Southend Pier Cultural Centre: Out on a limb', *Building*, 31 August 2012, www.building.co.uk, accessed 1 May 2019.

291 'Sculpted by Wind and Wave', www.whitearkitekter.com, accessed 1 May 2019.

292 'RIBA East Award 2013', www.pricemyers.com, accessed 1 May 2019.

293 Pearce, 'The end of the pier show'.

294 www.cromerpier.co.uk, accessed 10 December 2018.

295 Matthew Freeman, '40 years of Cromer's "Seaside Special"', *Sightline*, Autumn (2018).

296 City of Bangor Council, *Bangor Pier Centenary 1896–1996* (Bangor, 1996), p. 16.

297 'The History of Clevedon Pier', www.clevedonpier.co.uk, accessed 1 June 2019.

298 Keith Mallory, *Clevedon Pier* (Bristol, 1981), p. 19.

8. Prospect

299 Anthony Wills and Tim Phillips, *British Seaside Piers* (Swindon, 2014), pp. 218–221.

300 *The Times*, 2 June 2001.

301 www.southwoldpier.co.uk, accessed 2 May 2019.

302 www.felixstowe-pier.co.uk, accessed 3 June 2019; www.eadt.co.uk, 29 July 2017, accessed 3 June 2019.

303 www.milbank.co.uk, accessed 3 June 2019.

304 www.felixstowe-pier.co.uk, accessed 3 June 2019.

305 www.e-l-d.co.uk, accessed 3 June 2019.

306 www.theguardian.com, accessed 3 May 2019.

307 Anya Chapman, 'Pier pressure: Best practice in the rehabilitation of British seaside piers' in *REHAB 2015: Proceedings of the International Conference on Preservation, Maintenance and Rehabilitation of Historical Buildings and Structures,* ed. Rogerio Amoeda, S. Sérgio Lira and Cristina Pinheiro (Porto, 2015), pp. 67–76, p. 75.

308 www.guardian.com, 11 September 2013, accessed 1 May 2019.

309 'Hastings Pier wins the 2017 RIBA Stirling Prize for architecture', www.architecture.com, accessed 2 June 2019.

310 www.theguardian.com, 24 March 2019, accessed 3 May 2019.

311 www.piers.org.uk, accessed 3 May 2019.

312 www.northwalespioneer.co.uk, 20 December 2018, accessed 2 May 2019.

313 www.dailypost.co.uk, 10 March 2019, accessed 1 June 2019.

314 Fred Gray, *Designing the Seaside: Architecture, Society and Nature* (London, 2006), pp. 222–7.

315 Richard Morrice, 'A Report into Recent Practice Following Catastrophic Damage at Historic Places, with Particular Reference to Brighton's West Pier', English Heritage report, December, 2003, p. 18; English Heritage, 'Saving Brighton's Seafront Treasure', *Heritage Today*, June, 2004.

316 *The Daily Telegraph*, 31 July 2004.

317 Fred Gray, *British Airways i360: The Guide Book* (Brighton, 2016).

318 *The Daily Telegraph*, 2 August 2016.

319 www.westpier.co.uk, accessed 1 July 2019.

320 BACTA, *The Serious Business of Fun* (London, c.2017), p. 23.

321 www.theargus.co.uk, 8 April 2016, accessed 1 July 2019.

322 www.brightonpier.co.uk, accessed 1 May 2019.

323 Wills and Phillips, *British Seaside Piers*, pp. 206–7.

324 House of Lords, *Select Committee on Regenerating Seaside Towns and Communities, The Future of Seaside Towns*, HL Paper 320 (2019).

325 www.swanagepiertrust.com, accessed 12 June 2019.

326 Jess Steele, *People's Piers: Co-operative and Community Solutions for Heritage Assets* (Manchester, 2013); Anya Chapman, 'Pier pressure'.

327 Nigel Winterbottom, 'Brighton Pier, UK – innovation in renovation', *Proceedings of the Institution of Civil Engineers – Engineering History and Heritage*, 167, 2 (2014).

328 House of Lords, *The Future of Seaside Towns*.

329 Ibid.

330 Committee on Climate Change, *Managing the Coast in a Changing Climate* (London, 2018); Mary Zsamboky, Amalia Fernandez-Bilbao, David Smith, Jasper Knight and James Allan, *Impacts of Climate Change on Disadvantaged UK Coastal Communities* (York, 2011).

FURTHER READING

Martin Easdown's brilliant and extensive original research has developed our knowledge and understanding of British seaside piers. This book would have been slimmer and less certain without Martin's work. Simon H. Adamson's seminal 1977 book was the first in a steady stream of pier books. Tim Mickleburgh's publications, particularly his *Guide to British Piers*, have been hugely influential in charting the scope of the subject. The two best recent national-level surveys are by Chris Mawson and Richard Riding (covering lost piers as well as extant structures) and the collaboration between the National Piers Society and English Heritage, authored by Anthony Wills and Tim Phillips, detailing sixty-four surviving piers.

The list that follows does not reference accounts of individual piers or seaside towns; these may be found in the publications mentioned above. It does, however, include some of the many social histories of the British seaside published over the long post-war period. More recent trends include books about seaside architecture, photographic essays and pier travelogues.

Adamson, Simon H., *Seaside Piers* (London, 1977)

Anderson, Janice and Edmund Swinglehurst, *The Victorian and Edwardian Seaside* (London, 1978)

Bainbridge, Cyril, *Pavilions on the Sea: A History of the Seaside Pleasure Pier* (London, 1986)

Ball, Rob, *Funland: A Visual Tour of the British Seaside* (London, 2019)

Bounds, John, and Danny Smith, *Pier Review: A Road Trip in Search of the Great British Seaside* (Chichester, 2016)

Braggs, Steve, and Diane Harris, *Sun, Sea and Sand: The Great British Seaside Holiday* (Cheltenham, 2006)

Brodie, Allan, *The Seafront* (Swindon, 2018)

Brodie, Allan and Gary Winter, *England's Seaside Resorts* (Swindon, 2007)

Corbin, Alain, *The Lure of the Sea: The Discovery of the Seaside in the Western World 1750–1840* (Cambridge, 1994)

Dobraszczyk, Paul, *Iron, Ornament and Architecture in Victorian Britain: Myth and Modernity, Excess and Enchantment* (Farnham, 2014)

Easdown, Martin, *Piers of Kent* (Stroud, 2007)

Easdown, Martin, *Yorkshire's Seaside Piers* (Barnsley, 2008)

Easdown, Martin, *Piers of Sussex* (Stroud, 2009)

Easdown, Martin, and Darlah Thomas, *Piers of Wales* (Stroud, 2010)

Easdown, Martin, and Linda Sage, *Piers of Hampshire and the Isle of Wight* (Stroud, 2011)

Easdown, Martin, and Richard Riding, *A Guide to Collecting Seaside Pier Postcards* (National Piers Society, 2006)

Feigel, Lara, and Alexandra Harris, *Modernism on Sea: Arts and Culture at the British Seaside* (Witney, 2009)

Ferry, Kathryn, *The British Seaside Holiday* (Oxford, 2011)

Fischer, Richard, and John Walton, *British Piers* (London, 1987)

Girling, Richard, *Sea Change: Britain's Coastal Catastrophe* (London, 2007)

Gosling, Luci, *Images from the past: The British Seaside* (Barnsley, 2017)

Gray, Fred, *Designing the Seaside: Architecture, Society and Nature* (London, 2006)

Greenbury, Judith, *Piers and Seaside Towns: An Artist's Journey* (Bristol, 2001)

Hannavy, John, *The English Seaside in Victorian and Edwardian Times* (Oxford, 2008)

Hern, Anthony, *The Seaside Holiday: The History of the English Seaside Resort* (London, 1967)

Howell, Sarah, *The Seaside* (London, 1974)

Hylton, Stuart, *The British Seaside: An Illustrated*

History (Stroud, 2018)

Lindley, Kenneth, *Seaside Architecture* (London, 1973)

Mawson, Chris, and Richard Riding, *British Seaside Piers* (Hersham, 2008)

Mickleburgh, Timothy, *The Guide to British Piers* (National Piers Society, 1998)

Mickleburgh, Timothy, *Piers: Photographic Memories* (Salisbury, 2006)

Pearson, Lynn F., *The People's Palaces: Britain's Seaside Pleasure Buildings of 1870–1914* (Buckingham, 1991)

Pearson, Lynn F., *Piers and Other Seaside Architecture* (Oxford, 2008)

Roberts, Simon, *Pierdom* (Manchester, 2013)

Sandler, Nigel, *British Piers: The Postcard Collection* (Stroud, 2017)

Walvin, James, *Beside the Seaside* (London, 1978)

Walton, John, *The English Seaside Resort: A Social History* 1750–1914 (Leicester, 1983)

Walton, John, *The British Seaside: Holidays and Resorts in the Twentieth Century* (Manchester, 2000)

Wills, Anthony, and Tim Phillips, *British Seaside Piers* (Swindon, 2013)

ACKNOWLEDGEMENTS

Over many years I have benefitted greatly from conversations with other pier aficionados. Colleagues in the National Piers Society (NPS) including Martin Easdown, Tim Phillips, the late Richard Riding and Anthony Wills have helped in developing my understanding of piers. Founded in 1979, the NPS is a non-profit making charity with the aim 'to promote and sustain interest in the preservation, building and continued enjoyment of seaside piers'. The Society has an excellent website (www.piers.org.uk) with information on individual piers, both surviving and lost, publishes a quarterly journal, PIERS, and runs the annual 'Pier of the Year' competition.

Martin Easdown and Anthony Wills, Allan Brodie of Historic England and the architectural and seaside historian Kathryn Ferry commented on a draft of the book. Nigel Hosker commented on the chapter on making piers; remaining inadequacies and errors are my responsibility.

As civil and structural engineers with extensive pier experience, Jon Orrell and Nigel Hosker of HOP Consulting Ltd answered many of my pier engineering questions. Faye Davies provided me with fascinating new insights about the building and condition of the Brighton West Pier. Kathryn Ferry very usefully pushed me to think more critically about the design context of the mid-nineteenth century. Over several years Martin Easdown kindly commentated on my writing and provided valuable information. A group of friends and colleagues in Brighton aided and abetted my pier work: they include Rachel Clark, the late Andy Durr, Andy Garth, Olu Jenzen, Jackie Marsh-Hobbs and Geoffrey Mead. My understanding of the two important Hastings and St Leonards piers was enhanced by Hastings' wonderful historian Steve Peak. Nick Dermott was a font of knowledge about Margate and Ted Lightbown and, latterly, Carl Carrington did much to improve my knowledge about Blackpool's three magnificent piers. Wayne Walters was immensely generous in allowing me access to his extensive collection of pier photographs.

My enduring debt of gratitude is to my family, Carol, Holly and Jack, who indulged my passion for the seaside and helped with my various seaside projects. As she knows so well, this book would not have been completed without Carol's immense support.

Illustration Acknowledgements

INDEX